Justice and Peace in the Israeli–Palestinian Conflict

In this book, the late Prof. Yaacov Bar-Siman-Tov argues that the failure of the Israeli–Palestinian peace process so far has been mainly the result of the inability of both sides to reach an agreed formula for linking justice to peace.

The issues of justice and injustice are focused mainly on the outcomes of the 1947–49 first Arab–Israeli War and specifically in the creation of the Palestinian refugee problem. The conflicting historical narratives of the two sides regarding the question of responsibility for the injustice done to the Palestinians turn the Israeli–Palestinian conflict into a classic case of linking the issues of justice and peace. Yaacov Bar-Siman-Tov maintains that the narratives of justice and injustice in the Israeli–Palestinian conflict have proved to be formidable barriers to peace. Hence, he recommends that justice should be compromised for the sake of peace.

The link between justice and peace is an important issue requiring both sides' attention, but, given the wide and currently unbridgeable gap separating the two sides, it should be postponed to the phase of reconciliation rather than being included in the process of conflict resolution. The two-state solution is endorsed as the best and practical solution and as a first step for a "just peace" in this conflict, to be followed by reconciliation. Highly topical, this book is essential reading for scholars and researchers of International Relations, Peace Studies, and the Arab–Israeli conflict.

Yaacov Bar-Siman-Tov was Giancarlo Elia Valori Professor of International Relations for the Study of Peace and Regional Cooperation at the Hebrew University of Jerusalem and the Head of the Jerusalem Institute for Israel Studies. He was also the founding Director of the Swiss Center for Conflict Research, Management and Resolution at the Hebrew University. A noted expert in the fields of conflict management and resolution and the Arab–Israeli conflict, he was the author of several books, including *Israel and the Peace Process, 1977–1982: In Search of Legitimacy for Peace* (1994); *The Transition from War to Peace: The Complexity of Decisionmaking – The Israeli Case* (1996). He was also the editor and co-editor of several books, among them: *Stable Peace Among Nations* (2000); *From Conflict Resolution to Reconciliation* (2004); *The Israeli–Palestinian Conflict: From Conflict*

Resolution to Conflict Management (2007); and *Barriers to Peace in the Israeli–Palestinian Conflict* (2010).

Arie M. Kacowicz is the Chaim Weizmann Chair in International Relations and an Associate Professor at the Department of International Relations at the Hebrew University of Jerusalem. He is the author of *Peaceful Territorial Change* (1994); *Zones of Peace in the Third World: South America and West Africa in a Comparative Perspective* (1998); *The Impact of Norms in International Society: The Latin American Experience, 1881–2001* (2005); and *Globalisation and the Distribution of Wealth: The Latin American Experience, 1982–2008* (2013). His areas of interest include globalization and global governance, international relations of Latin America, peace studies, and the Arab–Israeli conflict.

UCLA Center for Middle East Development (CMED)

Edited by Steven Spiegel
UCLA
Elizabeth Matthews
California State University, San Marcos

The UCLA Center for Middle East Development (CMED) series on Middle East security and cooperation is designed to present a variety of perspectives on a specific topic, such as democracy in the Middle East, dynamics of Israeli–Palestinian relations, Gulf security, and the gender factor in the Middle East. The uniqueness of the series is that the authors write from the viewpoint of a variety of countries so that, no matter what the issue, articles appear from many different states, both within and beyond the region. No existing series provides a comparable, multinational collection of authors in each volume. Thus, the series presents a combination of writers from countries who, for political reasons, do not always publish in the same volume. The series features a number of sub-themes under a single heading, covering security, social, political, and economic factors affecting the Middle East.

1. **The Struggle over Democracy in the Middle East**
   Regional politics and external policies
   Edited by Nathan J. Brown and Emad El-Din Shahin

2. **Women in the Middle East and North Africa**
   Agents of change
   Edited by Fatima Sadiqi and Moha Ennaji

3. **The Israel–Palestine Conflict**
   Parallel discourses
   Edited by Elizabeth Matthews

4. **Gender and Violence in the Middle East**
   Edited by Moha Ennaji and Fatima Sadiqi

5. **Non-State Actors in the Middle East**
   Factors for peace and democracy
   Galia Golan and Walid Salem

6. **Regional Security Dialogue in the Middle East**
   Changes, challenges and opportunities
   Edited by Chen Kane and Egle Murauskaite

7. **Israeli Peacemaking Since 1967**
   Behind the breakthroughs and failure
   Galia Golan

8. **Justice and Peace in the Israeli–Palestinian Conflict**
   Yaacov Bar-Siman-Tov and Arie M. Kacowicz

Justice and Peace in the Israeli–Palestinian Conflict

Yaacov Bar-Siman-Tov

Edited by
Arie M. Kacowicz

Routledge
Taylor & Francis Group
LONDON AND NEW YORK

First published 2014
by Routledge
4 Park Square, Milton Park, Abingdon, Oxon OX14 4RN

and by Routledge
605 Third Avenue, New York, NY 10017

Routledge is an imprint of the Taylor & Francis Group, an informa business

British Library Cataloguing in Publication Data
A catalogue record for this book is available from the British Library

Library of Congress Cataloging-in-Publication Data
Bar-Siman-Tov, Yaacov, 1946-
Justice and peace in the Israeli-Palestinian conflict / Yaacov Bar-Siman-Tov; edited by Arie M. Kacowicz.
pages cm. – (UCLA center for Middle East development (CMED) series)
Includes bibliographical references and index.
1. Justice. 2. Arab-Israeli conflict–Peace. I. Kacowicz, Arie M., editor. II. Title.
JC578.B355 2014
956.9405'4–dc23
2014009890

ISBN: 978-1-138-02484-7 (hbk)
ISBN: 978-1-138-02485-4 (pbk)
ISBN: 978-1-315-77547-0 (ebk)

Typeset in Times New Roman
by Cenveo Publisher Services

In memory of Yaacov Bar-Siman-Tov and Ronit Bar-Siman-Tov

Contents

Preface

Professor Yaacov Bar-Siman-Tov completed a full draft of *Justice and Peace in the Israeli–Palestinian Conflict* about two years ago. Unfortunately, he died on 18 February 2013, several months after his beloved wife, Ronit Bar-Siman-Tov, passed away. Shortly before he died he sent a complete manuscript draft to his son, Ittai Bar-Siman-Tov. Upon Yaacov's death, Ittai contacted Routledge, which had offered Yaacov an advanced contract for his research. After Routledge reaffirmed their interest in publishing the book, Ittai asked me to edit his father's book and prepare it for production and publication.

I knew Yaacov Bar-Siman-Tov for over 30 years, first as his student in the Department of International Relations, and then as his colleague since 1993 at the Hebrew University of Jerusalem. We cooperated in editing *Stable Peace among Nations* in the late 1990s, and again in 2001–03 in an important oral history project that he coordinated at the Leonard Davis Institute for International Relations, tracing the causes for the failure of the Oslo peace process (or, in his own words, "what went wrong") (see Kacowicz 2005).

Yaacov Bar-Siman-Tov was an expert on conflict resolution and spent several decades of his career researching and teaching about the Arab–Israeli conflict in general, and the Israeli–Palestinian conflict in particular. This book can be considered as the concluding part of a research trilogy: Yaacov began with the search for the possibilities of peace and stable peace (Kacowicz *et al.* 2000), moved to the question of reconciliation (Bar-Siman-Tov 2004), and ended trying to understand the difficult relationship between justice and peace. He perceived that link to be one of the major obstacles for conflict resolution in general, and for the resolution of the Israeli–Palestinian conflict in particular. This research stems from his previous important work of scholarship on barriers to peace in the Israeli–Palestinian conflict (see Bar-Siman-Tov 2010).

In the last several years, Yaacov discussed his work in progress with me. We had several conversations about whether the Israeli–Palestinian conflict was regressing from conflict resolution to conflict management, and the possibilities of resolving it against formidable barriers, such as the insistence on justice narratives on both sides. In this context, this book presents the narratives of Israelis and Palestinians about their conflict in an objective way, getting into the basic issues and offering a clear and convincing summary of them.

Yaacov Bar-Siman-Tov's book embodies a careful and sensible exercise in empathy. In the words of his former doctoral supervisor, Prof. Alan Dowty, "it represents a lifetime of wisdom and it is remarkable for its ability to encompass the narratives of both sides, which is the most useful approach." In this book, Prof. Bar-Siman-Tov also follows the footsteps of his second doctoral supervisor, Prof. Yeoshafat Harkabi (1972), by clearly discerning the Palestinian attitudes towards Israel, especially in the context of their narratives of justice and injustice with respect to the outcomes of the 1947–49 war and the creation of the Palestinian refugee problem.

The argument of the book is simple yet powerful. Yaacov Bar-Siman-Tov maintains that the narratives of justice and injustice in the Israeli–Palestinian conflict have proved to be formidable barriers to peace. Hence, he recommends to the practitioners on both sides (and to the general public) that *justice should be compromised for the sake of peace*. Moreover, Yaacov stresses the argument that the two-state solution for the Israeli–Palestinian conflict is the only solution that might be an imperfect approximation of a "just peace," though the Palestinians will have to give up their claims for a "right of return" of the Palestinian refugees to the State of Israel.

Still, throughout his book, Yaacov Bar-Siman-Tov expresses sound skepticism with regard to the possibility of the Palestinians compromising on their narratives of justice and injustice, and recognizing Israel as a Jewish state. My own reading of this difficult conundrum is slightly different from his. Up until today, I am not completely sure whether the Palestinian insistence on the "right of return" is a sacred and untouchable component of their identity (as he argues), or it might be their ultimate "bargaining chip" to be exchanged in the peace negotiations for the fulfillment of their other claims, such as the territorial borders of the Palestinian state and their access and sovereignty over East Jerusalem, including the *Haram* Temple Mount.

I cannot think of a more topical and relevant piece of scholarship for students and practitioners alike than this book. This is particularly the case against the background of the Herculean (but not Quixotic) attempts of US Secretary of State John Kerry to bring the parties together in what seems to be perhaps the last serious attempt for a negotiated solution of the intractable Israeli–Palestinian conflict. I wish that the negotiators on both sides, as well as the general public in both societies, will learn from the wisdom and common sense that are clearly articulated throughout the book. In that sense, the book represents Yaacov Bar-Siman-Tov's final contribution, and an important concluding statement of his long academic career.

The academic editing of the book included preparing and revising the manuscript for production and updating it with several endnotes to the events of 2014. At times the academic labor was painful in a personal sense, since it reminded me of the dialogue with Yaacov that we shared for the last 20 years. Despite our scholarly disagreements, I tried the utmost to maintain the language and spirit of his arguments, without adding my own views. For the completion of the book I would like to thank Galia Press-Bar-Nathan, Orly Kacowicz, and

Keren Sasson, who commented on this Preface; to Daniel Schwartz, a political philosopher, for his suggestions on the first chapter; to Shaul Shenav, a political scientist and expert on narratives, for his advice on Chapter 2; to Ittai Bar-Siman-Tov, for his contribution throughout the manuscript of his late father; and particularly to Lior Lehrs, a brilliant PhD student who worked closely with Yaacov at the Jerusalem Institute for Israeli Studies, for his substantial comments and advice on the entire book manuscript. I also thank Yaacov's children, Keren, Ittai, and Yonatan, for bringing me into this project. This is in a vivid sense the best living memory I can think of to perpetuate the scholarship of Prof. Bar-Siman-Tov and perhaps make a practical contribution to peace. Finally, I want to thank James "Joe" Whiting, Editor, as well as Kathryn Rylance, Steven Speigel, Elizabeth Matthews, Emma Hudson, and Sheila Garrard for their valuable help and assistance in the production of the book.

Time is running out for the peaceful resolution of the Israeli–Palestinian conflict in a negotiated form of a two-state solution. I sincerely hope that Israelis, Palestinians, Americans, Europeans, and other citizens of the world, students and practitioners, politicians, and the general informed public will read this book and learn from its wisdom. The excruciating dilemma of choosing between peace and justice, prioritizing the former over the latter, reminds me of Hedley Bull's brilliant analysis of preferring order over justice (see Bull 1977). In our imperfect world, there are no absolute solutions but just approximations to the good (not necessarily the best). There is a saying in Hebrew that "it is better to be wise than to be just." I share Yaacov's conclusion that we should prefer peace rather than justice if we want to reach conflict resolution, without completely forgetting about justice but relegating it to the later phase of reconciliation. The outcome of the current Israeli–Palestinian negotiations in the foreseeable future will be the ultimate litmus test for Prof. Bar-Siman-Tov's lasting contribution to the theory and practice of international relations.

Arie M. Kacowicz, Jerusalem, Israel
February 2014

References

Bar-Siman-Tov, Yaacov (ed.). *From Conflict Resolution to Reconciliation* (New York: Oxford University Press, 2004).

Bar-Siman-Tov, Yaacov. "Justice and Fairness as Barriers to the Resolution of the Israeli–Palestinian Conflict." In *Barriers to Peace in the Israeli–Palestinian Conflict* (ed.) Yaacov Bar-Siman-Tov. (Jerusalem: The Jerusalem Institute for Israeli Studies, 2010), pp. 178–227.

Bull, Hedley. *The Anarchical Society: A Study of Order in World Politics* (London: Macmillan, 1977).

Harkabi, Yeoshafat. *The Arab Attitudes to Israel* (Jerusalem: Keter, 1972).

Kacowicz, Arie M., Yaacov Bar-Siman-Tov, Ole Elgstrom, and Magnus Jerneck (eds). *Stable Peace among Nations* (Lanham, MD: Rowman and Littlefield, 2000).

Kacowicz, Arie M. "Rashomon in Jerusalem: Mapping the Israeli Negotiators' Position on the Israeli–Palestinian Peace Process, 1993–2001," *International Studies Perspectives*, 6 (2005), pp. 252–73.

Abbreviations

AHC	Arab Higher Committee
DOP	Declaration of Principles
ICPR	International Commission for Palestinian Refugees
IM	International Mechanism (for Compensation of Palestinian Refugees)
NSU	Palestinian Negotiations Support Unit
PA	Palestinian Authority
PLO	Palestinian Liberation Organization
PN	Palestinian National Council
PPR	Permanent place of residence
UN	United Nations
UNGA	United Nations General Assembly
UNRWA	United Nations Relief and Works Agency for Palestine Refugees in the Near East
UNSC	United Nations Security Council

Introduction

The reasons for the failure of the Oslo process and the eruption of the Israeli–Palestinian violence in September 2000 have been explored in depth in the memoirs of participants in the peace process and in academic research. Several of these studies have characterized the Israeli–Palestinian conflict as intractable, uncontrollable, and insoluble. Others have attributed the failure of the talks to the parties' lack of readiness and ripeness to make the concessions necessary for resolving the conflict, and some have focused on psychological, cultural, and internal political barriers or the ineffectiveness of the US mediation.

In this book, I argue that the failure of the Israeli–Palestinian peace process so far has been mainly the result of the inability of both sides to reach an agreed formula for linking justice to peace. The relationship between peace and justice has been at the heart of the peace process. Actually, the peace process only exacerbated the wide gap between both sides' narratives and the difficulty if not the impossibility to bridge the gap between them. Both sides continue to be guided by their historical narratives, which became protected values; that is, sacred and mystical values intertwined with their national identities and therefore not subject to negotiation, bargaining, or compromise of any sort. Each side continues to invoke its perceived injustices committed by the other side, consumed by a high sense of justice and righteousness in its cause, while de-legitimizing the justice of the other side.

The peace process has only proved again the old and basic assumption that it is a clash between two narratives of justice. The issues of justice and injustice are embedded in the conflict and they have been reflected in their interactions. They probably will continue to remain for a long time if not permanently in the narratives of each side and in the current and future peace negotiations.

The basic conclusion of this political reality is that justice cannot be absolute, but relative at its best, and that it will be permanently incomplete. Any demand for linking justice to peace based on one's exclusive narrative is impossible and a formidable barrier to conflict resolution. The central problem in the case of two conflicting views of justice is that both sides are partly right, in terms of one or another aspect of their claims, and therefore it cannot be expected that a peace agreement will fully and satisfactorily address all of the problems related to justice. Therefore, justice has to be compromised if the parties have an interest to resolve the conflict in the first place.

The issues of justice and injustice are focused mainly on the outcomes of the 1947–49 first Arab–Israeli War and specifically in the creation of the Palestinian refugee problem. According to the Palestinian national narrative, throughout the 1947–49 war more than 700,000 Palestinians became refugees. Most of them (around two-thirds) became refugees in the West Bank and the Gaza Strip, while the rest fled to neighboring Arab states, including Jordan, Syria, and Lebanon. The Palestinians argue that the Palestinian flight was a deliberated "transfer" policy (i.e. ethnic cleansing) authorized by the Jewish–Israeli leadership in order to clean the Jewish state of its Arab local inhabitants. It was an active expulsion policy conducted by Jewish and later by Israeli troops. Throughout the years since the end of 1947 the Palestinian refugee population has massively grown, counting today (according to United Nations Relief and Works Agency for Palestine Refugees in the Near East – UNRWA) more than 5 million people. Moreover, the Palestinians claim that their demand for the right of return is recognized by various UN resolutions, first and foremost UN General Assembly Resolution 194.

The Israeli counter-narrative about the creation of the refugee problem is totally different. Although Israel recognizes the fact that hundreds of thousands of Palestinians (but less than 700,000) left during the war, this exodus was caused by a combination of several factors, including civilian flight from a war zone, orders from Arab leaders and commanders to leave temporarily until reaching a decisive victory, and increasing economic and social problems. The Palestinian refugee problem emerged as a natural consequence out of a war situation, which the Palestinians and the Arab states were responsible for initiating. No orders of expulsion were made and there was no deliberated "transfer" policy. Moreover, the war caused also the emergence of a parallel Jewish refugee problem. Hundreds of thousands of Jews who lived in neighboring Arab states were expelled or coerced to leave their homes and most of them were successfully absorbed in Israel. The findings of a group of Israeli historians, the so-called "New Historians," at the end of the 1980s, that active expulsion by Jewish forces also played a significant role in the flight of the Palestinians, did not change substantially the Israeli official narrative regarding the creation of the Palestinian refugee problem.

The narrative differences between the two sides regarding the Palestinian exodus from Palestine in 1947–49 refer directly to the question of the responsibility for its creation. However, there is no one single explanation for the Palestinian exodus, probably because it happened in different stages during the war and because of various causes and different versions. Historians mention the following causes for the Arab exodus: fear, anarchy, robberies, and intimidation of the Arab militias and irregulars; disunited and ineffectual leadership; unclear leadership instructions about what to do or expect; unwillingness to be under Jewish control; erosion of morale; society disintegration; psychosis of flight; orders by Arab commanders and the Arab Higher Committee (AHC) of evacuation in order to clear battle areas, while promising immediate return following a decisive victory; Jewish psychological warfare; Jewish retaliatory strategy against Arab military bases; reports on Jewish atrocities; Jewish direct and indirect attacks on Arab villages and cities; and direct expulsion by Jewish and Israeli forces. While there is no evidence that the AHC or Arab leaders outside of Palestine issued specific instructions to flee, there is also no evidence for a formal or official Jewish or Israeli decision or policy of expulsion of the Arab population.

In sum, both sides share part of the responsibility for the Palestinian exodus. However, the refugee problem cannot be separated from the broader context of the war that was initiated by the Palestinians and the Arab states, and was perceived by both sides as a total one, a zero-sum conflict, and an attempt at "politicide" by the Arab states and the Palestinians to undo the political creation of the State of Israel.[1]

The far-reaching outcomes of the 1947–49 war included not only the creation of the Palestinian refugee problem, but also the fact that an Arab state was never established alongside the State of Israel, as recommended by the UN Partition Plan of 29 November 1947. Instead, most of the territories allocated to an Arab state in Palestine were militarily occupied by Transjordan (the West Bank) and by Egypt (the Gaza Strip), whereas Israel extended its sovereign territory from 55 percent to 77 percent of the area west of the Jordan River (Western Palestine), following the Rhodes Armistices of 1949. The continuation of the conflict and its aggravation and the failure to conclude a comprehensive Arab–Israeli peace agreement prevented any prospect to resolve the Palestinian refugee problem. Following the 1967 war, between 200,000 and 300,000 Palestinians fled or were expelled from the West Bank and the Gaza Strip occupied now by Israel to Jordan, Syria, Egypt, and elsewhere, and they are nowadays considered displaced persons. Among them, 180,000 were first-time refugees, while the rest were 1947–49 refugees. However, the outcomes of the 1967 war, the occupation of the West Bank and the Gaza Strip by Israel, and the first *intifada* (1987–91) led to the Oslo peace process (1993–2001), which was the first Israeli–Palestinian attempt to resolve the conflict by peaceful means.

Palestinian negotiators and scholars claim that the conflict cannot be resolved unless Israel accepts the following Palestinian demands: recognition of its responsibility for the expulsion of Palestinians from the land of Palestine in the 1947–49 war and acceptance of the Palestinian demand for a just solution to the refugee problem through the implementation of Palestinians' "right of return" to their homes in Palestine (within the territory of the State of Israel), following UN General Assembly Resolution 194 of December 1948. Hence, a just solution to the conflict – or, in their view, a "just peace" – depends on Israeli acquiescence to these demands.

The Palestinians deny any responsibility for the rejection of the UN Partition Plan of November 1947 and their attempt together with Arab states to prevent by war the implementation of the Partition Plan and the establishment of the State of Israel ("politicide"). The Palestinians base their claims as legal rights and as protected values that were enshrined by UN General Assembly Resolution 194. Therefore, their demands for Israel's recognition of its responsibility for creating the refugee problem and accepting the right of return are not issues open for negotiation, bargaining, or compromise. The right of return is a "private (personal) right" of every refugee, and Palestinian leaders and negotiators have no authority or legitimacy to waive this right in the name of the refugees.

Israel, for its part, has refused so far to accept these Palestinian demands as preconditions for the resolution of the conflict. Its argument is that the Palestinians and Arab countries bear the responsibility for the outcomes of the 1947–49 war and for the Palestinian refugee problem. Israel argues that the Arabs' refusal to recognize the November 1947 Partition Plan and their initiation of a war intended to prevent, by force, the establishment of the State of Israel are the reasons for the historical injustice perpetuated against the Palestinians. Moreover, the Palestinians are aware that their demand for implementation of the right of return means the end of Israel as a Jewish state, and their insistence on this right is therefore a formidable barrier to the resolution of the conflict.

The conflicting historical narratives of the two sides regarding the question of responsibility for the injustice done to the Palestinians turns the Israeli–Palestinian conflict into a classic case of linking the issues of justice and peace. Given that the two sides often define the conflict in terms of injustice and unfairness, these issues have particular relevance for the peace process, and this is what makes dealing with them as barriers to the resolution of the conflict so problematic.

In this book, I argue that the link between justice and peace is an important issue requiring both sides' attention, but, given the wide and currently unbridgeable gap separating the two sides, it should be postponed to the phase of reconciliation rather than being included in the process of conflict resolution. The two-state solution is endorsed as the best and practical solution and as a first step for a "just peace" in this conflict, to be followed by reconciliation.

The arguments offered in the book will be examined in the following order. First, I present two theoretical chapters. Chapter 1, "Just peace: linking justice to peace" has three aims: First, to explore the reasons for the demand of linking justice to peace as they are presented in different approaches in the field of conflict and peace studies. Second, to examine the implications for linking justice to peace on peace negotiations, concluding a peace agreement, and its implementation, as well as on the stabilization of a peace agreement, its durability, and the prospects of reconciliation. Third, to explore alternative ways to balance the relationship between justice and peace, leading to a peace agreement that might become durable and stable over time.

Chapter 2, "Narratives of justice and injustice in peacemaking," aims to examine the process in which historical narratives, collective memory, myths, and ethos, emerge to be almost the sole criteria for defining "just peace" or for linking justice to peace, as well as their influence upon peacemaking and reconciliation.

Second, the next two chapters refer to the narratives of both parties in the Israeli–Palestinian conflict. Chapter 3, "The Israeli–Jewish narratives of justice and injustice," presents the Israeli meta-narrative of justice that justifies the establishment and the existence of the State of Israel as the national home of the Jewish people in terms of distributive justice, as well as in terms of correcting and compensating justice because of the injustice that happened to the Jewish people throughout its history that reached its peak at the Holocaust. The national narratives of justice focus on presenting the Israeli positions and behaviors throughout the Arab–Israeli conflict, while denying the Arab and the Palestinian justice and injustice narratives of the conflict.

Chapter 4, "The Palestinian narratives of justice and injustice," presents the Palestinian narratives of justice and injustice, which are perceived as the most necessary and legitimate means of expressing the justice of the Palestinian claims, the injustice inflicted on them, and the need to correct the injustice as one of the most effective and least evident forms of resistance. Over almost 70 years of lingering conflict the issues of justice and injustice had become the key discourse in official Arab and Palestinian statements and declarations, in Palestinian scholarly writings, and in Palestinian public debate. The main expression of the justice–injustice issues is the demand for the "right of return" that has gained the status of a sacred right and a protected value and principle.

Third, the next two chapters refer to the two rounds of the peace process, that of 1993–2001 (the "Oslo peace process") and 2007–08 (the "Annapolis process"). Chapters 5 and 6 are empirical chapters that present the sides' attempts to link justice to peace during the peace negotiations. Chapter 5, "Linking justice to peace in the Oslo process, 1993–2001," depicts the role of the Israeli and the Palestinian narratives of justice and injustice throughout the negotiations at Track I, i.e. the Oslo process since its beginning in January 1993 (at Oslo) to January 2001 (at Taba), as well as, in the Track II initiatives – the "People's Voice" and the Geneva Initiative. The historical narratives – and in particular the ethos of injustice and the Palestinian demands for justice, fairness, and equality – played a central role throughout the Oslo process. Although they did not prevent the initiation and pursuit of the process, these narratives did contribute significantly to its failure through the enormous gaps that they generated between the parties.

Chapter 6, "Linking justice to peace in the Annapolis process, 2007–08," presents the sides' attempts to link justice to peace in the resuscitated peace process after the second *intifada* and seven years without negotiations. Throughout the negotiations of 2007–08 both sides presented their traditional positions regarding issues of justice, especially regarding the problem of the Palestinian refugees. Two issues were discussed in depth, the question of responsibility and apology, and the right of return. Israel's negotiators, for the first time in the peace process, introduced its request for recognizing Israel as a Jewish state in accordance to justice claims.

Finally, in the concluding chapter, I offer some theoretical and practical conclusions. Chapter 7, "Linking justice to peace in the Israeli–Palestinian conflict: looking for solutions," has two aims. First, to summarize the role of the narratives of both parties in the peace process, arguing that the gap between both sides' justice narratives is the major barrier for resolving the conflict. Second, to look for alternative solutions for linking justice to peace, among them: linking justice to reconciliation, a two-state solution, and a one-state solution.

The empirical and theoretical materials used in this book draw on the documents of the Israeli–Palestinian negotiations (including the leaked *Palestinian Papers* published by *Al Jazeera* in 2011), interviews made with negotiators in the media, and the book memoirs of some of the participants. In addition, there is an extensive reference to books and articles of both sides to the conflict, and to the wide literature about the Israeli–Palestinian conflict in general and the Israeli–Palestinian peace process in particular.

This book is part of a larger research project on "Just and Durable Peace by Piece" funded by the EU's 7th Framework Programme, proposal no. 217589. I would like to thank Professors Karin Aggestam and Annika Bjorkdahl, both from Lund University in Sweden, for initiating the project and inviting me to participate in it.

Note

1 Editor's note: Yeoshafat Harkabi coined the term "politicide" to indicate the Arab and Palestinian intentions to politically (if not physically) destroy the new Israeli state declared on 14 May 1948. For a comprehensive summary of the literature discussing the creation of the Palestinian refugee problem, see Chiller-Glauss (2007). See also Morris (2004).

References

Al Jazeera. *The Palestinian Papers* (2011). Accessed at: http://transparency.aljazeera.net/files.

Chiller-Glauss, Michael. *Tackling the Intractable: Palestinian Refugees and the Search for Middle East Peace* (Bern: Peter Lang, 2007).

Morris, Benny. *The Birth of the Palestinian Refugee Problem Revisited*, 2nd edition (Cambridge: Cambridge University Press, 2004).

1 Just peace

Linking justice to peace

Introduction

The concept of *just peace* as proposed by Pierre Allan and Alexis Keller implies that it is a unique kind of peace that differs from other types, such as negative peace, positive peace, and stable peace (Allan and Keller 2006a; Allan 2006; Allan and Keller 2006b). The concept of just peace is based on the following assumptions:

1 Peace is just only when it is based on justice, or includes justice in it. Thus, "just peace" is a situation or a process "whereby peace and justice are reached together" (Allan and Keller 2006b, 195).
2 The parties mutually recognize that the peace agreement is just.
3 Peace is just only when it is not imposed on the sides and it is negotiated and accepted by them willingly, on a voluntary basis. "[Peace] is just, because it is based on conventions that are negotiated and accepted by the parties" (Allan and Keller 2006a, 1).
4 The parties accept the peace agreement as regulating their relations in a legitimate way and making them satisfied (Allan 2006, 115). Just peace makes the sides respect their commitments. They do not have any reason or motivation to violate the agreement (Keller 2006, 51).
5 Just peace is a precondition for the durability of peace.
6 A just peace is a requirement when one or both sides ask for it or even make it a condition for conflict resolution.
7 The call for just peace or linking peace to justice implies that peace and justice should live in harmony. At the same time, peace and justice may collide and a growing tension may develop between the two.

(Margalit 2010, 7)

The need to link peace with justice is obvious and desired. However, peace and justice may clash and contradict each other. In such a case the main questions are: How to reconcile between peace and justice and what to do when they clash, so that the two cannot be reconciled? Can peace be justified without being just? Can justice be justified without peace? There are no simple answers to these questions.

The ideas of linking justice with peace emerged in the last decade at the core of the theoretical and empirical literature of conflict resolution and peacemaking, including studies on reconciliation. Looking at the relevant studies in the field indicates that we can differentiate between two basic approaches that refer to the possible links between peace and justice.

The first approach calls for a strong link between justice and peace since issues of justice are considered to be a major cause of conflict, so that justice becomes a foundation for peace. Justice is required and necessary for peace, so that peace cannot be reached without reference to justice. Justice includes procedural and substantive dimensions and both should be included in peacemaking and in the peace agreement.

The second approach has two variants, a Realist and a Liberal version. First, there is a Realist approach to peacemaking that denies any necessary link between justice and peace. Second, the Liberal approach to peacemaking, although it does not negate this link in principle, objects to the absolute conditional demand for such a link because it may prevent peace, especially when justice and peace are not compatible and even confront each other. The insistence on this link may therefore become a barrier to conflict resolution. Hence, those who desire to end conflicts peacefully should be wary of absolute demands about the linkage between justice and peace.

This chapter has several aims. First, to explore the reasons for the demand of linking justice to peace as they are presented in different approaches in the field. Second, to examine the implications for linking justice to peace on peace negotiations, concluding a peace agreement, and its implementation, as well as on the stabilization of a peace agreement, its durability, and the prospects of reconciliation. Third, to explore alternative ways about how to balance the relationship between justice and peace, in order to bring about the completion of a peace agreement as well as to guarantee its durability over the long term.

I organize the discussion in the following order: First, I introduce the concepts of justice and injustice. Second, I discuss the approaches that endorse an explicit link between justice and peace. Third, I present the approaches that oppose linking justice with peace. Fourth, I examine different ideas about how to balance between justice and peace when the two concepts clash and contradict each other. Finally, I suggest linking justice to reconciliation instead of peacemaking because justice, although intrinsically related to reconciliation, is not essential to the earlier stages of conflict resolution, and the insistence of including justice in it becomes a barrier to reaching peace in the first place.

What is there between justice and injustice?

Justice is the quality of being just; the quality of being correct or right; righteousness, equitableness, or moral rightness; upholding the justice of a cause; the moral principle determining just conduct; fair representation of facts; vindictive retribution; conformity to right relationships; making things right; honesty; impartiality; rectifying the wrong; restitution; and fairness (the definitions are taken from Rh Value Publishing 1994, 776, 993; Lederach 1997, 28).

Justice and truth are the first virtues of human activities, as natural characteristics of human interactions. Justice is nevertheless a "contested concept," that is, not necessarily a universal, objective, and agreed concept, but a subjective and relative one, which has different understandings, interpretations, and applications (Gallie 1955–56; Garver 1987; Swanton 1985). As a contested concept, justice involves endless disputes about its proper uses on the part of its users, and these disputes "cannot be settled by appeal to empirical evidence, linguistic usage, or the canons of logic alone." Moreover, such disputes are "perfectly genuine," "not resolvable by argument," and "nevertheless sustained by perfectly respectable arguments and evidence" (Gallie 1955–56, 169; see also Gray 1977, 344). Indeed, the question of justice arises only where there are competing interests or competing claims. Each party tends "to defend its case with what it claims to be convincing arguments, evidence and other forms of justification" (Gallie 1955–56, 168).

Because of its contested characteristics we need a shared conception of justice, or at least some measure of agreement about its meanings and applications in order to cooperate among individuals and societies. The value and the procedures that define justice may develop by negotiations among the conflicting parties. In the absence of an agreement or shared understanding on what is just and unjust, individuals and societies will fail not only to cooperate, or to coordinate effectively their interaction, but will find themselves in a conflict situation (Deutsch 1985, 6–9; Rawls 1999a, 3–11).

The conceptualizations of justice are influenced by the specific context and situation, and by the interpretations and expectations in the initial situation. There are many interpretations of what a just situation is. Therefore, there is a need to formulate the criteria to identify what sort of situations can be defined as just or unjust (Rawls 1999a, 14 and 47; Campbell 2000). For instance, justice generally refers to a certain distribution of goods (distributive justice), and the way such distribution is effected (procedural justice). The relationship between the kind and the procedure of the distribution links justice with fairness or, in Rawls's terms, "justice as fairness." The principles of justice are then the result of a fair agreement or bargaining. Justice as fairness "conveys the idea that the principles of justice are agreed to in an initial situation that is fair" (Rawls 1999a, 11).

Justice requires the recognition of certain basic needs. The notion of needs tends to be controversial when it is culturally defined and when needs are converted into rights, imposing demands on other people. Therefore, the sense of "absolute needs or rights" ignores the differences in needs and rights between different people and different cultures (Solomon 1995, 187–93).

Although Rawls in his *Theory of Justice* applies the idea of justice mainly to individuals within a given society, in his book *The Law of Peoples* he extends his conceptions of right and justice to the relations between constitutional liberal democracies. These peoples are peculiar in that "their basic needs are met and their fundamental interests are fully compatible with those of other democratic peoples. There is a true peace among them because all societies are satisfied with status quo for the right reasons"(Rawls 1999b, 3).[1]

The major principles of *The Law of Peoples*, which are roughly similar to those enshrined by international law include the following:

1 Peoples are free and independent, and their freedom and independence are to be respected by other peoples.
2 Peoples are to observe treaties and undertakings.
3 Peoples are equal and are parties to the agreements that bind them.
4 Peoples are to observe a duty of non-intervention.
5 Peoples have the right of self-defense but no right to instigate war for reasons other than self-defense.
6 Peoples have to honor human rights.
7 Peoples are to observe certain specified restrictions in the conduct of war.
8 Peoples have a duty to assist other peoples living under unfavorable conditions that prevent them from having a just or decent political and social regime (according to Rawls, this principle is especially controversial).

(Rawls 1999b, 37)

All these principles must satisfy the criterion of reciprocity (Rawls 1999b, 41). In this context, Rawls maintains that the demands of distributive justice do not apply to the society of peoples (i.e. the international society). In his own words, "inequalities are not always unjust, and that when they are, it is because of their unjust effects on the basic structure of the Society of Peoples, and on relations among peoples and their members" (Rawls 1999b, 113).

Injustice is the quality or fact of being unjust; inequality; violations of rights of others; unjust or unfair action or treatment; an unjust act; a wrong; and unfairness (defined in Rh Value Publishing 1994, 733). People develop a sense of injustice when they have been wronged, or when they feel that they are denied promised benefits, or when they do not get what they believe that they deserve, or when they are deprived of their rights and needs.

The sense of injustice may develop as "a reaction to a perceived discrepancy between entitlements and benefits" (Lerner 1981, 12–13). In other words, a perceived discrepancy develops between what an individual obtains and what he or she is entitled to obtain. The greater the extent of relative deprivation the more intense will be the sense of injustice. "The intensity of the sense of injustice is also undoubtedly influenced by the prior experience and future anticipation of relative deprivation" (Deutsch 1985, 51).

People's feelings of injustice are not only a function of their objective situation, but also a result of psychological factors (Solomon 1995, 4–6, 30–33, 187–91; Deutsch 2000, 41–52). Awareness of the injustice consists of a constellation of feelings and is cultivated mainly from negative emotions such as outrage, anger, indignation, envy, resentment, depression, disappointment, humiliation, vengeance, a sense of helplessness, and all other passions that people feel when they have been deprived of their rights and basic needs. People are likely to feel humiliated both by the circumstances of the situation and by the inability to change it. Nevertheless, people may also develop in this adverse situation positive emotions such as self-esteem, a sense of power, and pride when they act to eliminate injustice and to correct it.

In a complex and often conflicting set of feelings that vary within the context of alternative normative judgments, justice "is not simply an application of a clearly defined, already established and internalized set of rational principles" (Solomon 1995, 172). When people feel that they are in an unjust situation they might develop a strong justice motive to correct it. This justice motive is defined as "the drive to correct a perceived discrepancy between entitlements and benefits" (Welch 1993, 20). For the justice motive to lead to an action, whether or not those perceptions are accurate is entirely a non-relevant issue. Even an unfounded perception may trigger the justice motive. The justice motive can move people to "extremes of self-sacrifice in order to promote justice"; sometimes they act even "out of raw-interest" regardless of the inherent costs to themselves (Lerner 1981, 13). Perceived claims of justice and injustice will focus on the satisfaction of these claims, even at the cost of the exclusion of other concerns, which might sometimes be even more crucial and immediate.

Welch mentions that the sense of injustice and the motive to correct it differs from an aversion of losses or securing gains in three significant aspects. First, it triggers a unique emotional response, which contains a powerful passion that increases the stridency of demands, amplifying intransigence, reducing sensitivity to threats and value-tradeoffs, and increasing the willingness to take risks including those of violence. Second, it differs prescriptively in terms of behavior. Third, it tends to be categorical and deontological rather than utilitarian; thus, nothing short of full satisfaction is accepted (Welch 1993, 20).

When people believe themselves wronged, they see this as the sole responsibility of others. They tend to see themselves as victims of injustice and blame others for their suffering and humiliation. They demand not only a recognition of the other side's responsibility for the injustice done to them, but also its acceptance of the validity of rights infringed and needs that were deprived, as well as the correction of the wrong. Victims of injustice tend to look for compensation and retaliation. The demands are perceived as just, fair, and honest, so victims are unwilling to negotiate or compromise about them. Compensation is likely to be the most popular demand because it not only benefits the victim for the loss, but it also restores to some degree a lost equality. When compensation is denied, the victim may look for extreme personal means to correct injustice and get satisfaction, including vengeful violence. For instance, retaliation is perceived as a legitimate way to redress the injustice. However, when the victim is not sufficiently powerful to obtain compensation or to retaliate, it justifies its weakness as an outcome of its victimization (Deutsch 1985, 22).

What makes the sense of justice regarding some rights so essential is the fact that it remains stable and it consolidates over time, and, the more it is discussed, mentioned, and stimulated, the more it is entrenched in people's minds. People become more committed to it and refuse to compromise over it. The sense of justice gives people a feeling of rightness about their case that others cannot reasonably reject, and justification for their attitudes and behavior. While people are keenly aware of their own concern for justice, they tend to ignore the other's concern for justice, showing lack of empathy. Thus, they regard the other's sense of justice as distorted by its self-interest, ideological motives, and other biases (Bland and Ross 2008).

Justice is often perceived as a deontological and imperative norm, as a protected value that does not accept any delay, deviation, negotiation, or compromise. Its demands must be met before any other objectives or values can be pursued.[2] The primacy of justice can neither be debated nor questioned.

Why link peace to justice?

Linking peace to justice is an old normative demand. It seems natural, normal, and necessary that peace and justice should coincide as is recalled in the Bible, in Psalms 85:10 "*Mercy* and *truth* are met together; *justice* and *peace* have kissed." Lederach, who refers to these four concepts as "a conceptual framework for reconciliation" (not as a conceptual framework for peace), maintains that justice represents the "search for individual and group rights, for social restructuring, and restitution" and it is linked with peace, "which underscores the need for interdependence, well-being, and security" (Lederach 1997, 29).

Article 3 of the UN Charter also emphasizes the link between peace and justice but adds to them the concept of security: "All members shall settle their international disputes by peaceful means, in such a manner that international peace and security, and justice are not endangered."

We can differentiate between two current approaches that insist on strongly linking peace with justice. The first approach places emphasis on *procedural justice*, while the second approach advances *transitional justice*.

The procedural justice approach

The procedural justice approach argues that peace negotiation and peace agreement should be managed by principles of justice, equality, and fairness. Negotiations and peace should be based on voluntary acceptance, without the use of threats or rewards, and without any coercion and imposition, and even without exploiting asymmetrical power relations, while applying the principles of procedural justice and distributive justice (Albin 2001; Deutsch 2000,

41–44). Justice and fairness are “what can freely be agreed on the equally well-placed parties,” in the sense of being able to veto an agreement (Barry 1995, 51).

Concerns about justice should be included in the negotiations and in the peace agreement, since “such concerns provide the lenses through which information is evaluated and preferences determined” (Bazerman and Neale 1995, 106). These concerns are especially raised by negotiations involving asymmetrical power relations, since they may enable the strong side to exploit its power for maximizing its gains at the expense of the weak side. Indeed, the weak side will often question whether the structure and the process of negotiations could produce anything fair and just, because of its inability to advance its interests and to guarantee a balanced agreement. Therefore, according to this view, the link of justice to peace is crucial in asymmetrical power relations, and it should be based on principles of procedural justice, distributive justice, and compliance to commitments taken in the agreement (Albin 2001; Deutsch 2000).

The principles of procedural justice include the following elements: fair treatment; respect and dignity; a freely agreed and balanced negotiation process, such as agenda-setting and the nature and ordering of issues to be negotiated; the structure of the negotiation (balancing power relations by a veto power of the weaker side, free choice of the participants); and fair negotiation procedures (freedom of introducing inputs, claims, and proposals, and rejecting proposals without being subjected to coercion).

Agreements are just and fair if and when they are based on terms agreed by the parties, and they must be mutually beneficial. According to Barry, “the rules of justice are those that would be advantageous to all if generally adhered to it” (Barry 1995, 48). Justice, therefore, is based on mutual advantage as well as on reciprocity. Reciprocity is an essential criterion for justice. “Justice as reciprocity” combines mutual advantage “as the criterion for rules with a motive for keeping them as a sense of fair play” (Barry 1995, 46; Gibbard 1990, 261–64). Reciprocity also requires mutual responsiveness to each other’s concessions.

Linking justice to peace is also based on principles of *distributive justice*, such as identical or comparable gains and costs (equal concessions, equal sacrifices, comparable exchange of concessions). Linking justice to peace refers also to the implementation phase of the agreement. Compliance with the commitments taken according to the content and the spirit of the agreement is an integral part of justice making (Albin 2001, 9–10, 25). In this regard, the weak side has a veto power over negotiations and over the signing of a peace agreement. Thus, without its willingness no agreement is possible.

The transitional justice approach

The transitional justice approach argues that linking justice to peace is required especially when one side’s or both sides’ basic rights, needs, and identity were violently deprived or violated by the other side throughout the conflict. The link between justice and peace is a necessary condition for coping with historical injustice. Without redressing the injustice of the past and correcting it, it is impossible to end a conflict and to make peace, or to stabilize peace relations and/or to secure reconciliation.[3]

When the issue of justice is at the core of the conflict and it is not dealt with, either substantively or procedurally, the conflict will continue and might escalate. While substantive ways to address a conflict mean resolving past and present grievances, procedural ways are mechanisms for handling mutual claims of justice through peaceful means (Zartman 2005a, 2). The demand for justice contains three necessary and sequent steps: recognition and taking responsibility for the injustice done; apology and asking for forgiveness; and correcting the injustice caused to the victim's side.

In sum, both approaches that promote linking justice to peace contain demands for procedural and corrective justice. Linking justice to peace is not limited only to principles of distributive justice such as equal share or equality of outcomes in a peace agreement, but it "represents the search for individual and group rights, for social restructuring, and for restitution" (Lederach 1997, 29).[4] Justice becomes also an issue of values, principles, and legitimacy. Linking justice to peace tends to be a part of one's identity and collective memory and interpretation of history. Linking justice to peace turns justice into a sacred or a protected value, a taboo value, and the only criterion for judging the quality of peace and justifying it over the long term. Therefore, it cannot be negotiated and compromised. A protected or a sacred value is defined as "any value that a moral community implicitly or explicitly treats as possessing infinite or transcendental significance that precludes comparisons, trade-offs, or indeed any other mingling with bounded or secular values" (Tetlock *et al.* 2000, 853).

The consideration of the justice and injustice narratives in peacemaking as protected values makes them sacred, resisting trade-offs with other competing values (Baron and Spranca 1997; Tetlock 2003; Atran *et al.* 2007; Atran and Axelrod 2008; Bazerman *et al.* 2008; Hanselmann and Tanner 2008). The literature suggests that such values arise from deontological rules concerning action; therefore, they are absolute ones. Absoluteness means resistance to trade-offs. In other words, people feel duty, moral obligation, and commitment to protect their justice values. They will be concerned that their participation in peace negotiations may bring them to trade off their justice values or to concede them in return for other values (peace, independence). Thus, people may refuse any action that will endanger the sanctity of their values of justice mainly because they are the sources of their social and national identity, and because they believe that protecting them enhances their image in their own eyes and in the eyes of others. People may refer to their justice values as protected values also because they mistrust others or their own political leadership to be strong enough not to concede them, so that protecting them will avoid some form of "moral contamination" (Baron and Spranca 1997; Tetlock 2003; Margalit 2010).

Why not to link justice to peace

The theories that deny any particular link between peace and justice or make that link conditional upon more important considerations include Realist and Liberal approaches to negotiations and to peacemaking. While a Realist approach to negotiations and peacemaking denies any necessary link between peace and justice, a Liberal approach sees the link as a reasonable and logical one. However, Liberals (or at least some strands of Liberalism), have serious doubts and reservations about the concept of "just peace" and making the link between peace and justice conditional for concluding peace in the first place.

The Realist approach to negotiations and to peacemaking

The Realist approach to negotiations and to peacemaking refers mainly to the arguments of procedural justice rather than to those of transitional justice. It argues that the concept of justice used between individuals or between groups in a society is not necessarily relevant or applicable in international (i.e. interstate) relations. In the anarchical realm of international relations, justice and fairness are far from being agreed concepts, so there are no objective criteria for clearly establishing them. Moreover, parties have conflicting conceptions of justice and fairness, and it is almost impossible to reach a consensus about their meaning and about their link with peace. Thus, the Realists' main claim is that parties may agree to conclude an agreement because of their (national) interests and for reasons other than justice or fairness.

For Realists, the natural motivation of actors in international negotiations is to act according to their own interest, while taking advantage of their power resources in order to maximize gains, without sharing expected outcomes in an equal or symmetrical basis. At the same time, when agreements are freely and voluntarily concluded they should be implemented and respected by the parties concerned. Thus, adherence to voluntary agreements becomes a significant dimension of procedural justice (Snyder and Diesing 1977; Zartman 1995; Albin 2001). Moreover, there is not necessarily a contradiction between self-interest, asymmetrical distribution of power, and justice in negotiated agreement. It is just and fair that the management of negotiations and its outcomes reflect the interests and the bargaining power of the sides (Gauthier 1986). Brian Barry defines this behavior as acting according to the principles of justice as a theory of mutual advantage, which "prescribes that the amount received by the parties under the settlement must reflect their relative bargaining power" (Barry 1995, 33, 39–40).

The Realist approach is a rational and self-interested one, so that the concept of justice might be relevant only to sides who are more or less equal in their power. Nevertheless, if the negotiations are free of coercion and do not reflect appeasement, in asymmetrical power relations even a weak party has the veto power to reject an unfair solution according to its views. Therefore, it is not necessarily true that the strong side always succeeds in maximizing its gains in international agreements. Studies prove that the weak side succeeds in gaining even more than the strong one, especially when it exploits effectively its veto power (Zartman and Rubin 2000). Moreover, when conflicting justice principles are at the core of the negotiations, power asymmetries tend to be less relevant in the bargaining because the weak side's commitment to its principles augments its power (Albin 2001, 38).

The Liberal approach to negotiations and to peacemaking

In contrast to the Realist approach, the Liberal approach to negotiations and to peacemaking perceives peace and peacemaking as essential values in human and international relations. However, Liberals tend to reject the terminology of "just peace" and any conditional link between peace and justice making the former subservient to the latter. The Liberal approach recognizes that a tension may emerge between peace and justice; however, in case of a potential clash between these two it is preferable to gain peace and to pay with justice because peace should have precedence over justice (Margalit 2010, 1).

Margalit maintains that, while political philosophers have dealt with the notion of a lasting and durable peace, they hardly refer to the notion of just peace, probably because they feel that the "idea of just peace may be the enemy of the notion just (i.e., simply) a peace."[5] Thus, Liberals realize that peace does not need justification. While war needs justification "peace is by that very fact justified" (Margalit 2010, 79). Peace and peacemaking "seem so good and just in and of themselves [and], there is no need for justification" (Margalit 2010, 9).

The attempt to differentiate between just and unjust peace departs from the differentiation between just and unjust war. There is no necessary parallel between the opposite terms of war and peace. Thus, "we should not view the theory of just peace as the mere flip side of the theory of just war" (Margalit 2010, 80). Any attempt to create an independent debate between just and unjust peace is wrong and may damage the idea of peacemaking and peace in the first place. The use of the concept of just peace is especially wrong because it frames peace with a prescriptive sense that means an "ideal type of peace."

Since there is not an ideal type of just peace, any attempt to frame it as such and to impose it will be a further source of conflict (Beilin 2006, 130; Roberts 2006, 58; Margalit 2010, 1). Thus, separating between peace and just peace diminishes the value of peace. The use of the language of "just peace" makes the conduct of international relations more difficult and even more dangerous to deal with. Throughout the course of history and into the present, states as well as non-state actors, such as terrorist organizations, often justify their decisions to employ force by using the language of justice and acting in the name of just peace (Roberts 2006, 58; Beilin 2006, 130–31).

Furthermore, the evaluation of what is considered "just" is often biased by self-interest. The resulting conflict in perceptions of what constitutes a just agreement may create barriers to the formulation and implementation of peace. In various circumstances, it may appear to one or both sides that not making peace because it seems unjust is justified; however, later on it becomes clear that greater injustice lay in not making peace. Thus, "the price paid by both sides for abstaining from making peace at junctions where such an act was possible, because it seemed unjust, was too dear and demonstrated the danger that lies in using the expression unjust peace" (Beilin 2006, 131).

The insistence on unilateral interpretations of justice may become a significant barrier for conflict resolution, if not an excuse for not concluding peace. Insistence on justice may cause a missed opportunity for peace. Therefore, "the more ambitious goal of linking justice with peace can lead to smaller chances for success. Indeed, it may derail the whole enterprise and keep the flames of violent conflict active through the search for justice" (Allan and Keller 2006a, 2). Insistence on justice may cause a war or its escalation, "striving for justice may imply a just war or at least 'justifiable' violence" (Allan and Keller 2006a, 1). Indeed, as Margalit maintains, "there is a difference between just peace and *justifiable* peace; not every injustice justifies going to war" (Margalit 2010, 9; see also Kamm 2001).

Nevertheless, the question remains as to how far one side or both (or more) sides in a conflict will be ready to go for peace by giving up on justice. Margalit answers "quite a distance … but not the whole way" (Margalit 2010, 8). Some injustice must be tolerated to maintain peace and prevent war (Margalit 2010, 79; Kamm 2001). Similarly, Bland and Ross (2008) sustain that

> while a minimal sense of justice is [a] significant aspect of any durable peace, the struggle for justice by one or both sides is apt to be counterproductive. In our experience, it is best to direct initial attention away from conflicting claims about history and the entitlements that arise from past losses.

However, there are some cases in which one should prefer justice to peace: "Only crimes against humanity … crimes against the possibility of morality, should trump peace in all circumstances and should never be recognized in a compromise" (quoted in Margalit 2010, 8 and 67).

Based on findings from psychological experiments, experts on negotiations warn that concerns about justice and fairness can promote irrationality in the way that peacemakers make decisions and in implementing and deepening the peace process. Such concerns can also lead to inefficiency, such that both parties are worse off as a result of justice considerations (Bazerman and Neale, 1995). Historical data confirm these findings. Justice motives of decision makers tend to be cognitive-simple in an analysis of a conflict situation. They are insensitive to new information, so they tend to make cognitive errors. They are less responsive to negotiations, more difficult to persuade, and less likely to compromise in finding solutions to conflicts based on value trade-offs, since their demands that entitlements be respected are absolute and categorical ones. Thus, motivations of justice become a significant factor for the continuation of the conflict (Welch 1993, 31–32).

The real danger is making justice holy, sacred, and a protected value (a taboo). When the relation between justice and peace is presented as a relation between holiness and peace, then "peace is incompatible with the acceptance of injustice. Temporary peace can suffer injustice, but permanent peace should not" (Margalit 2010, 80). Moreover, the question is how can we be sure whether the demands for justice are sincere or an excuse for not concluding a peace agreement? Thus, a party who is not ripe for peaceful resolution may exploit the injustice caused to it in order to prolong the conflict.

Linking justice to peace becomes even more problematic when two historical injustices confront each other, each bearing opposite historical interpretations and narratives about what happened and with opposite conceptualizations about how to correct the past injustice. The real problem in most historical conflicts is precisely that both sides are actually right in one way or another (or at least, they are partially right in their conflicting claims). No negotiated settlement will correct all such injustices to the satisfaction of the parties. Therefore, looking for an agreement that satisfies entirely both sides' sense of justice and injustice is entirely hopeless (Bland and Ross 2008).

Welch summarizes his remarkable study *Justice and the Genesis of War* with the same conclusion:

> The justice motive cannot be harnessed to the cause of peace until the norms of international justice are strong enough to determine entitlements and obligations authoritatively, and until states begin to internalize those determinations and adjust their own claims and expectations accordingly. Until such time … the justice motive, then, will continue to be part of the problem until it can become part of the solution.
>
> (Welch 1993, 210)

Thus, justice in international relations and its link to peace can be significant and play a positive role only when the parties agree about a common meaning. Therefore, "in an absence of agreement on the meaning of justice in a given case, there is no justice or injustice" (Welch 1993, 216).

Similarly, Zartman finds that looking-backward negotiations about past injustices not only are a significant barrier to conflict resolution but they might even lead to war (Zartman 2005b, 291). Therefore,

> it is clear that in many cases forward-looking peace and justice have been achieved by ignoring demands for backward-looking justice, and that in other cases provisions for handling backward-looking justice have been the price paid for the establishment of forward-looking outcomes.
>
> (Zartman 2005b, 294)

Among other interesting findings there is the priority of concluding peace over accomplishing justice, and making peace as a precondition for justice. In most of the successful peace negotiation cases, the need for peace came first. However, when peace is the promise of justice it "cannot come in such a way as to preclude attention to justice later on," at the stage of reconciliation (Zartman 2005b, 297).

Balancing justice with peace

Reviewing the different approaches that consider linking justice to peace suggests that a concern for justice must be included in the peace negotiations and in the final peace agreement. Thus, considerations of justice cannot be excluded from a successful peace process. Although including the issue of justice in the peacemaking can undermine the prospects of concluding peace, it cannot be simply ignored altogether.

At the same time, both sides should be aware that there is no ideal solution to the question of justice in peacemaking, especially when two claims of justice confront each other, whereas in many historical conflicts both sides are actually partially right "at least in the bill of particulars they offer in support of the injustice they claim to have suffered" (Bland and Ross 2008). Moreover, in such a case no one has the monopoly on the justice issue and no one has the only truth about it.

Since justice is also perceptual and socially constructed, much depends on how decision makers politically and socially value the peace negotiations and agreement. In this sense, the relevant question remains: How to find a common formula and fair balance that satisfies both sides' conception of justice, while recognizing that both have to compromise some of their just claims for the sake of peace? In the absence of a certain measure of agreement between the sides on what is just and unjust, it is clearly more difficult, if not impossible, for the sides to conclude a peace agreement. Without a shared conception of justice, the sides may fail to resolve a conflict. In such a case, linking justice to peace may foil the possibility of concluding a peace agreement, so justice becomes a barrier to conflict resolution.

Yet, there is a major difference between the requirements for procedural justice and those for corrective (or transitional) justice. It seems that the demands for procedural justice are easier to handle than those of corrective and transitional justice, because they are limited mainly to questions of asymmetrical power relations. Both sides can design together a fair procedure regarding the process, structure, and outcomes of negotiations. The sides are more able to negotiate a just and fair agreement if they have cooperative rather than a competitive orientation toward each other, and if both have a shared interest in concluding a peace agreement. The involvement of a mediator may balance the power relations and may secure the principles of procedural justice, even when the situation is usually more competitive. In order for the negotiations to be viewed as just and fair, the mediator should effectively use its role in the process by introducing its own proposals (Albin 2001; Deutsch, 1985).

The requirements for corrective justice are, however, much more difficult to reconcile because they are too demanding emotionally, symbolically, and materially, especially when the injustice claim is not recognized by the other side or where injustice claims confront each other. As Said maintains, it is impossible to reach a formula for just peace, in the form of a sentence, "a just peace is so and so," that will be accepted by both sides. He proposes instead to look for "a method for thinking about just peace as a way of getting beyond the usually bipolar oppositions that lock collective antagonists together in conflicts" (Said 2006, 176). Said acknowledges that any conception of a just peace must reflect the differences between the parties, recognizing that these differences are all "based on actual but widely divergent experiences, and this is one reason why a just peace which in its meaning suggests the stability of something finally achieved is a contradictory or at least fluid, rather than stable concept" (Said 2006, 179).

Bland and Ross share the concern that linking justice to peace may foil the prospects of concluding a peace agreement. They maintain that the real problem lies in a situation of asymmetrical power relations, when the weaker side perceives that every agreement that does not answer its conception of just peace is negative by definition, and only perpetuates its perceived unjust situation. Although the weaker side has to realize that it is difficult, if not impossible, to accomplish completely its own conception of justice, unaddressed injustice feelings and humiliation prevent it from viewing positively the benefits of peace agreement. The feelings of humiliation and indignation cannot be repaired "until considerations of material interest loom larger than such affective considerations" (Bland and Ross 2008).

Since almost every negotiated peace agreement imposes losses and injustices on both parties, the crucial question, as Bland and Ross maintain, is not whether peace is completely just but whether the benefits of peace outweigh the limitations of imperfect justice. In other words, how should we reconcile and legitimize the necessary idea of trading off some justice for the benefits of peace? What are the moral limits for such a trade-off? Is it legitimate to trade some justice, which is part of one's values and identity, for the sake of material needs that only a peace agreement can provide? These are indeed complex questions with no simple answers. Much depends on the characteristics of the injustice perpetrated to one or more of the parties concerned, its current operational implications, such as suffering and humiliation, and the promised and expected benefits of peace.

Margalit (2006, 2010) draws the line between legitimate and illegitimate deals by focusing on the humiliation issue. Humiliation is a formative experience, which shapes the way that people view themselves as humiliated and having failed. Margalit actually sets a very high bar for rejecting peace proposals that look unjust. In his view, unless such an agreement treats one of the parties as less than equal, or perpetuates its humiliation and even inhuman status, a peace agreement should merit positive consideration. Negotiated agreement that can secure a better status and improve everyday lives of people legitimizes the need to compromise on some injustice (Margalit 2002). Hence, compromises made for the sake of peace even at the expense of justice are necessary because of the high moral significance of peace (Margalit 2010).

Bland and Ross also suggest that, when there are different types of injustices at different times, the parties should seek to correct the most serious current injustices instead of those of the past because the current ones are probably more painful and require immediate solutions. An additional creative solution available to the rival parties is to present a more modest goal of linking justice to peace that will correct some of the injustice, but will not resolve it entirely. Thus, parties that cannot accept, in principle, the requirements of entirely correcting past injustices can at least recognize the other's suffering as just, and may even agree to reduce some of the suffering rather than resolving the issue of injustice entirely.

Bland and Ross's suggestions are creative and reasonable. They are based on some cost-benefit calculations that perceive the benefits of peace as exceeding the costs of justice, particularly in a situation of conflicting claims of justice, within a lingering situation of suffering and humiliation. However, this reasonable way of calculation is possible only when one or both parties agree to reframe their conceptualization of justice in terms of interests rather than a sacred value. Whereas justice as a protected value cannot be negotiated or compromised, the reframing of justice in terms of interests can be indeed negotiated and compromised. Once the issue turns from just entitlement to deal making, then the matter becomes one of cost–benefit calculation and a practical, pragmatic transaction.

Another potential solution is trading injustice claims that are presented as protected values. Although trading protected values is very difficult to realize, the fact that both sides make crucial sacrifices may reassure both of them that the value trading is just and fair. The parties are more willing to give up on a claim of injustice that is defined as a taboo value or a protected value when they realize that the other side does the same. When each side sees the other's losses as real and painful, then it may be able to accept its own losses. When losses of claims of injustices are perceived as mutual and balanced, then the agreement may be seen as a more just and fair (Bland and Ross 2008).

The idea of justice as a balanced settlement of conflict claims requires a measure of mutuality and reciprocity not necessarily of the same size but of roughly similar value. Framing the peace negotiations and agreement as a mutually agreed trade-off of losses between the parties (alongside a sharing of potential benefits), and developing commitment to the agreement as the most reasonable alternative for both sides can influence the balance of satisfaction in the direction of durable peace. A better way of linking justice to peace is probably when the sides recognize each other's identities, renounce some basic demands, and accept to abide by common rules jointly developed (Allan and Keller 2006b, 195).

Mutual satisfaction tends to guarantee the maintenance of peace. Aron defines this condition as *peace by satisfaction* (Aron 1966, 144). Mutual satisfaction does not necessarily require equal or symmetrical outcomes, especially where individual and joint outcomes are evaluated separately. Each side may perceive satisfaction based on its earlier expectations and on discrepancy between earlier expectations and the negotiations' outcomes.

Satisfaction should not be limited only to the decision makers or to the ruling political or military elites, but should also include most of the political, economic, and social elites, as well as other sectors of the population. Wide satisfaction with the negotiating process and with the agreement will legitimize the peace agreement and minimize the influence of those who are less or not satisfied with the agreement. However, the failure of decision makers to require the necessary legitimacy for an agreement that requires conceding what is termed as justice for the sake of peace may foil the prospects of peacemaking (Bar-Siman-Tov 1994; Kacowicz 1998; Rothstein 1999). When there is no consensus in the society as to the need to concede justice for peace because it is perceived as an act of betrayal of a protected value, then there is not much room for conflict resolution. Compromising justice for the sake of peace because of weakness or historical necessity will not secure a durable peace in the long term. When the sole justification of a peace agreement is that there was "no other alternative" or "no other choice" then there is no real satisfaction to respect and carry on such an agreement. This kind of a peace agreement will be liked more as a truce rather than a genuine peace (Margalit 2010, 77–79).

Linking justice to reconciliation

The failure of the parties to share a common concept of justice, or sacrificing some justice for the sake of peace, or reframing their just values, or trading them will foil the prospects of concluding a peace agreement. If in this case the sides are still interested in reaching a peace agreement, they should consider the possibility of leaving the issue of justice to the later reconciliation stage in their relations, after formal peace is achieved.

In order to guarantee dealing with the injustice issue in the reconciliation stage, the sides should consider its formal inclusion in the peace agreement itself. A paragraph stating the mutual commitment to look for a compromise solution to the justice issues later on, following the implementation of the peace agreement, may help the sides to overcome the barrier to a peace agreement. The conclusion of a peace agreement and its implementation to the satisfaction of both sides will enable the sides to build trust and to ease the process of reconciliation that will require them to cope with the issue of justice later on. Nevertheless, even at the reconciliation stage, it is unrealistic to expect that one side's justice concept will be accepted as the single and objective truth, and the sides probably will need to negotiate different kinds of justice: substantive (fundamental needs of both sides), future (just institutions, arrangements, and relationships), procedural (fair and reciprocal process of negotiations), and emotional (a significant degree of a just outcome) (Kelman 2004, 123).

Reconciliation will also require consideration by each side of its responsibility for the wrong done to the other in the course of the conflict, as well as the need for an acknowledgment of the injustice, and its implications in terms of apology and compensation. Nevertheless, as Kelman maintains, "the acknowledgment of responsibility cannot be based entirely on an objective set of legal or moral norms, but requires a process of negotiation in which different types of responsibility are identified and agreed upon" (Kelman 2004, 124). This is quite true especially when both sides are responsible for the injustice done, in one way or another, and they share the blame. Therefore, a mutual process of reconciliation based on mutual acknowledgment and apology is required.

A failure to reach a reconciliation agreement to the satisfaction of both sides may endanger the peace agreement, and the sides should consider this possibility as a constraint on the peace durability. This may encourage them to moderate or to reduce claims of injustice or to be more responsive to the other's claims in order not to endanger the peace. Much depends also on the material benefits of the peace relations. If these appear to be substantial, then the sides will prefer not to endanger them. However, if the dividends of peace are low and they do not satisfactorily answer their initial expectations, the issue of the past injustice may serve as an excuse for ending the peace relations, or leaving them at the initial stages of negative or precarious peace only.

Conclusions

Linking justice to peace or the demand for "just peace" is necessary in conflicts where one or two sides were deprived of their needs and rights, especially in protracted conflicts. Even when the sides to a protracted conflict have an interest in peacefully resolving their conflict, they sometimes fail to satisfy one or both sides or overcome the bitterness and grievances inherent in a protracted conflict because of perceived feelings of injustice.

Although the sides cannot ignore the past injustice and it should be part of the peace negotiations, linking justice to peace as a precondition for concluding a peace agreement tends to be a barrier to conflict resolution, especially in cases where both sides present conflicting claims of injustice. In such cases, there are alternative ways for balancing justice and peace requirements; however, most of them cannot entirely resolve the injustice problem, and sometimes they may perpetuate the feelings of injustice.

This study suggests that the issue of the past injustice should be included within the framework of the peace agreement, but its implementation should be deferred to the reconciliation phase only, after formally making peace. This should be the case at least when it seems that, because of the bitterness and the grievances, the sides are not emotionally mature enough to deal with the issue of the injustice in the peacemaking stage. Indeed, the literature on reconciliation regards the coping with past injustice as a basic and elementary part of the reconciliation process and not of the peacemaking. The implied assumption behind this conception is not only the fact that the sides are not ripe enough to deal with the injustice in the peacemaking stage, but also that there is a need to resolve the conflict and to put an end to the continued suffering of the sides. Building peace and producing benefits of peace make peace more attractive and ease the process of coping with the past injustice in the aftermath of the peace agreement. The case of Western Europe after World War II, in which past injustices were left aside while increasing the cooperation and the exchange among the parties, is an effective model of dealing with past injustice. After 1945, insisting on linking justice to peace could have foiled not only the establishment of peace in Europe but also the prospects of building the European community.

Notes

1 Rawls elaborates here upon Raymond Aron's concept of "peace by satisfaction." See Aron 1966.
2 Editor's note: Thus, it is a precondition to any further action, a "first principle." See Arkes 1986.
3 Editor's note: The author uses the concept of "traditional justice" by clearly drawing the distinction between "procedural justice" and "transitional justice." At the same time, "transitional justice" in broader terms refers to a whole field in international relations, political science, and law with a vast literature that assesses the mechanisms and procedures of coping with past injustices, including gross violations of human rights, especially in domestic conflicts and civil wars. It includes the establishment of international and national tribunals and courts of justice, reconciliation committees, reparations, and apologies. The field of transitional justice generally refers to five components: justice, truth, reconciliation, reparations, and (political) reforms. See among others Teitel 2000; Bell, Campbell and Ní Aoláin 2004; Roht-Arriaza and Mariezcurrena 2006; Sikkink 2012. The editor thanks Lior Lehrs for his comments on this point.
4 Editor's note: In general, a good agreement is one that restores a previous situation (status quo) before an aggression takes place, rather than the one that distributes half and half what is under dispute. The editor thanks Daniel Schwartz for his comments on this point.
5 Editor's note: Some political philosophers have addressed the important issue of the justice related to the conclusion of peace treaties. See for instance Schwartz 2011.

References

Albin, Cecilia. *Justice and Fairness in International Negotiations* (Cambridge: Cambridge University Press, 2001).
Allan, Pierre. "Measuring International Ethics: A Moral Scale of War, Peace, Justice, and Global Care." In *What is a Just Peace?* (eds) Pierre Allan and Alexis Keller. (Oxford: Oxford University Press, 2006), pp. 90–129.
Allan, Pierre and Alexis Keller. "Introduction: Rethinking Peace and Justice Conceptually." In *What is a Just Peace?* (eds) Pierre Allan and Alexis Keller. (Oxford: Oxford University Press, 2006a), pp. 1–11.

Allan, Pierre and Alexis Keller. "The Concept of a Just Peace, or Achieving Peace Through Recognition, Renouncement, and Rule." In *What is a Just Peace?* (eds) Pierre Allan and Alexis Keller (Oxford: Oxford University Press, 2006b), pp. 195–215.

Arkes, Hadley. *First Things: An Inquiry into the First Principles of Morals and Justice* (Princeton, NJ: Princeton University Press, 1986).

Aron, Raymond. *Peace and War: A Theory of International Relations* (New York: Doubleday, 1966).

Atran, Scott and Robert Axelrod. "Reframing Sacred Values," *Negotiation Journal*, Vol. 24, 3 (2008), pp. 221–46.

Atran, Scott, Robert Axelrod, and Richard Davis. *Science*, Vol. 317, 5841 (2007), pp. 1039–40.

Baron, Jonathan and Mark Spranca. "Protected Values," *Organizational Behavior and Human Decision Processes*, Vol. 70, 1 (1997), pp. 1–16.

Barry, Brian. *Justice as Impartiality* (Oxford: Clarendon Press, 1995).

Bar-Siman-Tov, Yaacov. *Israel and the Peace Process: In Search of Legitimacy to Peace* (Albany: SUNY Press, 1994).

Bazerman, M. H. and M. A. Neale. "The Role of Fairness, Considerations and Relationship in a Judgmental Perspective of Negotiation." In *Barriers to Conflict Resolution* (eds) Kenneth Arrow *et al.*, (New York: Norton, 1995), pp. 87–106.

Bazerman, M. H., Ann Tenbrunsel, and Kimberly Wade-Benzoni. "When Sacred Issues Are at Stake," *Negotiation Journal*, Vol. 24, 1 (2008), pp. 113–17.

Beilin, Yossi. "Just Peace: A Dangerous Objective." In *What is a Just Peace?* (eds) Pierre Allan and Alexis Keller (Oxford: Oxford University Press, 2006), pp. 130–48.

Bell, Christine, Colm Campbell, and Fionnuala Ní Aoláin. "Justice Discourse in Transition," *Social and Legal Studies*, Vol. 13, 3 (2004), pp. 305–28.

Bland, Byron and Lee Ross. "Relational Barriers: Reflections on Peacemaking" (unpublished article, August 27, 2008.)

Campbell, Tom D. *Justice: Issues in Political Theory* (New York: Palgrave-Macmillan, 2000).

Deutsch, Morton. *Distributive Justice: A Social-Psychological Perspective* (New York: Yale University Press, 1985).

Deutsch, Morton. "Justice and Conflict." In *The Handbook of Conflict Resolution: Theory and Practice* (eds) Morton Deutsch and Peter T. Coleman (San Francisco, CA: Jossey-Bass Publication, 2000), pp. 41–64.

Gallie, W. B. "Essentially Contested Concepts," *Proceedings of the Aristotelian Society Series*, Vol. 56 (1955–56): pp. 167–98.

Garver, Eugene. "Paradigms and Princes," *Philosophy of the Social Sciences*, Vol. 17, 1 (1987), pp. 21–47.

Gauthier, David. *Morals by Agreement* (Oxford: Clarendon Press, 1986).

Gibbard, Allan. *Wise Choices, Apt Feelings: A Theory of Normative Judgment* (Oxford: Clarendon Press 1990).

Gray, J. N. "On the Contestability of Social And Political Concepts," *Political Theory*, Vol. 5, 3 (1977), pp. 331–48.

Hanselmann, Martin and Carmen Tanner. "Taboos and Conflicts in Decision-Making: Sacred Values, Decision Difficulty, and Emotions," *Judgment and Decision Making*, Vol. 3, 19 (2008), pp. 51–63.

Kacowicz, Arie M. *Zones of Peace in the Third World* (Albany: SUNY Press, 1998).

Kamm, F. M. "Making War (and its Continuation) Unjust," *European Journal of Philosophy*, Vol. 9 (2001), pp. 328–43.

Keller, Alexis. "Justice, Peace, and History: A Reappraisal." In *What is a Just Peace?* (eds) Pierre Allan and Alexis Keller (Oxford: Oxford University Press, 2006), pp. 19–51.

Kelman, Herbert C. "Reconciliation as Identity Change." In *From Conflict Resolution to Reconciliation* (ed.) Yaacov Bar-Siman-Tov. (New York: Oxford University Press, 2004), pp. 111–24.

Lederach, John P. *Building Peace: Sustainable Reconciliation in Divided Societies* (Washington: USIP, 1997).

Lerner, Melvin J. "The Justice Motive in Human Relations." In Melvin J. Lerner and Sally C. Lerner (eds) *The Justice Motive in Social Behavior: Adapting to Times of Scarcity and Change* (New York: Plenum Press, 1981), pp. 1–13.

Margalit, Avishai. *The Ethics of Memory* (Cambridge, MA: Harvard University Press, 2002).

Margalit, Avishai. *The Decent Society* (Cambridge, MA: Harvard University Press, 2006).

Margalit, Avishai. *On Compromise and Rotten Compromise* (Princeton, NJ: Princeton University Press, 2010).

Rawls, John. *A Theory of Justice* (Cambridge, MA: Harvard University Press, revised edition, 1999a).

Rawls, John. *The Laws of Peoples* (Cambridge, MA: Harvard University Press, 1999b)

Rh Value Publishing. *Webster's Encyclopedic Unabridged Dictionary of the English Language* (New York: Gramercy Books, 1994).

Roberts, Adam, Sir. "Just Peace: A Cause Worth Fighting For." In *What is a Just Peace?* (eds) Pierre Allan and Alexis Keller (Oxford: Oxford University Press, 2006), pp. 52–89.

Roht-Arriaza, Naomi and Javier Mariezcurrena (eds). *Transitional Justice in the Twenty-First Century: Beyond Truth versus Justice* (New York: Cambridge University Press, 2006).

Rothstein, Robert L. "In Fear of Peace: Getting Past Maybe." In *After the Peace: Resistance and Reconciliation* (ed.) Robert L. Rothstein (Boulder, CO: Lynne Rienner, 1999), pp. 1–25.

Said, Edward W. "A Method for Thinking about Just Peace." In *What is a Just Peace?* (eds) Pierre Allan and Alexis Keller (Oxford: Oxford University Press, 2006), pp. 176–94.

Schwartz, Daniel. "The Justice of Peace Treaties," *Journal of Political Philosophy*, Vol. 20, 3 (2011), pp. 273–92.

Sikkink, Kathryn. *The Justice Cascade: How Human Rights Prosecutions are Changing World Politics* (New York: W. W. Norton, 2012).

Snyder, Glenn H. and Paul Diesing. *Conflict Among Nations: Bargaining, Decision Making and System Structure* (Princeton, NJ: Princeton University Press, 1977).

Solomon, Robert C. *A Passion for Justice* (Lanham, MD: Rowman & Littlefield, 1995).

Swanton, Christine. "Essentials Contestedness of Political Concepts," *Ethics*, Vol. 85, 4 (1985), pp. 811–27.

Teitel, Ruti. *Transitional Justice* (New York: Oxford University Press, 2000).

Tetlock, Philip E. "Thinking the Unthinkable: Sacred Values and Taboo Cognitions," *Trends in Cognitive Sciences*, Vol. 7, 7 (2003), pp. 320–24.

Tetlock, Philip E., O. V. Kristel, S. B. Elson, M. C. Green, and J. S. Lerner. "The Psychology of the Unthinkable: Taboo Trade-Offs, Forbidden Base Rates, and Heretical Counterfactuals," *Journal of Personality and Social Psychology*, Vol. 78 (2000), pp. 853–70.

Welch, David A. *Justice and the Genesis of War* (Cambridge: Cambridge University Press, 1993).

Zartman, I. William (ed.). *Elusive Peace: Negotiating to End Civil Wars* (Washington, DC: Brookings, 1995).

Zartman, I. William "Negotiating Forward- and Backward-Looking Outcomes." In *Peace Versus Justice: Negotiating Forward- and Backward-Looking Outcomes* (eds) I. William Zartman and Victor Kremenyuk (Lanham, MD: Rowman & Littlefield, 2005a), pp. 1–8.

Zartman, I. William "Looking Forward and Looking Backward on Negotiations Theory." In *Peace Versus Justice: Negotiating Forward and Backward-Looking Outcomes* (eds), I. William Zartman and Victor Kremenyuk (Lanham, MD: Rowman and Littlefield, 2005b), pp. 289–301.

Zartman, I. William and Jeffery Z. Rubin. "The Study of Power and the Practice of Negotiation." In *Power and Negotiation* (eds) I. William Zartman and Jeffrey Z. Rubin (Ann Arbor: The University of Michigan Press, 2000), pp. 3–28.

2 Narratives of justice and injustice in peacemaking

Introduction

In the absence of universal, objective, and accepted criteria for defining just peace or for linking justice to peace in a definitive way, the parties in a protracted conflict develop their own criteria for defining just peace or for linking justice to peace. These criteria are based mainly on each side's historical narratives, collective memories, myths, and ethos. This combination of criteria is a socially constructed phenomenon, which each side develops throughout the conflict according to its own experience, interpretation of the conflict, goals, and needs.

This chapter aims to examine the process in which historical narratives, collective memories, myths, and ethos, emerge to become major criteria for defining just peace or linking justice to peace. Moreover, it assesses the impact of these factors upon peacemaking and reconciliation.

The concept of historical narratives

A narrative

> is a way of organizing episodes, actions, and accounts of actions; it is an achievement that brings together mundane facts and fantastic creations; time and place incorporated. The narratives allow the inclusion of actors' reasons for their acts, as well as the causes of [their] happening.
>
> (Sarbin 1986, 9)

The most essential characteristic of a narrative is the structuring of events in a way that demonstrates coherence and a sense of movement through time. A narrative is successful if it presents a "goal state or valued endpoint" and then "select[s] and arrange[s] events in such a way that the goal state is rendered more or less probable" (Gergen and Gergen 1986, 25–26). People think, perceive, imagine, and make their decisions based on their narratives (Sarbin 1986, 8). The narratives link between a situation and the story schema. Creating a story out of experience "is a heuristic process, one which requires skill, judgment, and experience" (Robinson and Hawpe 1986, 111).

Historical narratives are "a social construction that coherently interrelate a sequence of historical and current events; they are accounts of a community's collective experiences, embodied in its belief system and represent the collective's symbolically constructed shared identity" (Bar-Tal and Salomon 2006, 20). Historical narratives are composed of a unique sequence of events and experiences, whether true or fictitious, real or imaginary. They address issues not only about what happened but also about why it happened and who or what was responsible (White 1978; Shenhav 2005; Tessler 2006).

Narratives are not intended to provide an objective history of the past. They are selective and distorted in ways that meet societal present needs. They offer an intentional interpretation of the events in the past in order to be functional and instrumental, which is the basic rationale for their acceptance. The historical narratives are shared by the society and treated by it as a truthful account of the past and valid history (Brunner 1986, 1990; Jameson 1981; Mink 1978).

The past is a social and political construction due to the concerns of the present and the future. The beliefs, interests, and hopes of the present and the future shape the various perceptions of past history. The conception of the past is aimed to cope with and resolve present and future problems. The past is not preserved just for itself but it is reconstructed on the basis of the present. The understanding of the past is always instrumental to the solution of the current problems (Brunner 1991; Halbwachs 1992; Hutton 1993). The historical narratives revise, select, and order past details in such a way that will serve as justification of one's present conditions and situation (Polkinghorne 1988). Hence, historical narratives provide knowledge and belief (Margalit 2002, 16).

The historical narratives focus on the society's memories of its past and they are aimed at adjusting the current basic needs, claims, rights, and interests of the society. They are shared by the society and they are treated as the only truthful and valid description of the past. Any questioning of their validity may trigger immediate anger and objection. The historical narratives are then the traditional and the legitimate sources that shape perceptions, attitudes, beliefs, arguments, claims, and behaviors. They provide the epistemic foundation of the society's existence and continuity (Bar-Tal and Salomon 2006, 23–24, 33). Thus, the national identity is defined and maintained through the use of the narrative configuration (Polkinghorne 1988; Sarbin 1986; Gillis 1994).

The historical narratives are also a form of organizing human experiences into meaningful episodes, guiding emotions and actions (Sarbin 1986). They provide a symbolized account of human actions; they introduce the historical barriers that need to be to overcome, and the plans created to cope with these barriers. The narratives focus on meaning and intention and represent a cultural and political discourse (Polkinghorne 1988; Shiff 2006). They serve as a kind of rationale for political decisions and they are used to justify societal attitudes and actions both in the present and towards the future.

The historical narratives serve even as a paradigmatic way of thinking (Brunner 1986, 12). They highlight the social group's distinct identity. They contribute to the formation, maintenance, and strengthening of the social and the political identity. Thus, they are the "cement that holds thick relations together" (Margalit 2002, 8). They also provide an overall sense of the party's historical development by offering a holistic framework that creates a certain picture of the past. The party reconstructs its own history from a current ideological and political stance. The core of these historical narratives is founded upon its ideological commitment. Hence, history becomes a tool for the ideological and political needs of the society. The significance of the historical narratives does not lie in their accurate mapping of the past, but in establishing a basic concept that reinforces a particular dimension of ideology and political position (Zerubavel 1995). For instance, the historical narratives may depict a catastrophic event, giving it a special meaning and significance for the present, so that traumatic memories tend to overreact in present events (Margalit 2002, 3).

The historical narratives may turn out to be a myth, which present the past story in a dramatic form. A myth is an expression of collective feelings and emotions, and it is understood as a true narrative of events. The myth is believed to be true not because of historical evidence but because it makes sense of a group's present situation. The myth, like the historical narratives, tells the past story of how it came about. The historical events are selected partly because they are compatible with what people believed ought to have happened, and because they are consistent with the dramatic story (Tudor 1972; Gedi and Elam 1996; Margalit 2002, 65–66). The practical aim of a myth is to justify the acceptance of a certain state of affairs and to advocate a given course of action. It offers an account of the past for the needs of the present and the future and provides the explanation for the present behavior and arguments for claims of a group for rights such as sovereignty, independence, or an extension of territory. A political myth

> may help strengthen the solidarity of the group in the face of a challenge, it may serve to encourage the resistance of an oppressed minority [and] it may inspire its members with confidence in their destiny and glorify their achievements.
>
> (Tudor 1972, 139)

Kenneth and Mary Gergen (Gergen and Gergen 1986) have developed a framework in which narratives are classified according to the kind of change that the protagonist undergoes in relation to his or her desired goal, as designed by the narrative. The framework includes three types of narratives: the stable narrative, in which the protagonist remains essentially consistent with respect to the goal; the progressive narrative, in which there is an active movement towards the goal; and the regressive narrative, in which the protagonist ends up further removed from his or her goal. According to this framework, the parties to a conflict conceive their behavior within a given historical narrative framework. That framework affects their planned action and desired goals, which are based on the present and future implications of their historical narratives.

The functions of historical narratives in a protracted conflict

Parties in a conflict tend to use their historical narratives alongside their collective memory as the main criteria for the historical truth in the conflict, particularly regarding its origins and development over time. The historical narratives can transform historical events into political myths and ethos, shaping protected values as a fixed prism, in which the parties in a conflict perceive the past, the present and the future, and refuse to accept any alternative views.

There is a fascinating dialectic between the historical narratives and the shaping of social and political identities. While historical narratives become part of one's social and political identity, the social and political identity is founded upon and justified by the historical narratives in the first place. Especially significant in this regard are *historical meta-narratives.*

Historical meta-narratives "are the all-encompassing, interpretive frameworks which incorporate the basic symbols, values, beliefs, and behavioral codes of a collective, and serve, therefore, as the symbolic representation of the national ethos" (Auerbach 2009, 297). The meta-narratives are the most basic and fundamental historical narratives and the most ancient ones, which are deeply rooted in the social and national identity of a nation. Meta-narratives refer to the most crucial events that relate to the birth of the people as a nation, to the ancient history of their statehood, to the events that present the origins and the sources of the national identity, and to the claims for a nationhood, statehood, territory, and historical rights.

The salience of meta-narratives is especially expressed in an intractable conflict, when both parties use them for justifying and legitimizing their historical rights and claims. Meta-narratives tend to be few and protected, resistant to change, non-negotiable, and non-compromised. Meta-narratives are usually the source of defining subsequent national historical narratives that highlight other significant historical events in the long history of a given people (Auerbach 2009).

To sum up, historical narratives influence the perception of a conflict, its origins and causes, its management, and its potential resolution, as well as the interactions with the rival party. The literature identifies the following instrumental functions for historical narratives in conflict relations:

1 They provide a coherent and meaningful description of the history of the conflict, its causes, development, and possible outcomes.
2 They justify and legitimize one's goals, attitudes, and behavior in the conflict. Thus, they justify the outbreak of the conflict and its crucial events,

including decisions of initiating violence and war against the other party, presenting those decisions as just, right, and only for self-defense.
3 They glorify one's goals, needs and rights, and the commitment to their fulfillment, while stressing that a failure to accomplish them or compromising them is a severe threat to the very existence of the nation, people, or social group.
4 They provide a sense of unity and solidarity and the rationale for mobilization of the members of society for the sake of legitimate causes in the conflict, including making the necessary sacrifices.
5 They de-legitimize the goals, attitudes, and conflict behavior of the other party, while defining them as unjustified and unreasonable.
6 They present each party as the sole victim of the conflict, unlike the rival one. A sense of self-collective victimhood is perceived to be an outcome of continuously intentional harm inflicted by the rival party throughout the protracted conflict. This harm is always viewed as unjust and immoral. The historical narratives emphasize and keep the sense of self-victimhood and its outcomes as well as the emotions of being a victim, including injustice, suffering, traumatic experiences, human losses, anger, fear, and hatred. The historical narratives stress the willingness of revenge, and deny calls for apology, forgiveness, resolution of the conflict, and ulterior reconciliation. The sense of collective victimhood is kept as part of the collective memory and of the national identity, and it serves as a means to project soft-power in the just struggle against the rival party, as well as a tool to acquire sympathy, legitimacy, and support from the international community (Bar-Tal *et al.* 2009; Caplan 1999).
7 They tend to memorize and sustain the injustice done by the other party, emphasizing the undoing of the injustice as a precondition for any positive and peaceful change in the conflict relations with the other side. There is a frequent use of phrases such as "we shall never forget" and "we shall never forgive."
8 They may play as the only prism to accept, process, and interpret any incoming information in the management of the conflict.

(Bar-Tal and Salomon 2006)

Historical narratives of justice and injustice

Historical narratives are especially significant in defining and describing justice and injustice in conflict relations. On the one hand, historical narratives are the most significant sources of presenting the origins of justice, especially the claims for historical rights and needs, nationhood, statehood, and territory. On the other hand, historical narratives are also the most significant sources for presenting injustice caused by the other party in the conflict, and making its correction the only way for concluding a just peace. Thus, historical narratives and justice are linked together. Justice is a form of remembrance; it is the institutionalized remembrance of the past, and the key dimension of the memory of an evil past (Booth 2001, 777–79). Thus, "memory and justice [give] voice to the past and its victims and [insist] on the restoration of justice in the world against the oblivion of forgetting" (Booth 2001, 780). The historical narratives emphasize the restoration of justice as a moral responsibility and accountability of peoples and leaders. It is a moral debt and part of the national identity that cannot be forgotten or ignored (Booth 1999, 249).

The historical narratives develop the sense of injustice and victimhood as they contain beliefs, attitudes, emotions, and behavioral tendencies. The beliefs focus on various types of injustices perpetrated, such as massacres, ethnic cleansing, destructions, occupation, oppressions, and humiliations, which are inflicted by the rival party throughout the conflict. These beliefs also ascribe full responsibility for the injustices to the other side. The emotions consist of intense hatred, hostility, mistrust, fury, anger, outrage, disgrace, self-pity, and vulnerability. They also provide a sense of moral responsibility for seeking justice against any attempt of the rival party to justify and legitimize the injustice done, to ignore it, or to run away from taking responsibility for it.

The emotional attitudes contain negative and hostile feelings, including calls for revenge and clear-cut, absolute, and uncompromising demands from the other party, such as demanding full responsibility for the injustice, apologizing for it, asking for forgiveness, and righting the injustice by returning refugees in cases of ethnic cleansing and providing financial compensation. The behavioral tendencies may include intensified violent reactions that are viewed as punishment and vengeance against the injustice caused by the other party and aimed to coerce the rival party to right the injustice. The status of being a victim of injustice also rationalizes and justifies immoral and illegitimate acts against the other side, including the use of violence, such as in acts of terrorism (Bar-Tal *et al.* 2009; Booth 1999, 2001).

This combination of beliefs, emotions, and behavioral tendencies included in the historical narratives develops into a syndrome of injustice that will guide not only the society's attitudes and behaviors in the conflict, but also the prospects for its future conflict resolution and ulterior reconciliation. Defending and maintaining the syndrome of injustice tends to become a holy and obsessive devotion of leaders and peoples. Moreover, once a party views itself as a victim of injustice, it makes an active effort to mobilize international sympathy, legitimacy, and support for its own concept of injustice and the need to right it to its full satisfaction. Thus, historical narratives legitimize the justice requested and place it orthogonally to the claim of the other (Bar-Tal *et al.* 2009).

Parties in a conflict tend to believe that their views of the history of the conflict and their request for a just peace are truthful and legitimate, while the views of the other side are always distorted by self-interest, ideological motives, and other biases. When a party (or both sides) to a conflict strongly adhere to their own historical narratives and this becomes the sole value and moral authority for defining justice and rights in the conflict, then any decision, policy, or action may be conditional on their adjustment to the content and the spirit of the historical narratives (Devine-Wright 2003).

Historical narratives of the parties tend to attribute all the responsibility for the historical injustice to the rival side. The adversary imposed the conflict, not only fighting for unjust goals, but also using immoral means to accomplish them. The conflict magnifies the sense of the past injustice and interlocks it with the present unjust situation. Historical narratives tend to identify injustice as a major single traumatic event (such as a massacre, ethnic expulsion, or occupation) or as a series of traumatic events that caused a severe harm to the social group by the rival party.

A major traumatic event is considered sometimes as a "chosen trauma" that leads the society to memorize it as the critical event that shapes its national identity (Volkan 1997).[1] Historical narratives emphasize that certain tangible individual and collective rights were removed or violated, such as the right of self-determination, the right for a territory, and free expression of the national identity. Societies may decide to internalize past injustices and to make them into powerful historical narratives, which become part of the national identity, and this is maintained throughout generations (Robben and Suarez-Orozco 2000).

The use of the term "right" and linking it to narratives of justice and injustice is typical and relevant to both domestic and international conflicts. It empowers the symbolic aspects of controversial claims in a conflict and makes it a protected value. Thus, "rights first and foremost raise the bar for what is at stake. At least rhetorically, it removes the debate onto a higher moral plateau" (Barkan 2005, 88). The historical narratives become a cause for a competition of rights and for a national struggle for accomplishing the rights and correcting the injustice.

Historical narratives as protected values

Historical narratives tend to be a major criterion for defining the parties' concepts of justice and injustice. Parties in a conflict tend to perceive their historical narratives, especially those of justice and injustice as protected values or even as sacred values.

The consideration of narratives of justice and injustices as protected values makes them sacred and taboo, resisting trade-offs with other values (Baron and Spranca 1997; Tetlock 2003; Atran *et al.* 2007; Atran and Axelrod 2008; Bazerman *et al.* 2008; Hanselmann and Tanner 2008). The literature suggests that such values arise from deontological rules concerning action and, therefore, they are absolute ones. Absoluteness means resistance to trade-offs and to compromise. In other words, people feel a high moral obligation and commitment to protect their narratives of justice. People are concerned in respect of their participation in peace negotiation that it may bring them to trade off their justice narratives or to concede them in return for other values, such as peace, security, and economic benefits.

In negotiations to manage and resolve conflicts, people may refuse any action that will endanger the sanctity of their historical narratives mainly because they are the sources of their social and national identity, and because they believe that protecting them enhances their self-image and their international stature. People may prefer to present their justice and injustice narratives as protected values also because they mistrust everybody else, including their own leaders, to be strong enough not to concede them and protect those "first principles," in order to avoid "moral contamination" (Baron and Spranca 1997; Tetlock 2003; Margalit 2010).

People become angry and unforgiving when they discover that their own leaders or other members of their society have compromised their narratives of justice and injustice. Defining those narratives as protected values may cause problems in conflict resolution because they are more important and significant than other alternative values, inhibiting certain actions that could be interpreted as compromising them. When narratives of justice defined as protected values derive from deontological prohibitions of action, then they become barriers to conflict resolution because they do not allow any flexibility or compromise. Therefore, parties in a conflict who are interested in resolving their dispute should refrain from defining their narratives of justice and injustice as protected values.

Narratives of justice and injustice as barriers to conflict resolution

Historical narratives tend to present the issues of justice and injustice as the most significant moral, ideological, and political commitments. Parties in a protracted conflict are apprehensive that any change in their narratives of justice, even a small one, or, alternatively, accepting a small portion of the rival's narrative will shatter their national identity. When narratives of justice and injustice are profoundly religious ones, it makes them even more fundamental and uncompromised. The parties are deeply embedded in their own beliefs, and it is pointless to challenge them, because any such an attempt will be perceived as a threat to their religion (Holmes 1997, 303; Barkan and Karn 2006, 14). Political leaders are indeed especially careful not to make such a change in the historical narratives because it will immediately trigger domestic criticism that may endanger their leadership role.

The use of narratives of justice and injustice is motivated sometimes by normative considerations, such as the need to remember and not to forget the injustice, as well as the commitment to correct the past injustice. However, it is also manipulated by leaders and elites who would like to gain political power or to remain in power, or as a way of mobilizing people to action, or as a strategy for long term political gains, or to discredit political adversaries (Forsberg 2001, 65; Atran and Axelrod 2008, 227). Indeed, as Barry Schwartz argues, "given the constraints of a recorded history, the past cannot be literally construed; it can only be selectively exploited" (Schwartz 1982, 393). Sometimes, the adversaries even use the historical injustice as a bargaining leverage in their political negotiations (Barkan and Karn 2006, 9).

Narratives of justice and injustice are usually subjective and do not necessarily reflect the objective truth. Hence, making them the only criteria for defining justice and linking it to peace is highly problematic, especially when this collides with the other side's narrative, which is also subjective and socially constructed. Indeed,

> even if factual truth is established, facts do not speak for themselves … it is the interpretation that the facts are given that is more important; and if the different interpretative frameworks do not converge; facts alone will not help to form a shared past.
>
> (Forsberg 2001, 63)

Moreover, every alleged injustice by one side is countered immediately with an alleged injustice perpetrated by the other; the result being a chain of accusations and mutual recriminations, and a ceaseless debating of the past that only maintains the past contested, exacerbating the narrative gaps. In most conflict situations, historical narratives clash with each other, especially on justice and injustice issues, and in most of them there is no way of settling or bridging the gap between contradictory narratives. Thus, "each party incorporates the historical facts within its own cognitive schema of the conflict, and discussions of these facts lead only to irresoluble clashes of narratives that will highlight the differences and leave the parties frustrated" (Rouhana 2004, 178). In the absence of any shared agreement about the past injustice, any attempt to accept one side's injustice claims will be seen by the rival party as an injustice, ending any chance for compromise and peace. This is not to claim that narratives of justice are not important or that there is equal justice or injustice on both sides' narratives. The argument is that insisting on adhering to those narratives builds strong barriers for conflict resolution (Holmes 1997, 301; Rouhana 2004, 177–78).

Narratives of justice create limits and constraints for any flexibility in potential negotiations that requires making some concessions that refer to the historical narratives. They even prevent any showing of respect for the rival's protected values, because they may be interpreted as compromising one's core values. Although eliminating the narratives of justice is impossible because they are indeed part and parcel of people's tradition and identity, considering any peace negotiations only through the prism of the past, and making the correction of the past a precondition for concluding peace may foil the prospects for peace (Biggar 2001a; Caplan 1999).

As long as the parties are locked in their narratives of justice regarding the injustice done to them they fail to make the necessary concessions for conflict resolution. Narratives of justice and collective memories may then become barriers for any change in the structure of the conflict. Those who adhere to the historical memory of injustice may find themselves prisoners of the past, enabling the past to control the present and future (Margalit 2002, 6; Holmes 1997, 301). Moreover, "those who only remember the past are also condemned to repeat it. To live exclusively with [the] past is to become the past." (Rosenblatt 1982, 47).

While forgetting or ignoring the unjust past is impossible, the relevant question becomes how to deal with it in peace negotiations in a way that it will not prevent conflict resolution. The unsettled past cannot be simply forgotten, but it cannot be resolved immediately either. Indeed, as Biggar correctly maintains, the burden of the past in many protracted conflicts is so big and heavy that it cannot easily be managed and resolved. It requires a long process of reconciliation, over years if not generations. Any delaying of the peace process because of that past will only exacerbate the role of justice and injustice in conflict resolution and may even escalate the conflict (Biggar 2001b, 271–72).

Furthermore, reframing of the historical narratives and the collective memories as the basic pillars for linking justice to peace is also necessary in order to advance a peace process. Adjustment of certain historical narratives is requested. Representing the past injustice in a different way is necessary. Thus, "there is no point in [dealing] with many faces of injustice. Instead, it is much more economical to concentrate on the one positive idea of justice, and thereby gain coherent unity, rather than rely on scattered anecdotes about injustices" (Margalit 2002, 117). Indeed, since almost any depiction of the injustice issue in a conflict is characterized by tragic elements, "justice will have to include the recognition of tragedy and to take into account that any peace arrangement will contain elements of injustice since the tragedy is permanent" (Belaief 1997, 331). In this view, making peace *is* justice by itself, because it will not only stop the current suffering and will prevent another war, but it will also bring positive outcomes such as ending occupation, the establishment of an independent state, peaceful secession, and acquiring independence.

Historical narratives: from conflict resolution to reconciliation

Any move towards conflict resolution requires the re-evaluation of the justice of the historical narratives and their role in the peace process. Acknowledging the past, particularly the injustice and the harm each side has done to the other, is crucial for reconciliation, but it may prevent a resolution of the conflict in the short term. An expectation of both sides' mutual legitimization of each party's historical narrative is not realistic at the conflict resolution stage. At this stage, conflicting historical narratives may actually prevent conflict resolution.

Since addressing conflicting historical narratives about justice is probably unavoidable, this study suggests differentiating between two stages in dealing with the issue of justice narratives in conflict resolution and in reconciliation. Indeed, while justice is

> central to reconciliation it is not a central part of the applied or theoretical conflict resolution discourse … justice was not taken as a frame of

> reference for the conflict resolution approach, perhaps because such a framework was assumed to compromise the conflict resolution effort.
>
> (Rouhana 2004, 176)

In other words, justice may foil the possibility of conflict resolution. However, since justice is still a basic need of one or the two parties in a conflict, I suggest that, at the conflict resolution stage, the parties should agree that the issue of justice is significant for their future relations and that they cannot avoid it. At the same time, because of fundamentally different versions of the historical injustice, and the need for a mutual legitimization of each side's historical narrative, the parties should also agree to defer coping with their past injustices to a later stage in the peace building, as a precondition for reconciliation and after peace is formally reached.

A successful conflict resolution and building of mutual trust following it may enable the parties to account for the past more easily, reaching a common ground. Adopting this strategy is not a call for forgetting or burying the past injustice, but laying them to wait for a ripe time (Biggar 2001a, 9). For instance, in the German–Czech Declaration on Mutual Relations and Their Future Development, concluded in January 1997, which may be defined as a reconciliation agreement, both sides agreed that "injustice inflicted in the past belongs in the past, and will therefore orient their relations towards the future ... . Both sides therefore declare that they will not burden their relations with political and legal issues which stem from the past."[2]

When attempts to do justice based on one's historical narrative "begin to threaten the negotiated peace," then the dilemma is what to choose: "a peace built upon the public suppression of the victim's memories, or a justice that risks bringing war back to life again?" (Biggar 2001a, 10). Therefore, in this critical situation a compromise is required, so there is also a moral and a political need to conclude peace and to avoid further sufferance (Biggar 2001b, 275).

Yehudit Auerbach suggests seven stages of a reconciliation pyramid that refers directly to conflicting historical narratives that the parties should consider if they would like to reach reconciliation. However, some of them may also refer to parties who would like to resolve the conflict but they are not ripe enough yet for reconciliation.

The first stage refers to an acquaintance with clashing narratives. It emphasizes the importance of not only acknowledging the other's narrative but also acknowledging that its narrative has some validity. The significance of this stage lies in the shift from a full adherence to one's own historical narrative at the expense of ignoring and denying the other's narrative, to some willingness to acknowledge the existence of the other's historical narrative. The two sides should acknowledge each other's narrative and show some willingness to listen to the other, not necessarily to agree, but to try to understand its basic beliefs. This is indeed a quite revolutionary step in the conflict relations; however, a willingness to do so is not so simple and easy because it may raise some questions as to the validity of one's own historical narratives.

The second stage calls for acknowledging the other's narrative, without necessarily accepting it as true. However, this stage is more difficult than the previous one because it implies understanding and recognizing the other's justice narrative as an authentic and legitimate one; this could be interpreted as compromising one's own legitimate claims and rights. It seems that in a protracted conflict the sides will resist that possibility until they reach formal peace.

The third stage requires expression of empathy for the other's plight. Although Auerbach argues that this is most difficult to reach in identity conflicts, it seems that this stage is easier to reach than the initial two because it does not require acknowledging the validity of the other's justice narrative or taking any responsibility for its suffering, but only expressing some form of empathy to the physical and non-material conditions of the other party as a result of the lingering conflict. Therefore, I would consider this stage to be preliminary to the other two stages mentioned above, because it is less demanding.

The fourth stage calls for assuming at least partial responsibility for the other's alleged plights, which means not only a formal recognition of the other's injustice narrative but also some readiness to take responsibility for the injustice claim. This is indeed a most difficult step in conflict relations that may be equivalent to pleading guilty, which makes it very sensitive for each party to accept in a protracted conflict. Moreover, any acceptance of such a step may lead to an immediate call for future reparations and compensation for the injustice and this may prevent any consideration of any partial responsibility for the injustice claim. It seems that, in a case of conflicting narratives of justice, this stage can be accepted only on a mutual basis. It means that both parties will take joint responsibility for the conflict and its injustice outcomes.

The next three stages refer indeed only to the reconciliation phase and they are less relevant to the conflict resolution phase because the sides are not psychologically, cognitively, and emotionally ripe for considering them. The fifth stage suggests expressing readiness for restitution or reparation for past wrongs. The sixth stage requires publicly apologizing and asking for forgiveness for past wrongs. Finally, the seventh stage calls for incorporating opposite narratives into accepted mutual accounts of the past (see Auerbach 2009).

Conclusions

Narratives of justice and injustice are significant values for parties in a protracted conflict. These narratives are part of the collective memory of the sides and frame their national identity. Justice and injustice narratives play a paramount role in shaping the attitudes, beliefs, and behavior of the rival parties. Yet, when these historical narratives become protected values they may become formidable barriers to conflict resolution. While remembering that the past is crucial for the definition of one's identity, parties who have an interest in making peace should be careful not to be prisoners of the past, since that may prevent peacemaking.

Notes

1 Examples of such "chosen traumas" are the destruction of the two Jewish Temples, the Holocaust of European Jewry in 1942–45, and the Palestinian *Nakba* (catastrophe), following the First Arab–Israeli War.

2 In their bilateral agreement, Germany acknowledged responsibility for the crimes of Nazi Germany, while the Czech Republic expressed regret for the expulsion of Sudeten Germans immediately after World War II that led to the death of millions of Germans. See http://law.gonzaga.edu/library/ceedocs/cz/decz.htm.

References

Atran, Scott and Robert Axelrod. "Reframing Sacred Values," *Negotiation Journal*, Vol. 24, 3 (2008), pp. 221–46.

Atran, Scott, Robert Axelrod, and Richard Davis. *Science*, Vol. 317, 5841 (2007), pp. 1039–40.

Auerbach, Yeudith. "The Reconciliation Pyramid – A Narrative-Based Framework for Analyzing Identity Conflicts," *Political Psychology*, Vol. 30, 2 (2009), pp. 291–318.

Barkan, Elazar. "Considerations Toward Accepting Historical Responsibility." In *Exile and Return: Predicaments of Palestinians and Jews* (eds) Ann Lesch and Ian Lustick. (Philadelphia: University of Pennsylvania Press, 2005), pp. 85–105.

Barkan, Elazar and Alexander Karn. "Group Apology as an Ethical Imperative." In *Taking Wrongs Seriously: Apologies and Reconciliation* (eds) Elazar Barkan and Alexander Karn. (Stanford, CA: Stanford University Press, 2006), pp. 3–30.

Baron, Jonathan and Mark Spranca. "Protected Values," *Organizational Behavior and Human Decision Processes*, Vol. 70, 1 (1997), pp. 1–16.

Bar-Tal, Daniel and Gavriel Salomon. "Israeli-Jewish Narrative of the Israeli–Palestinian Conflict: Evolution, Contents, Function, and Consequences." In *Israeli and Palestinian Narratives of Conflict* (ed.) Robert I. Rotberg. (Bloomington: Indiana University Press, 2006), pp. 19–46.

Bar-Tal, Daniel, Lily Chernyak-Hai, Noa Schori, and Ayelet Gundar. "A Sense of Self-Perceived Collective Victimhood in Intractable Conflicts," *International Review of the Red Cross*, Vol. 91, 874 (2009), pp. 229–58.

Bazerman, Max H., Ann Tenbrunsel, and Kimberly Wade-Benzoni. "When Sacred Issues Are at Stake," *Negotiation Journal*, Vol. 24, 1 (2008), pp. 113–17.

Belaief, Lynne. "Tragic Justice." In *Philosophical Perspectives on the Israeli–Palestinian Conflict* (ed.) Tomis Kapitan. (Armonk, NY: M. E. Sharpe, 1997), pp. 331–42.

Biggar, Nigel. "Making Peace or Doing Justice: Must We Choose?" In *Making the Past: Making Peace and Doing Justice after Civil Conflict* (ed.) Nigel Biggar. (Washington, DC: Georgetown University Press, 2001a), pp. 6–22.

Biggar, Nigel. "Concluding Remarks" In *Making the Past: Making Peace and Doing Justice after Civil Conflict* (ed.) Nigel Biggar. (Washington, DC: Georgetown University Press, 2001b), pp. 270–85.

Booth, James W. "Communities of Memory: On Identity, Memory, and Debt," *American Political Science Review*, Vol. 93, 2 (1999), pp. 249–63.

Booth, James W. "The Unforgotten: Memories of Justice," *American Political Science Review*, Vol. 95, 4 (2001), pp. 777–91.

Brunner, Jerome. *Actual Minds, Possible Worlds* (Cambridge, MA: Harvard University Press, 1986).

Brunner, Jerome. *Acts of Meanings* (Cambridge, MA: Harvard University Press, 1990).

Brunner, Jerome. "The Narrative Construction of Reality," *Critical Inquiry*, Vol. 18, 1 (1991), pp. 1–21.

Caplan, Neil. "Victimhood and Identity: Psychological Obstacles to Israeli Reconciliation with the Palestinians." In *Israeli and Palestinian Identities in History and Literature* (eds) Kamal Abdel-Malek and David C. Jacobson. (New York: Macmillan, 1999), pp. 63–86.

Devine-Wright, Patrick. "A Theoretical Overview of Memory and Conflicts." In *The Role of Memory in Ethnic Conflict* (eds) Ed Cairns and Michael D. Roe. (New York: 2003), pp. 9–34.

Forsberg, Thomas. "The Philosophy and Practice of Dealing with the Past: Some Conceptual and Normative Issues." In *Making the Past: Making Peace and Doing Justice after Civil Conflict* (ed.) Nigel Biggar. (Washington, DC: Georgetown University Press, 2001), pp. 57–72.

Gedi, Noa and Yigal Elam. "Collective Memory – What Is It?," *History and Memory*, Vol. 8, 1 (1996), pp. 30–50.

Gergen, Kenneth J. and Mary M. Gergen. "Narrative Form and the Construction of Psychological Science." In *Narrative Psychology: The Storied Nature of Human Conduct* (ed.) Theodore R. Sarbin. (New York: Praeger, 1986), pp. 22–44.

Gillis, John R. "Introduction: Memory and Identity: The History of a Relationship." In *Commemorations: The Politics of National Identity* (ed.) John R. Gillis. (Princeton, NJ: Princeton University Press, 1994).

Halbwachs, Maurice. *On Collective Memory.* Edited, translated, and with Introduction by Lewis A. Coser (Chicago: Chicago University Press, 1992).

Hanselmann, Martin and Carmen Tanner. "Taboos and Conflicts in Decision-Making: Sacred Values, Decision Difficulty, and Emotions," *Judgment and Decision Making*, Vol. 3, 19 (2008), pp. 51–63.

Holmes, Robert L. "Beyond Justice and Rights: Competing Israeli and Palestinian Claims." In *Philosophical Perspectives on the Israeli–Palestinian Conflict* (ed.) Tomis Kapitan. (Armonk, NY: M. E. Sharpe, 1997), pp. 297–308.

Jameson, Frederic. *The Political Unconscious: Narrative As A Socially Symbolic Act* (London: Methuen, 1981).

Hutton, Patrick H. *History as an Art of Memory* (Hanover: University of Vermont, 1993).

Margalit, Avishai. *The Ethics of Memory* (Cambridge, MA: Harvard University Press, 2002).

Margalit, Avishai. *On Compromise and Rotten Compromise* (Princeton, NJ: Princeton University Press, 2010).

Mink, Louis. "Narrative Form as a Cognitive Instrument." In *The Writing of History: Literary Form and Historical Understanding* (eds) Robert H. Canary and Henry Kozisky. (Madison: The University Press of Wisconsin Press, 1978), pp. 129–49.

Polkinghorne, Donald. *Narrative Knowing and the Human Sciences* (Albany: SUNY Press, 1988).

Robben, Antonius and M. Suarez-Orozco. *Culture under Siege: Collective Violence and Trauma* (Cambridge: Cambridge University Press, 2000).

Robinson, John A. and Linda Hawpe. "Narrative Thinking as a Heuristic Process." In *Narrative Psychology: The Storied Nature of Human Conduct* (ed.) Theodore R. Sarbin. (New York: Praeger, 1986), pp. 111–25.

Rosenblatt, Roger. "Israel: How Much Past is Enough?," *Time*, September 20, 1982, p. 47.

Rouhana, N. Nadim. "Identity and Power in the Reconciliation of National Conflict." In *The Social Psychology of Group Identity and Social Conflict: Theory, Application and Practice* (eds) Alice H. Eagly, Reuben M. Baron and V. Lee Hamilton. (Washington, DC: American Psychological Association, 2004), pp. 173–87.

Sarbin, Theodore R. "The Narrative as a Root Metaphor for Psychology." In *Narrative Psychology: The Storied Nature of Human Conduct* (ed.) Theodore R. Sarbin. (New York: Praeger, 1986), pp. 3–21.

Schwartz, Barry. "The Social Context of Commemoration: A Study in Collective Memory," *Social Forces*, Vol. 61, 2 (1982), pp. 374–402.

Shenhav, Shaul. "Thin and Thick Narrative Analysis: On the Question of Defining and Analyzing Political Narratives," *Narrative Inquiry*, Vol. 15, 1 (2005), pp. 75–99.

Shiff, Brian. "The Promise (and Challenge) of an Innovative Narrative Psychology." In *Narrative Psychology: The Storied Nature of Human Conduct* (ed.) Theodore R. Sarbin. (New York: Praeger, 2006), pp. 27–36.

Tessler, Mark. "Narratives and Myths about Arab Intransigence toward Israel." In *Israeli and Palestinian Narratives of Conflict* (ed.) Robert I. Rothberg. (Bloomington: Indiana University Press, 2006), pp. 174–93.

Tetlock, Philip E. "Thinking the Unthinkable: Sacred Values and Taboo Cognitions," *Trends in Cognitive Sciences*, Vol. 7, 7 (2003), pp. 320–24.

Tudor, Henry. *Political Myth* (London: Macmillan, 1972).

Volkan, V. *Blood Lines: From Ethnic Pride to Ethnic Terrorism* (Boulder, CO: Westview Press, 1997).

White, Hyden. "The Historical Text as Literary Artifact," in *The Writing of History: Literary Form and Historical Understanding* (eds) Robert H. Canary and Henry Kozisky. (Madison: The University Press of Wisconsin Press, 1978), pp. 41–62.

Zerubavel, Yael. *Recovered Roots: Collective Memory and the Making of Israeli National Tradition* (Chicago: Chicago University Press, 1995).

3 The Israeli–Jewish narratives of justice and injustice

The Jewish–Israeli side in the Arab–Israeli conflict, and especially in the Israeli–Palestinian conflict, combines three sets of narratives of justice and injustice. The first is the meta-narrative, which is more basic and foundational, while the other two are national narratives that refer to the development of the Arab–Israeli and the Israeli–Palestinian conflicts, and especially to the 1947–49 war and the Six Day War of 1967 and their outcomes.

The meta-narrative of justice and injustice presents and justifies the establishment and the existence of the State of Israel as the national home of the Jewish people in terms of distributive justice, as well as in terms of corrective and compensating justice, because of the profound injustice perpetrated against the Jewish people throughout its history, which reached its peak in the Holocaust during World War II. The national narratives of justice focus on presenting the Israeli positions and behaviors throughout the Arab–Israeli conflict, while denying the validity of the Arab and the Palestinian narratives of it.

The meta-narrative of justice

The Israeli–Jewish meta-narrative is best reflected in the Zionist ideology and in the Declaration of Israel's Independence of 14 May 1948, which provide the justness of the establishment and the existence of Israel as the state of the Jewish people, as well as fulfilling the Jewish national goals. The following historical, theological, national, existential, political, societal, and cultural arguments were used to *justify* these goals:

1. The Land of Israel (*Eretz Israel*) was the birthplace of the Jewish people, where their spiritual, religious, and political identity was shaped, and where they first attained independence and statehood, creating cultural values of national and universal significance.
2. After being forcibly exiled from their land, the Jewish people remained faithful to it. During the long exile years, the Jewish people never gave up their unique relation to the Land of Israel, which remained the Jewish homeland, so the Jews maintained close spiritual and physical ties with their land, and continuously aspired to return to it.

3 The continuity of Jewish life never ceased in the Land of Israel for the last 3,000 years.
4 The persistence of anti-Semitism, humiliation, and the persecution of the Jewish people in the Diaspora, and especially in Europe, resulting ultimately in the Holocaust of 1941–45, stressed the urgent need of resolving the problem of the Jewish people's homelessness, by re-establishing the Jewish State in the Land of Israel for a secure existence in their national homeland.[1] The establishment of a Jewish state will return Jews to conditions of "normalcy" as a nation among all nations.
5 The Jewish people's national aspiration to adhere to their own identity and establish their homeland can be fulfilled only in the Land of Israel. Jewish self-determination is conditioned on the Jews' realization of their "historical rights" to their homeland in *Eretz Israel.*
6 Since the end of the nineteenth century several waves of Jewish immigration to Palestine expressed their national aspiration to build a state for the Jewish people in their ancient homeland. The Jews did not return as colonizers, but rather as pioneers and redeemers of the land. They did not intend to disrupt or destroy the lives of the local inhabitants of the Land of Israel. All land for Jewish settlement was legally bought.
7 By the beginning of the twentieth century, the Zionist claim to a historic right to the land gained international political endorsement. The right of the Jewish people to a national home in their own country was recognized first in the Balfour Declaration on 2 November 1917, and re-affirmed in the Mandate of the League of Nations (1922), which, in particular, gave an international legitimacy to the historical link between the Jewish people and the Land of Israel and the right of the Jewish people to rebuild their National Home. This right was re-affirmed by the November 1947 UN Partition Plan, calling for the establishment of an independent Jewish state in Palestine.[2]
8 The existence of Israel as a Jewish nation-state is a necessary condition for the security of the Jewish people and for the continuation of the Jewish civilization.
9 Although the whole Land of Israel, including East Jordan, is the historic homeland of the Jewish people, the Zionist movement accepted that they would fulfill the Jewish national self-determination in only part of Palestine, west of the River Jordan (Western Palestine).
10 The Zionist movement is a just national political movement, which acted in a very positive way for the Jews because it provided a pragmatic solution to the Jewish problem.
11 Israel's birth in 1948 was just and legitimate. The fact that a Palestinian state was not established and the emergence of the Palestinian refugee problem were the result of the Arab rejection of the UN Partition Plan of November 1947 and the aggression of the 1947–49 war.

(See Israel's Independence Declaration, May 14, 1948; Bar-On 2006; Bar-Tal and Salomon 2006; Gans 2004, 2006, 2007, 2008; Gavison 2003; Kimmerling 1983; Scham *et al.* 2005, Shimoni 1995; Zerubavel 1995)

The Israeli–Jewish justice argumentation emphasizes the normative historical link between the Jews and the Land of Israel and the understanding that Jewish national self-determination is viable only within the historical homeland as recognized by the international community. The justification for the establishment of a Jewish state in the Land of Israel is based on the principles of distributive justice, self-determination, historical rights, and correcting and compensating for past injustices.

The justification for establishing a Jewish state in the Land of Israel is based on distributive justice considerations regarding the division of territory among nations for the purpose of implementing their right of self-determination. Thus, the principle of distributive justice justifies the Jewish right of self-determination, nationhood, and statehood like other nations. Thus, the Jewish people constitute a nation that has legitimate rights to nationhood, self-determination, and statehood (Gans 2004, 2007).

The Zionist movement justifies the establishment of a Jewish state in the Land of Israel also on historical and formative rights. The Jewish people enjoyed self-determination and statehood in the Land of Israel, during Biblical times and the Second Temple, and were uprooted by force from their land. The Jewish people never gave up their willingness to resume their political self-determination there. The commitment to their formative territory is valid regardless of whether they always occupied the territory.

The right of the Jewish return to the Land of Israel and the establishment of the State of Israel are also justified by considerations of corrective and compensating justice. The persecution of Jews throughout the history, primarily in Europe, that culminated in the Holocaust during World War II justifies the compensation of the Jewish people for all its suffering, by allowing them to establish their own independent state in the Land of Israel. This could also correct and compensate for the injustice that occurred to them throughout history since their expulsion from the land (Gans 2004, 2006, 2007, 2008; Gavison 2003).

The Jewish Agency expressed this claim for justice in the following way:

> If there was justice in the general concept of self-determination, there was also justice in the particular expression of that concept in terms of the 'historic reparation' to Jewry. No man of liberal spirit could deny that it was justice long-delayed. Nor could he gainsay the right of his people to find its way once more into the society of nations.
>
> (Jewish Agency 1947, 110, quoted in Kapitan 1997, 23)

Similarly, Gans defines the need for self-determination as a "remedial justification for seeking to protect their physical integrity and retain their dignity by means of realizing their right to self-determination in their historical homeland" (Gans 2007, 88–89).

The meta-narrative of injustice

The Israeli–Jewish meta-narrative of injustice is influenced profoundly by the suffering of the Jewish people throughout the Jewish history, including the destruction of Jewish historical independence several times, the exile from the land, anti-Semitism, and especially the Holocaust.

> Nowhere in the world is there a people who better know the meaning of personal, familial, and national suffering than the Jewish people. We are a nation of refugees. In our collective memory we carry the history of exile from our country, twice taken from ancestors.
>
> (Peres 1993, 183)

The meta-narrative of injustice is also based on the Israeli suffering in the Arab–Israeli conflict in general, and in the Israeli–Palestinian conflict in particular. The meta-narrative of injustice presents the wrong that the Arab states and the Palestinians caused to Israel throughout the Arab–Israeli conflict. The Arab wrong done against Israel combines both negative and hostile attitudes, as well as aggressive and violent behavior. These negative and hostile attitudes include the following elements:

1 the total and absolute Arab and Palestinian opposition to any independent Jewish political entity in Palestine;
2 the refusal to accept the UN Partition Plan of 1947 and the establishment of the State of Israel;
3 the refusal to recognize the existence of the Jewish people, their right of self-determination as a nation and as a state, as well their right to build a Jewish state in *Eretz Israel*;
4 the political and ideological declarations that called for correcting the Palestinian injustice by the destruction of Israel, such as the Palestinian National Covenant of 1968;
5 the attribution to Israel of all the responsibility for the emerging of the conflict over Israel, including the creation of the Palestinian refugee problem;
6 the Palestinian and Arab insistence on forcing Israel to admit responsibility for the refugee problem, which aims to raise doubts and to undermine Israel's legitimacy;
7 the Palestinian and Arab demands that Israel accepts the "right of return" of the Palestinian refugees to Israel, which aims to destroy Israel's existence as a Jewish state;
8 the Arab refusal to resolve peacefully the conflict with Israel, with the exception of Egypt and Jordan, which signed peace agreements with Israel in 1979 and 1994 respectively;
9 the Egyptian and the Jordanian refusal to keep warm the peace agreements with Israel;

10 the incitement and the propaganda against Israel that aim to de-legitimize it in the international arena, especially at the United Nations.

The Israeli narrative of Arab aggression and violent behavior towards Israel refers to border military incidents, terrorist actions, guerrilla war, and conventional wars. The continued violent confrontation from 1948 until the present caused Israel thousands of casualties and severe material damage, forcing Israel to invest much of its resources in security in order to face the permanent threat to its existence. In addition to that, the Arab trade boycott caused Israel a tremendous economic cost. There is not any historical precedence for the case where one state faces so many neighboring enemies as in the case of Israel. Israel stands alone not only versus the Arab states but also their many allies that included even a superpower in the past (the former Soviet Union) and other regional actors (Iran).

Because of the unique situation of asymmetrical conflict (one versus many), Israel tends to perceive itself as the permanent victim of Arab hostility, facing existential threats, and struggling for security and survival. This constant state of war made Israel insecure and therefore very reticent and suspicious about taking risks for peace. Indeed, for many years most Israelis did not believe that the Arabs would be ready to accept the existence of a Jewish state in the Middle East, if only Israel would adopt a more appeasing strategy. Any attempt to blame Israel as responsible for the conflict is doomed to be rejected or, at best, not taken seriously by the majority of the Israeli public. Paradoxically, the Israeli victories in the wars and its military superiority did not diminish the enduring self-perceptions of victimhood and powerlessness (Caplan 1999).

The 1947–49 war as a just war

The 1947–49 war is defined by Israel as a just war and as the War of "Independence" or "Liberation." The Israeli narrative of the 1947–49 war justifies Israel's war objectives and puts all the responsibility for the eruption of the war and its consequences on the Palestinians and the Arab states. The Palestinians, as well as the Arab states, opposed any political compromise to settle the conflict in the first place. In November 1947 not only did they reject the UN Partition Plan, but they also initiated a war that was aimed to prevent by force the implementation of the Partition Plan and to destroy Israel as a state ("politicide") and annihilate its people (genocide).

The Arabs imposed the war upon Israel, which had to defend itself in order to maintain its existence and prevent its destruction. The Arab rejection of the UN Partition Plan and the initiating of a total war aimed at destroying Israel made the Palestinians lose their right to their own state within the Partition Plan lines. The additional territories occupied by Israel in the war beyond the Partition Plan lines were justified and legitimized because they were captured in a defensive war. If only the Palestinians had agreed to accept the Jews and live in peace with them since the beginning of Zionist settlement in 1882, all of Mandatory Palestine, whether divided politically into two states or not, could have been a peaceful and prosperous land.

The Israeli narratives of the 1947–49 war disregard the tragedy of the Palestinians caused by the war, blaming them for their plight. The Palestinians and the Arab leadership were solely responsible for the war outcomes, including the fact that a Palestinian state was never established, and the emergence of the Palestinian refugee problem. Those who were responsible for initiating the war were also responsible for its outcomes.

Israel denies any responsibility for creating the Palestinian refugee problem. The Palestinians voluntarily left their homes because of fear or because of orders from Arab and Palestinian leaders promising them that they could return after the liberation of Palestine by the Arab armies, after the extermination of the Jews. Israel had no deliberate policy to expel the Palestinians and even asked them throughout the war to remain in their places and not to run away. Israel's decision makers opposed the Palestinian flight, especially before the establishment of the State of Israel because it might prevent the implementation of the Partition Plan and the establishment of the state. Moreover, the war created a refugee problem not only for the Palestinians, but also for the Jews in neighboring Arab countries. Hundreds of thousands of Jews in Arab and Muslim states were compelled to leave and move to the newly established State of Israel (Gelber 2001; Lorch 1968; Morris 1987; Peres 1993; Sela 2005; Teveth 1990; Alpher *et al.* 1999).

The emergence of a new Israeli historiography in the late 1980s caused an invigorated debate regarding the Israeli official and traditional narratives of the 1947–49 war. This new historiography emerged not only from the release of new archival documents about the first Arab–Israeli war, but also from the frustration following the escalation of the Israeli–Palestinian conflict with the 1982 Lebanese War and the eruption of the first *intifada* in December 1987 (Morris 1988; Sela 2005).

Simha Flappan (1987); Benny Morris (1987, 1988); Ilan Pappé (1992, 1999, 2004) and Avi Shlaim (1988, 1995), the so-called "new historians," led this revisionist historiography.[3] In their writings they questioned the traditional Israeli narratives of the war and claimed that Israel was also responsible for the creation of the refugee problem (Morris 1987) and for the prevention of the establishment of a Palestinian state via collusion with Jordan (Shlaim 1988). In their view, Israel's acceptance of the Partition Plan was tactical rather than strategic because it never gave up its dreams of establishing a Jewish state in the whole of Western Palestine (*Eretz Israel*). The partition lines were only transitional ones and Israel intended to change them (Shlaim 1988). In addition, Israel was also responsible for missing the opportunity for peace at the end of the war (Shlaim 1988, 1995; and Pappé 1992, 1999).

As for the creation of the refugee problem, Morris argued that there were no indications that the Palestinians were called upon by the Arab leaders to run away from Palestine. They did so for a combination of reasons: economic pressure, psychological warfare, intimidation, fear of Jewish indirect and direct attacks, and actual Jewish attacks including various cases of massacre. Some of these attacks, in certain places and at certain times, actually were executed by military orders. Although there were some past Zionist plans of "transfer" (ethnic cleansing) of the Palestinians from those parts of the land that were supposed to become part of the Jewish state, there was not any deliberate Israeli plan to expel Palestinians. Morris maintains that the tragedy of the Palestinian refugees was born out of the war and became inevitable because of the special circumstances of the war, the geographical intermixing of the Arab and Jewish populations, the mutual Jewish and Palestinian fears, and the structural weakness of Palestinian Arab society. The war also created a Jewish refugee problem of a similar magnitude because of the flight of Jews from the Arab states (Morris 1986, 1987, 1988, 1994, 2004, 2008).[4]

The new Israeli historiography created a heated debate among Israeli scholars; however, it did not change substantially the official Israeli narrative. Israel's leadership continued to argue that Israel had no responsibility for the creation of the Palestinian refugee problem. According to this view, the Palestinians and the Arab states, which rejected the Partition Plan and aimed to destroy Israel by a total war, were responsible for creating the refugee problem (Shapira 1999; Ben-Joseph Hirsh 2007).

In an interview with Ari Shavit (*Haaretz*, January 6 2004a), Morris justified the Palestinian expulsion because, without it, Israel could not have won the war and be established as a homogeneous Jewish state. In certain conditions such as in the 1947–49 war, the expulsion was not a war crime:

> From the moment the *Yishuv* [pre 1948 Jewish community in Palestine] was attacked by the Palestinians and afterward by the Arab states, there was no choice but to expel the Palestinian population … the need to establish this state [Israel] in this place overcame the injustice that was done to the Palestinians by uprooting them.

Morris even blamed David Ben-Gurion, Israeli Prime Minister and Defense Minister in the war for not expelling more Palestinians and defined it as "a serious historical mistake."

The fact that an increasing number of Israelis acknowledge that Israel played a significant part in creating the Palestinian refugee problem has not changed the general Israeli attitude to the Palestinian and Arab states' overall responsibility for the plight of the Palestinian refugees (Bar-On 2006; Morris 2001, 2004b).

Denial of the Palestinian rights

The greatest moral challenge to the Jewish–Israeli meta-narrative of justice has been the Arab and Palestinian claims that the establishment of the State of Israel in Palestine was an act of injustice because it came at the expense of the Palestinians. Since the establishment of the Zionist movement, throughout the Arab–Israeli conflict, Jewish–Israeli leaders confronted the Arab and Palestinian arguments with several counter-arguments:

1 Palestine was an empty land ("a land without a people"), being sparsely populated by Arabs. Until the arrival of the Zionists by the end of the nineteenth century Palestine was a neglected land, non-cultivated, and underdeveloped. The history of the land under Muslim rule was a story of continuous decline. Only with the return of Jewish settlers did it bloom again.
2 Palestine was never populated by indigenous Arab-Palestinians. The Arabs who moved to Palestine in recent centuries were largely from what are nowadays Syria, Lebanon, and Jordan, and they had no any authentic ties to the Land of Israel. Many of them came for economic reasons, especially after the Zionist movement made the land fruitful and the economy thrive.
3 The Palestinian national identity was also denied or at most described as a very recent political development, in reaction to the Zionist movement and to the Jewish claims of self-determination. Thus, the Palestinian identity is a by-product of the emergence of the Zionist movement as the Jewish national movement.
4 The Arabs never established an independent state in Palestine and the Palestinian Arabs never constituted a separate and distinctive national group. They never stood up as a unique nation with collective claims. That is why the League of Nations, in 1921, without any moral hesitation, approved the right of Jews to establish their homeland in Palestine.
5 Even if the Palestinians constituted a distinctive people and a nation and had a right for self-determination, including the establishment of an independent Palestinian state, they actually lost that right when they rejected the UN Partition Plan of 1947 and went to war against Israel.

(Bar-Tal and Salomon 2006; Gorny 1987; Kapitan 1997; Pappé 1992)

The Palestinian national identity was also denied after the 1947–49 war. The occupation of the West Bank by Jordan and the Gaza Strip by Egypt only strengthened the political denial of the Palestinians as a distinctive people. This denial did not change following the occupation of the West Bank and the Gaza Strip in the 1967 war by Israel. For the first time, after 1967, the Palestinian problem became an Israeli problem, since Israel got control over most of the Palestinian people. However, most of the Israeli leaders and people still denied the fact that the Palestinians were a people and a nation, who deserve self-determination and statehood.[5] Most of the Israeli decision makers and people perceived these territories as part of *Eretz Israel* that were liberated by the 1967 war, so that the territories, and in particular the West Bank, was considered "disputed" or "unallocated" rather than occupied territory because it had been illegally occupied by Jordan in 1948. Only a few perceived the territories as occupied ones and as bargaining cards for negotiating a peace agreement.

For many years until 1988, when Jordan announced its formal political disengagement from the West Bank, Jordan was perceived by the Labor Party in Israel as the only potential partner for negotiations about the final status of the West Bank. The "Jordanian option," as it was termed in Israel by the Labor Party, was considered the only political negotiating option with an Arab partner. However, Israel refused to negotiate the future of the West Bank (including East Jerusalem), which was defined as "Judea and Samaria," in order to reach a peace agreement with Jordan. Thus, negotiating East Jerusalem and the West Bank became a taboo in Israel's policy, especially with the coming of the *Likud* Party to power in 1977.

Nevertheless, with the exception of East Jerusalem that was annexed to Israel in June 1967, making its Palestinian population Israeli residents, Israel never formally annexed the West Bank and the Gaza Strip. Yet, this fact did not prevent the policy of establishing Jewish settlements in these territories immediately after 1967, which was augmented by subsequent *Likud* governments after 1977 and has continued until the present day.

The first change of Israeli policy vis-à-vis the Palestinians was made in the peace process with Egypt in 1977–79, when Israel accepted in the Camp David Agreements of September 1978 the granting of autonomy to the Palestinians in the occupied territories as a first step for deciding the future political status of these territories. The refusal of the Palestinians to join the autonomy talks left Israel and Egypt to negotiate the issue alone. However, in a short time, the autonomy negotiations failed because of the wide disagreements between the parties, and the Israeli reluctance to implement autonomy in the early 1980s.

It was only the first *intifada* (1987–93), in which the Palestinians in the West Bank and in the Gaza Strip violently resisted and rebelled against the Israeli occupation, that brought Israeli decision makers to reconsider the occupation of the territories and the resuming of the idea of granting autonomy to the Palestinians. This led to a political crisis and to the breakdown of the *Likud* and Labor coalition. The Labor Party under Yitzhak Rabin won the parliamentary elections of 1992 mainly because of the promise to look for some kind of political solution with the Palestinians that would change the status quo and formally end the *intifada*. Rabin still considered the option of autonomy as the only viable one; however, the initial success of the informal stage of the Oslo process at the beginning of 1993 to reach a draft agreement convinced him to endorse the Oslo peace process with the Palestinians.

The Oslo Accord (The "Declaration of Principles on Interim Self-Government Arrangements") of September 13, 1993, was the first clear Israeli indication of recognizing the Palestinians as a people with legitimate political rights, although that recognition did not necessarily mean a willingness to establish a Palestinian state. Rabin was thinking in terms of establishing a Palestinian entity that would be less than a state and only in the Gaza Strip and in parts of the West Bank. Only at the Camp David Summit in July 2000 did Israel formally accept the idea of Palestinian self-determination in the form of establishing an independent Palestinian state in about 91 percent of the West Bank and the entire Gaza Strip, though the talks ultimately failed.

Denial of Palestinian claims for justice

The Palestinian demands that Israel will acknowledge its responsibility for the creation of the refugee problem and that Israel will accept the Palestinian "right of return" to their original homes within the State of Israel have been utterly rejected by the Israeli leadership. Since 1949 and throughout the long conflict years, the Israeli leadership has denied any responsibility for the creation of the refugee problem; it has blamed the Arabs for it, and it has refused to recognize the "right of return" mainly because of political, ideological, security, and especially demographic reasons.

Israel argues that the entry of a massive influx of Palestinian refugees to its sovereign territory would pose a serious existential threat to its security, law, and order. Moreover, it will endanger Israel as a Jewish state by disrupting its demographic basis. In addition, a massive return will trigger motivation for Palestinian irredentism, as well as ownership problems because Palestinian homes were occupied by Jewish immigrants or destroyed altogether. Any recognition of the "right of return" would also be interpreted as admitting responsibility for creating the refugee problem in the first place. Israel, therefore, denies any responsibility even if there were no practical demand for a return of refugees (Gazit 1995; Alpher *et al.* 1999; Klein 2007).

Since mid-1948, the Israeli government has adopted an official policy of preventing the return of Palestinian refugees to their homes in Israel, justifying it because of the continuation of the state of war and perceiving the Palestinian refugees as enemies. By the end of September 1948 Israel adopted a new policy that a final settlement of the refugee problem would be reached only as part of a general agreement when peace comes. Israeli leaders argue that as long as a general comprehensive peace has not been achieved with all the Arab states, the Palestinians' return could endanger it (Morris 2008).

Yet, at the Lausanne Conference that was convened in 1949 immediately after the 1947–49 war with the participation of Israel and the Arab states, the Israeli government pressured by the United States accepted in principle to repatriate 100,000 Palestinian refugees, but only as part of a peace agreement and a final settlement, in which all other refugees would be absorbed by Arab states (see Caplan 1994). The Arab refusal of this proposal brought Israel to cancel its offer. Since then, Israel has refused to take any responsibility for the creation of the Palestinian refugee problem and to accept any return of the Palestinian refugees to their homes in Israel based on the Palestinian concept of the "right of return." Nonetheless, from the early 1950s until 1967, Israel established a family reunification program that enabled 40,000–50,000 refugees to return to Israel; several additional thousands returned also between 1967 and 1994 (Morris 2004b; Alpher *et al.* 1999).

The massive Jewish immigration from the Arab states in the 1950s and 1960s only enhanced Israeli opposition to the return of Palestinian refugees; they argued that the war had resulted in an exchange of population between Israel and the Arab states. Israel had dealt with its Jewish refugees from neighboring Arab countries, so it expected that the Arab states would deal with the Palestinian refugees likewise. Thus, the Palestinian refugees had to be resettled in their locations within the Arab states, whereas the confiscated and abandoned Palestinian property was a practical and just compensation for the property left by Jews who had to flee the Arab states.[6]

Israel's position regarding the compensation payment to the Palestinian refugees has been conditional. Since 1949–50 Israel stated that Israel was not responsible for the fate of the Palestinian refugees during the war. Israel also insisted that Palestinian property confiscated from exiled refugees had been exchanged for the sequestered property of Jewish immigrants from Arab states and that the Jewish–Israeli loss and the damage of property during the 1947–49 war should be calculated as well (Klein 2007). The status of the Palestinian refugees is a humanitarian issue of global concern largely because the Arab states exploited their misery for political reasons, perpetuating their plight.

The compensation funds for the refugees should be raised internationally and administered by an international organization. Israel would contribute voluntarily through the international fund compensation. The compensation should be calculated not on an individual basis but on a collective basis, and it should aim to resettle the refugees in their host countries. Traditionally, this position was based on the Israeli perspective that the Palestinian refugees were not part of a nation that deserves self-determination (Klein 2007, 467). In addition to that, Israel linked the compensation to the Palestinian refugees to a comprehensive peace with Arab states, end of the Arab boycott, and similar compensation for Jews from Arab countries who settled in Israel (Zureik 1996, 65–66; Tamari 2007).

Most Israeli scholars also deny the Palestinian claim for the "right of return" based on legal arguments. The main argument is that, according to international law, Palestinians have no legal right to repatriate to the State of Israel. None of the United Nations resolutions, including UN General Assembly (UNGA) Resolution 194, establishes a binding legal right or obligation for Palestinians to repatriate to Israel. Thus, the State of Israel is under no legal obligation to enable the repatriation of Palestinians to its territory. The UN resolutions are considered no more than recommendations, rather than a binding legal norm (Lapidoth 2002; Sabel 2004; Singer 2001; Zilbershats 2007; Zilbershats and Goren-Amitai 2011).

For instance, UNGA Resolution 194 does not state that the Palestinian refugees have a legal right to return, but only that they should be permitted to do so; hence, apparently, with Israel's authorization. The resolution also permits return only to those refugees who wish to live in peace with their neighbors. Actually, Israel, the Palestinians, and the Arab states rejected the resolution immediately after it was adopted. While Israel refused to repatriate the refugees, the Palestinians and the Arab states negated the legitimacy of the resolution for decades because it indirectly forced them to recognize the existence of the State of Israel by demanding that the Palestinian refugees who return will live peacefully with their Israeli neighbors.

Furthermore, Israeli scholars argue that, in addition to the fact that UNGA Resolution 194 is not legally binding, the norms of customary international law that it expresses are not binding because, when the resolution was adopted, there were no such customary norms. Moreover, the resolution does not mention that the return of Palestinians is based on principles of international law and equity (Lapidoth 2002; Sabel 2004; Zilbershats 2007; Zilbershats and Goren-Amitai 2011). The resolution only bases the requirement of compensation on the principles of international law and equity.

Israeli scholars also emphasize that the UN Security Council presents a different approach to the refugee problem to that of the General Assembly. For instance, UNSC Resolution 233 of 6 June 1967 refers only to a proposal to "facilitate return" of refugees from the West Bank and the Gaza Strip who fled the area because of the 1967 war. The UNSC Resolution does not refer to the refugees of the 1947–49 war. Furthermore, the famous UNSC Resolution 242 of 22 November 1967, which calls for resolution of the Arab–Israeli conflict based on the formula of peace for land, mentions also achieving "a just settlement of the refugee problem." The resolution refers to refugees in general, and does not mention Palestinian refugees in particular; nor does UNGA resolution 194 (III). This formula also includes the issue of Jewish refugees from Arab and Muslim states.[7]

The issue of the Palestinian refugees was also mentioned in the peace treaties that Israel signed with Egypt (in 1979) and with Jordan (1994), as well as in the Oslo Agreement with the Palestinians (1993). These agreements contain clauses regarding the possibility for Palestinian refugees who had fled the West Bank and Gaza Strip in 1967 to return to these areas. However, these agreements do not provide the refugees of 1947–49 and 1967 with the option to return to the State of Israel (Lapidoth 2002; Sabel 2004; Singer 2001; Zilbershats, 2007; Zilbershats and Goren-Amitai 2011). Indeed, the Palestine Liberation Organization (PLO) accepted that in the Oslo Agreement only UN Security Council Resolutions 242 and 338 were referred to, while UNGA Resolution 194 (III) was not mentioned at all.

Yeoshaft Harkabi presents a different Israeli attitude towards the Palestinian request for justice. Although Harkabi does not accept the Palestinian demand that the refugees will return to the State of Israel, he expresses his understanding of (and even empathy for) that request. In his words,

> there is a considerable element of truth and justice in the ideology of the Arabs; one can understand their feeling that Arab nationalism has suffered an injustice by losing the territory of Palestine to Israel. Their burning pain is sincere. The Arab indictment against Zionism partly

consists of correct charges, though in part it is distortion. To understand the Arab attitude, the Israelis must understand what they would do were they be Arabs, and what attitudes they would adopt towards Israel; hence, they should try to visualize the depths of the Arab conviction of injustice. Let them imagine that they are Palestinian refugees, who have been uprooted from the neighborhood where they lived, who have been deprived of their property by strangers, and who regard its restitution as a matter of fundamental right and justice.

(Harkabi 1972, 449)

Conclusions

The Israeli narratives of justice and injustice are old and established along the lines of Jewish history. They reflect mainly the Jewish rights for self-determination as a people and as a nation. They emphasize the historical rights of the Jewish people to *Eretz Israel*, and the Jewish suffering throughout history, as well as the need for establishing a Jewish independent state as a solution to the Jewish problems. The Israeli narratives include also the Israeli attitudes and emotions that were built throughout the Arab–Israeli conflict. While legitimizing the Israeli attitudes in the conflict, these historical narratives tend to de-legitimize the Palestinian narratives of justice and injustice, blaming the Palestinians and the Arab states for initiating the conflict, its escalation, and for the failure to resolve it so far.

The Israeli narratives have also guided the Israeli negotiators and decision makers throughout the peace process with the Palestinians in the last 20 years, especially regarding the issues of responsibility for creating the Palestinian refugee problem and the "right of return." Their actual impact in the peace negotiations will be presented in the following chapters.

Notes

1 Scholars are divided on whether the Holocaust had any tangible influence upon the establishment of the State of Israel. There are those who argue that there is no historical link whatsoever between the Holocaust and the establishment of Israel, and those who assign a great significance to the efforts of Holocaust survivors to mobilize public opinion in favor of the establishment of the State of Israel. See Friesel 1996; Bauer 1996; Ofer 2005.

2 By accepting the Partition Plan, the Jewish leaders compromised their territorial aspirations. This compromise was the outcome of a clear realization that, due to the international and regional limitations, the Jewish people could accomplish their national goals only in part of *Eretz Israel*. However, there were those who argued that the historical rights of the Jews to the Land of Israel justified political sovereignty over Greater Israel, namely, the whole of the Land of Israel, so the Jewish people could not compromise on this right. Following the occupation of the West Bank in the 1967 war, the aspirations for Greater Israel were revived again.

3 Excluding the book of Simha Flappan (1987), a veteran activist of Mapam's Party, the three others were young Israeli academics.

4 Both Palestinian and Israeli scholars criticized Morris's studies. While the former found his studies progressive as compared to Israeli official and traditional narratives, they denied his findings that the Palestinian refugee problem was a direct outcome of the war and not a deliberate Israeli plan to expel the Palestinians and conduct ethnic cleansing. Conversely, Israeli scholars dismissed his arguments that the idea of transfer of the Palestinians was embedded in Zionist thinking. See Khalidi 1988; Masalha 1991; Teveth 1990; Karsh 1997, 1999.
5 In this context, especially remarkable was the former Israeli Prime Minister Golda Meir's statement that there never existed a Palestinian people.
6 It is estimated that between 800,000 and 1 million Jews left or were forced to leave their homes in Arab countries from 1948 until the early 1970s.
7 UN Security Council Resolution 338 of 22 October 1973 that followed the 1973 October War called for the implementation of UN Security Council Resolution 242, without referring to the Palestinian refugees.

References

Alpher, Joseph, Khalil Shikaki, Gabriel Ben-Dor, Moshe Maoz, Ibrahim Dawrak, Yezid Sayigh, Yossi Katz (MK), Ze'ev Schiff, Ghassan Khatibi, and Shimon Shamir. "Concept Paper: The Palestinian Refugee Problem and the Right of Return," *Middle East Policy*, February 1999, pp. 167–89.

Bar-On, Mordechai. "Conflicting Narratives or Narratives of a Conflict: Can the Zionist and Palestinian Narratives of the 1948 War Be Bridged?" In *Israeli and Palestinian Narratives of Conflict* (ed.) Robert I. Rotberg. (Bloomington: Indiana University Press, 2006), pp. 142–73.

Bar-Tal, Daniel and Gavriel Salomon. "Israeli-Jewish Narrative of the Israeli–Palestinian Conflict: Evolution, Contents, Function, and Consequences." In *Israeli and Palestinian Narratives of Conflict* (ed.) Robert I. Rotberg. (Bloomington: Indiana University Press, 2006), pp. 19–46.

Bauer, Yehuda. "The Impact of the Holocaust on the Establishment of the State of Israel." In *Major Changes within the Jewish People in the Wake of the Holocaust* (ed.) Yisrael Gutman. (Jerusalem: Yad Vashem, 1996), pp. 545–52.

Ben-Joseph Hirsh, Michal. "From Taboo to the Negotiable: The Israeli New Historians and the Changing Representation of the Palestinian Problem," *Perspectives on Politics*, Vol. 5, 2 (June 2007), pp. 241–58.

Caplan, Neil. *The Lausanne Conference, 1949: A Case Study on Middle Eastern Peacemaking* (Syracuse, NY: Syracuse University Press, 1994).

Caplan, Neil. "Victimhood and Identity: Psychological Obstacles to Israeli Reconciliation with the Palestinians." In *Israeli and Palestinian Identities in History and Literature* (eds) Kamal Abdel-Malek and David Jacobson. (New York: Macmillan, 1999), pp. 63–86.

Flappan, Simha. *The Birth of Israel: Myths and Realities* (New York: Pantheon Books, 1987).

Friesel, Evyatar. "The Holocaust: Factors in the Birth of Israel?" In *Major Changes within the Jewish People in the Wake of the Holocaust* (ed.) Yisrael Gutman. (Jerusalem: Yad Vashem, 1996), pp. 519–44.

Gans, Chaim. "The Palestinian Refugees and the Right of Return: Theoretical Perspectives," *Theoretical Inquiries in Law*, Vol. 5, 2 (July 2004), pp. 269–304.

Gans, Chaim. *From Richard Wagner to the Palestinian Right of Return: A Philosophical Analysis of Israeli Public Affairs* (Tel Aviv: Am Oved, 2006) [Hebrew].

Gans, Chaim. "Is there a Historical Right to the Land of Israel?," *Azure*, Vol. 19 (2007), pp. 80–111.
Gans, Chaim. *A Just Zionism: On the Morality of the Jewish State* (Oxford: Oxford University Press, 2008).
Gavison, Ruth. "The Jews' Right to Statehood: A Defense," *Azure*, Vol. 15 (2003), pp. 70–108.
Gazit, Shlomo. "The Palestinian Refugee Problem," *Final Status Issues Study*, 2 (Tel Aviv: Jaffee Center for Strategic Studies, 1995).
Gelber, Yoav. *Palestine 1948: War, Escape, and the Emergence of the Palestinian Refugee Problem* (Brighton: Sussex Academic Press, 2001).
Gorny, Yosef. *Zionism and the Arabs* (Oxford: Clarendon Press, 1987).
Harkabi, Yeoshafat. *Arab Attitudes to Israel* (Jerusalem: Keter, 1972).
Kapitan, Tomis. "Historical Introduction to the Philosophical Issues." In *Philosophical Perspectives on the Israeli–Palestinian Conflict* (ed.) Tomis Kapitan. (Armonk, NY: M. E. Sharpe, 1997), pp. 3–47.
Karsh, Efraim. *Fabricating Israel's History: The "New Historians"* (London: Frank Kass, 1997).
Karsh, Efraim. "Benny Morris and the Reign of Error," *Middle East Quarterly*, Vol. 6 (1999), pp. 15–28.
Khalidi, Walid. "Plan Dalet: Master Plan for the Conquest of Palestine," *Journal of Palestine Studies*, Vol. 18 (1988), pp. 3–19.
Kimmerling, Baruch. *Zionism and Territory: The Socio-Territorial Dimensions of Zionist Politics* (Berkeley: University of California Press, 1983).
Klein, Menachem. "The Negotiations for the Settlement of the 1948 Refugees." In *Israel and the Palestinian Refugees* (eds) Eyal Benvenisti, Chaim Gans, and Sari Hanafi (Berlin: Springer, 2007), pp. 465–91.
Lapidoth, Ruth. "Legal Aspects of the Palestinian Refugee Question," *Jerusalem Letter/Viewpoints*, No. 485, September 1, 2002.
Lorch, Netanel. *The Edge of the Sword: Israel's War of Independence, 1947–1949* (Jerusalem: Massada Press, 1968, Revised Edition).
Masalha, Nur. "A Critique of Benny Morris," *Journal of Palestinian Studies*, Vol. 21 (1991), pp. 90–97.
Morris, Benny. "Yosef Weitz and the Transfer Committees, 1948–49," *Middle Eastern Studies*, Vol. 22 (1986), pp. 522–61.
Morris, Benny. *The Birth of the Palestinian Refugee Problem, 1947–1949* (Cambridge: Cambridge University Press, 1987).
Morris, Benny. "The New Historiography: Israel Confronts Its Past," *Tikkun*, Vol. 4 (November–December, 1988), pp. 19–23, 99–102.
Morris, Benny. *1948 and After, Israel and the Palestinians* (Oxford: Clarendon Press, 1994).
Morris, Benny. *Righteous Victims: A History of the Zionist–Arab Conflict, 1881–2001* (New York: Vintage Books, 2001).
Morris, Benny. Interview of Ari Shavit, *Haaretz*, 6 January 2004a.
Morris, Benny. *The Birth of the Palestinian Refugee Problem Revisited* (New York: Cambridge University Press, 2004b).
Morris, Benny. *1948: A History of the First Arab–Israeli War* (New Haven, CT: Yale University Press, 2008).
Ofer, Dalia. "The Holocaust, the Creation of Israel, and the Shaping of Israel Society." In *Shared Histories: A Palestinian-Israeli Dialogue*) (eds) Paul Scham, Walid Salem, and Benjamin Pogrund. (Walnut Creek, CA: Left Coast Press, 2005), pp. 135–47.

Pappé, Ilan. *The Making of the Arab–Israeli Conflict, 1947–1951* (London: I. B. Tauris, 1992).

Pappé, Ilan. *The Israel–Palestine Question* (London: Routledge, 1999).

Pappé, Ilan. *A History of Modern Palestine: One Land, Two Peoples* (Cambridge: Cambridge University Press, 2004).

Peres, Shimon. *The New Middle East* (New York: Henry Holt and Company, 1993).

Sabel, Robbie. "The Palestinian Refugees, International Law, and the Peace Process," *Refugee*, Vol. 21, 2 (2004), pp. 52–61.

Scham, Paul, Walid Salem, and Benjamin Pogrund. *Shared Histories: A Palestinian–Israeli Dialogue* (Walnut Creek, CA: Left Coast Press, 2005).

Sela, Avraham. "Israeli Historiography of the 1948 War." In *Shared Histories: A Palestinian–Israeli Dialogue* (eds), Paul Scham, Walid Salem, and Benjamin Pogrund. (Walnut Creek, CA: Left Coast Press, 2005), pp. 205–19.

Shapira, Anita. "The Failure of Israel's 'New Historians' to Explain War and Peace: The Past is not a Foreign Country," *The New Republic*, 29 November 1999.

Shimoni, Gideon. *The Zionist Ideology* (Hanover, NH: Brandeis University Press, 1995).

Shlaim, Avi. *Collision across the Jordan: King Abdullah, the Zionists and Palestine, 1921–51* (New York: Columbia University Press, 1988).

Shlaim, Avi. *War and Peace in the Middle East: A Concise History* (London: Penguin, 1995).

Singer, Joel. "No Palestinian 'Return' to Israel," *Human Rights Brief*, Vol. 8, 5 (2001).

Tamari, Salim. "Palestinian Refugee Property Claims: Compensation and Restitution." In *Israel and the Palestinian Refugees* (eds) Eyal Benvenisti, Chaim Gans, and Sari Hanafi. (Berlin: Springer, 2007), pp. 309–22.

Teveth, Shabtai. "The Palestinian Refugee Problem and Its Origins," *Middle Eastern Studies*, Vol. 26 (1990), pp. 214–49.

Zerubavel, Yael. *Recovered Roots: Collective Memory and the Making of Israeli National Tradition* (Chicago: Chicago University Press, 1995).

Zilbershats, Yaffa. "International Law and the Palestinian Right of Return to the State of Israel." In *Israel and the Palestinian Refugees* (eds) Eyal Benvenisti, Chaim Gans, and Sari Hanafi (Berlin: Springer, 2007), pp. 191–218.

Zilbershats, Yaffa and Nimra Goren-Amitai. *Return of Palestinian Refugees to the State of Israel* (Jerusalem: The Metzilah Center, 2011).

Zureik, Elia. *Palestinian Refugees and the Peace Process* (Washington, DC: Institute for Palestine Studies, 1996).

4 The Palestinian narratives of justice and injustice

The Palestinian narratives of justice and injustice are perceived by the Palestinians as the most necessary and legitimate means of expressing the justice of their claims, the injustice that happened to them, the need to correct the injustice, and one of the most effective and least evident forms of resistance against Israel (Rouhana 2006, 124). The historical narratives are the basis of their claims for political, ideological, and human rights. The issue of justice has become over the years of conflict the key discourse in official Arab and Palestinian statements and declarations, in Palestinian scholarly writings, and in Palestinian public argumentation.

The main expression of the justice–injustice issue is the Palestinian "right of return" that has gained the status of a sacred right and a protected value. It is an inalienable and basic human right, as protected by international law. The right of return (*haq al-'awda*) of the Palestinian refugees to their homes has a central place in Palestinian political narrative and mythology. The term "right of return" has become the basis of Palestinian nationalism and identity. It is probably the most significant symbol that unifies all the Palestinians. The continued existence of the refugee problem symbolizes for the Palestinians the nature of their unique tragedy and the historical injustice done to them. The issue of the refugees in the Palestinian narrative is not only a humanitarian problem; it is rather, first and foremost, an issue of justice (Abu Zayyad 1995; Zureik 2007).

The framing of the Palestinian refugee problem as injustice and defining the return of the refugees to their homes as a just right make the issue a sacred and protected value. The claim for a "right of return" has a symbolic power, a moral duty that cannot be negotiated and compromised. It also turns the conflict and its resolution into a "higher moral plateau" (Barkan 2005, 88). Acknowledgment of the right of return is perceived also as expressing the fact that the Palestinians are a people with national rights, including the natural right to live in their ancestral homeland, and the injustice done to them by the Israelis by preventing them from return. The denial of this inalienable right is perceived as rejecting their peoplehood and nationhood (Tamari 1995). Moreover, if the Palestinians have a legitimate claim to Palestine, there is no logic to deny their intrinsic right to return (Khalidi 1992, 31–32).

The Palestinians construct their narratives sometimes independently of the Zionist narratives and sometimes in juxtaposition to them (Abdel Jawad 2006, 73). The Palestinian narratives combine meta-narratives of justice and injustice. The basic sources of the Palestinian meta-narratives of justice and injustice, as well as those that deny the Israeli meta-narrative of justice and injustice, are presented in two official documents: The Palestinian National Covenant of 1968 and the Palestinian Declaration of Independence of 1988, as well as in many Palestinian declarations, statements, and academic publications.

The meta-narratives of justice

The core of the Palestinian meta-narratives of justice includes the following principles:

1 The right of self-determination should be implemented in Palestine because

> Palestine is the homeland of the Palestinian Arab people; it is an indivisible part of the Arab homeland, and the Palestinian people are an integral part of the Arab nation. Palestine, with the boundaries it had during the British Mandate, is an indivisible territorial unit.
>
> (The Palestinian National Covenant, 1968, Articles 1 and 2)

2 "The Palestinian identity is a genuine, essential, and inherent characteristic" (The Palestinian National Covenant, 1968, Article 4).
3 The Arab right in Palestine derives from the fact that the Arabs constituted not only the majority of its current inhabitants (up to 1948), but also that they had maintained that majority since the Arab conquest in the seventh century.
4 The Palestinians are a people whose ancient and deeply rooted history in the Land of Palestine existed long before the Jews appeared on the scene, given their descent from ancient Canaanites, Hittites, and Philistines.
5 The dominant culture and language in Palestine even under the Ottoman rule was Arab and Arabic.
6 Even before the appearance of the Zionist movement, at the end of the nineteenth century, a local Palestinian national identity emerged in a formative process. Moreover, the challenge of Zionism played a central role in the emergence and articulation of Palestinian nationalism (Hassassian 2005; Nassar 2005).
7 If it were not for the Zionist project of colonization, Palestine under the British mandate could have become an independent state of Palestine like the other neighboring Arab states.

The Palestinian National Council adopted the Palestinian Declaration of Independence in Algiers on 15 November 1988. It proclaimed the establishment of the State of Palestine and kept intact the narratives of justice that link the historical relation between the Palestinian people and Palestine.[1] It emphasized the historical rights, including the right of self-determination of the Palestinian people that had been recognized by the international community.

The Palestinian Declaration of Independence elaborated the principal national narratives similarly to Israel's Declaration of Independence in the following way:

1 In Palestine the Palestinian people were born, grew, developed, and excelled.
2 The Palestinian people was never separated from or diminished in its integral bonds from Palestine.
3 Throughout its history, the Palestinian people forged its national identity and kept its strong connection with the Land of Palestine, although they were deprived of political independence.
4 The Palestinian right of self-determination was recognized by the Covenant of the League of Nations (1919) and by the UN General Assembly Resolution 181 (1947), the Partition Plan.[2]
5 The UN Resolutions, which were enshrined upon principles of international law and legitimacy, recognized the Palestinian national rights, including also the right of return, the right to independence, and the right to sovereignty over territory and homeland that were violated by the Zionist/Israeli incursion.
6 Finally, the declaration proclaims the establishment of the State of Palestine "on our Palestinian territory with its capital Jerusalem (*Al-Quds Ash-Sharif*)." The borders of the declared State of Palestine were not specified (similarly to the Israeli Declaration of Independence). Interestingly, the population of the state referred to in this statement as The State of Palestine is Palestinians wherever they may be.

The meta-narratives of injustice

The Palestinian meta-narratives of injustice present the injustice inflicted on the Palestinians since the arrival of the Jewish-Zionists to Palestine by the end of the nineteenth century, which reached its peak with the establishment of the State of Israel in May 1948 and the *Nakba* or the Palestinian catastrophe of the 1947–49 war that prevented the establishment of the Palestinian state and created the refugee problem. The Palestinian suffering, from the *Nakba* until the lingering Israeli occupation of the Palestinian territories since 1967, is embedded within the meta-narratives of injustice. These narratives include the following arguments:

1 The international community, the superpowers, and especially Great Britain are responsible for the creation of the Palestinian problem. "The Balfour Declaration, the Mandate of Palestine and everything that has been based upon them, are deemed null and void" (The Palestinian National Covenant, 1968, Article 20).

> The partition of Palestine in 1947 and the establishment of the State of Israel are entirely illegal, regardless of the passage of time, because they were contrary to the will of the Palestinian people and to their natural right in their homeland, and inconsistent with the principles embodied in the Charter of the United Nations, particularly the right of self-determination.
>
> (The Palestinian National Covenant, 1968, Article 19)

There was not any moral justification for establishing a Jewish state in Palestine at the expense of the Palestinians; therefore, all the land belongs to them and they do not have to share it with the Jews (Cattan 1969; Khalidi 1992; Salem 2005).

2 The Arab rejection of the UN partition plan was right and just, because the UN plan was based on injustice. Similarly, the 1947–49 war was a "just war." It was a defensive action necessitated by the demands of self-defense. Palestinians' resistance to the takeover of their homeland by the Zionists was a natural and human reaction to injustice. Moreover, since violence has been always embedded in the Zionist credo and behavior, violent resistance to Zionism by Palestinians is a legitimate, just, and humane response to injustice. Resistance includes also rejecting peace proposals that were perceived as *unjust* mainly because they stemmed from extreme power asymmetry and imbalance between Palestinians and Israelis. The 1947–49 war then became inevitable because of Zionist intentions to build an exclusively Jewish state.

3 The establishment of a Jewish state is unjust and immoral because it brought about the dispossessing of the Palestinian people. The Palestinians view the Zionist claim to their homeland and its implementation as an enormous injustice. The Palestinians firmly deny the Zionist claim that Palestine was "a land without a people for a people without land." They consider themselves as the victims of this claim, which justified the Jewish immigration to Palestine. Thus, the Zionist ideology and its implementation were disastrous for the Palestinians (Masalha 2002; Yahya 2005).

4 The Jews are responsible for the emergence of the conflict because they had settled in the land of somebody else.

5 The Jews planned the 1947–49 war and they were better organized both politically and militarily for it, compared to the Palestinians.

6 Israel has been fully responsible for the expulsion of hundreds of thousands of Palestinians from their homes in Palestine, making them refugees. Israel aimed to conduct ethnic cleansing in its war of aggression against Palestinians. Immediately after the adoption of the UN Partition Plan, the Jews began to expel Palestinians. The Jews realized that Israel could not be established as a Jewish state without a great Jewish majority (Abdel Jawad 2007, Khaladi 1997–98; Masalha 2002; Qurei 2008; Rouhana 2006). The Palestinians deny Israeli claims that the refugees left because of calls by Arab leaders to them to leave their homes, although they agree that some of them left out of fear but they intended to return after a short term (Yahya 2005).

7 Israel has been fully responsible for all Palestinian suffering from 1947–49 until the present. The Palestinians have been victims in the conflict with Israel. The Palestinian victimhood includes humiliation and damage to dignity at the collective and individual levels (Said 2006).
8 Israel's refusal to let the refugees return to their homes was and still is a basic and crucial example of injustice (Said 2006; Khalidi 1997–98).
9 The Palestinians deny any responsibility for the eruption of the conflict, as well as for the injustice that happened to them because of their attitudes and behavior throughout the conflict.
10 The Palestinian narratives of injustice emphasize the emotions of permanent victimhood, people who were exiled, looking for "redemption through return" and reconstitution of an idealized past (Tamari 1999).
11 The sense of historical injustice is amplified by a conviction that the majority of Palestinians, including most of the refugees, had no control whatsoever over the initiating of the 1947–49 war and its developments, so they felt only victims of it (Rabinowitz 2007, 413).

The Palestinian Declaration of Independence emphasizes the injustice inflicted on the Palestinians who were deprived of their political independence by "a hostile array of local and foreign powers," and the Israeli occupation since 1967. It praises the Palestinian resistance and especially the massive national uprising, the first *intifada*.

De-legitimizing Israel's rights and justice

In the context of justifying their rights, the Palestinians tend to deny, devalue, and de-legitimize the rights of the Jewish people to nationhood and statehood in Palestine. Palestinians perceive the Jewish-Zionist narratives as the cause of their suffering and threatening their own existence. The Palestinians introduce the following arguments:

1 *Judaism is a religion.* The Jews are not a nation but rather a community of believers. Judaism as a world religion cannot attach itself to one particular place. Thus, "Judaism, being religion, is not an independent nationality. Nor do Jews constitute a single nation with an identity of its own; they are citizens of the states to which they belong" (The Palestinian National Covenant, 1968, Article 20).
2 *There is no Jewish people* but only [an] "imagined Jewish people that did not exist but was created, but also – and primarily – in the process through which this [Zionist] dream collided with the Palestinian reality, and in the process of employing violence and racism as two means of dealing with this collision" (Zoabi 2009, 2).
3 *The Jews do not have any historical rights in Palestine.* "Claims for historical or religious ties of Jews with Palestine are incompatible with the facts of history and the true conception of what constitutes statehood"

(Palestinian National Covenant, 1968, Article 20). Actually, the Jewish presence in Palestine was marginal even during Biblical times. The ancient Jews controlled Palestine only for a short time and their control was never complete, since it was limited only to a part of the country, and other nationalities shared it with them. The Jews conquered Palestine from the Arabs, who had lived there before them. Arab tribes inhabited Palestine since pre-historic days. The Jews left no lasting cultural and historical traces. The Arabs conquered the country from the Byzantines and not from the Jews, so the Jewish cannot demand its restoration from the Arabs (Harkabi 1972, 193). Moreover, the history of Palestine indicates that the Arabs have lived in Palestine longer than the Jews (Harkabi 1972, 194).

4 *The validity of the divine promises to the Jews has expired over time.* The divine promises were given to the Children of Israel on the condition they remained faithful to their Covenant with God, but the Jews, despite the numerous and repeated warnings of the prophets, violated the Covenant and, therefore, the promises have expired (Harkabi 1972, 196).

5 *Zionism is a European colonialist enterprise*, similar to other European projects in the late nineteenth century. It is a racist ideology of expansion aimed at stealing Arab land. Arabs have been systematically expelled by Zionist settlers from the beginning of their arrival to Palestine until now (Salem 2005).

6 *Denial or devaluation of the horror and the outcomes of the Holocaust.* Arabs and Palestinians argue that the Germans did not really exterminate six million Jews, so the Jews and Israel exaggerate the dimensions of the Holocaust in order to stress their suffering and to gain international sympathy for their claims for statehood. Moreover, the Jews abuse and misuse the Holocaust, not only to justify Israel's aggression against the Palestinians, but also to diminish the empathy towards Palestinian suffering. The Jews tend to monopolize their suffering in order to assume their image of being the ultimate victims.

The Palestinians believe that Jews had used the Holocaust to justify mass immigration of Jews into Palestine after 1945, while deliberately causing mass exodus of the Palestinians from their land (Alpher *et al.* 1999) The Palestinians were not the cause of the Jewish suffering. Rather, the opposite, they became the victims of Jewish suffering. Moreover, the same Jewish people who experienced such terrible suffering in human history caused so much injustice, suffering, and pain to the Palestinians. The Palestinians perceive the *Nakba* as their own holocaust, which is not much different from the Jewish Holocaust, so they adopt a similar approach in commemoration and historiography to the Jewish and Israeli one (Harkabi 1972; Qaymari 2005).

From the Palestinian standpoint, the Israelis will not be ready for peace and reconciliation unless they overcome their Holocaust trauma. If the Jews had a right to statehood because of their suffering and especially because of the Holocaust, this should have been carried out not in Palestine, which was the national home of the Palestinians, but elsewhere.

Moreover, while the Jews after the Holocaust had succeeded in establishing a state and had prospered, the Palestinians after the *Nakba* did not succeed in establishing their own state and continue to be the victims of the establishment of the State of Israel (Abdel Jawad 2007; Rouhana 2006).

7 *There will never be de jure recognition of Israel because of the displacement of the Palestinians by Israel.* Even when a Palestinian state is established, the relationship with Israel will remain only a pragmatic, de facto one ("We will never accept Israel") (Abu Sway 2008, 110–11).

8 *Palestinians recognized Israel as a state with the Declaration of Principles (Oslo Accord) of September 1993*, though this recognition was made conditional on implementing an Israeli promise to accept the establishment of a Palestinian state alongside it.

9 *The Palestinians will never recognize Israel as a Jewish state.* In their view, "the Jewish state in the Palestinian homeland must be denied legitimacy. This narrative is shared by all segments of Palestinian society, including Palestinians in Israel" (Rouhana 2006, 124–25). The Palestinians regard the Israeli claim to their homeland and its successful implementation as an enormous injustice done to them. "If Palestinians were to recognize Israel as a Jewish state, they would be accepting the principle that Jews are superior to Arabs. They would also be acknowledging the right to establish a Jewish state in Palestine, which is tantamount to recognizing the legitimacy of the Zionist project" (Rouhana 2006, 138).

Moreover, recognition of Israel as a Jewish state by the Palestinians implies that the right of return is rejected with Palestinian approval, so it will legitimize the victimizers and what the Zionists have done to Palestinians (Rouhana 2006, 126; Rouhana 2009; Nusseibeh 2011). Moreover, the Palestinians cannot recognize Israel as a Jewish state, since that recognition will make one fifth of the Israeli population (Muslim, Christian, Druze, or Bahai Arabs) second-class citizens and entitle full citizenship to any member of world Jewry outside of Israel. In addition to that, recognizing Israel as a Jewish state means also recognizing Jerusalem as the "eternal and undivided [Jewish] capital" of Israel, completely ignoring the fact that Jerusalem is as holy to 2.2 billion Christians and 1.6 billion Muslims (Nusseibeh 2011).

10 *The Palestinians cannot accept Israel's insistence on the issue of finality of the conflict* because "once the Palestinians accept a [final] settlement they cannot later [raise] questions about rectifying the injustices that have been perpetrated" (Rouhana 2006, 126).

11 *Zionism is a culture of force.* From the very moment Zionism was conceived, force, violence, and aggression have been central in its relationship with the Palestinians. A Jewish state could not be established in a homeland inhabited by another people except through the use of force. Israel used guns, terror, and massacre to bring about the expulsion of Palestinians during the 1947–49 war. Without that expulsion, Israel could not

have been established as a state with a significant Jewish majority (Rouhana 2006, 118–20).

The Palestinian Declaration of Independence of November 1988 referred to the injustice perpetrated on the Palestinians because of the establishment of the State of Israel: "The historical injustice inflicted on the Palestinian Arab people resulting [from] their dispersion and depriving them of their right to self-determination," and mentioned that "the Palestinian people, already wounded in its body, that was submitted to yet another type of occupation over which floated the falsehood that 'Palestine was a land without people.'"

The declaration did not recognize explicitly the State of Israel. However, it became the platform for the Palestinian acceptance of the idea of a two-state solution.[3] The declaration's reference to Palestine as being the "land of the three monotheistic faiths" has been interpreted as recognizing also the Jewish historical link to the land, instead of denying the validity of the Palestinian National Covenant.

Correcting the injustice by punitive and retributive justice

Immediately after the 1947–49 war, the Arabs and the Palestinians developed not only their deep concepts and perceptions of injustice but they also expressed their passionate desire, commitment, and determination to correct the wrong and the injustice done to them. The terms "wrong," "harm," and "injustice" have special and unique meaning in the Arab culture and in Arabic language. As Harkabi mentions: "There are grounds for the belief that the Arabic words for wrong, harm and injustice (*zulm, daym, jawr*) have a stronger connotation than their equivalents in other languages. It is not only a matter of iniquity but also a personal injury and a sense of disgrace that cries out for vengeance. Moreover, refusal to acquiesce in injustice or robbery is the characteristic that the Arabs ascribe to themselves as part of their self-image" (Harkabi 1972, 62).

Justice is a matter of moral principle, honor, and dignity. Justice is therefore indivisible and incompatible with compromise. Justice is a supreme moral value, even more than peace and overrides it. Justice refers to rights, and the notion of rights is the determining factor in conflict resolution and peacemaking (Sabet 1998). Codes of justice, honor, dignity, and shame are the main components of any conflict resolution (Abu-Nimer 1996). The Arab sense of injustice transcends tangible terms. It "has triggered intense emotional responses that cannot be quantified solely in tangible terms or reduced simply to an aversion of loss" (Sabet 1998, 8).

The issue of the rectification of the injustice done to the Palestinians was presented as the most important Arab and Palestinian objective in the conflict with Israel. The conflict was defined as a dispute over justice and the need for correcting the injustice. The conflict is a categorical one, between a party who is absolutely right (the Arabs and the Palestinians) and a party who is totally wrong (Israel). There is, therefore, no room for a settlement that will compromise the Arab and the Palestinian concept of justice (Harkabi 1972, 108).

Essentially, the Arabs and the Palestinians have used the terminology of punitive, retributive, and corrective justice in their claims for justice in their statements and declarations throughout the years of conflict. The leading figure until 1970 was Egypt's President Gamal Abdel Nasser.[4] Both retributive justice and corrective justice were simultaneously used and combined the demand for punishing Israel for the injustice done to the Palestinians and to the Arabs, and correcting the injustice by destroying Israel.

"Just peace" defined also as "just solution" became then the annulment of the wrong involved in the existence of Israel and restoration of Palestine to its legal owners. Peace cannot be based on wrong and injustice. Liquidation of Israel was termed as an expression of justice. Israel's existence is an injustice by itself and a violation of the legal rights of the Palestinians. Peace can be established only after the wrong is rectified and justice is done by the disappearance of Israel from the map and the restoration of the Palestinian people's rights. The wrong must be rectified; that is, the refugees must have their property restored and be given the right to decide whether to return or not to their original homes in Palestine (nowadays Israel). Therefore, Israel must disappear in order to make this possible. Hence, just peace can be established and endured only after the disappearance of Israel.

Although the Arabs and the Palestinians realized that the liquidation of a state is an unusual solution for an international conflict, they justified it by arguing that the conflict itself was also unusual since it had been founded on an unusual and enormous injustice. Israel was created through a terrible crime. Israel committed the greatest crime in modern history. For the first time in modern history an entire people has been expelled by force from its homeland. There must be no acquiescence in a historic wrong, even if it has become an accomplished fact. The war against Israel is for self-defense and a "just war." Thus, the liquidation of injustice, imperialism, or colonialism is a major aim of progressive humanity (Harkabi 1972, 60–70).

The Palestinian National Covenant of 1968 subsumed the right of return with the demand for the total liberation of Palestine. For instance, "the liberation of Palestine, from an Arab point of view, is a national (*qawmi*) duty and it attempts to repel the Zionist and imperialist aggression against the Arab homeland, and aims at the elimination of Zionism in Palestine" (Article 15). "Armed struggle is the only way to liberate Palestine." (Article 9). "The Palestinian people possess the fundamental and genuine legal right to liberate and retrieve their homeland" (Article 29). "The liberation of Palestine, from a humane point of view, will restore to the Palestinian individual his dignity, pride, and freedom" (Article 17).

The concept of the "right of return," which became a central ethos and a myth in the Palestinian national identity, was first formulated in 1974, at the 12th session of the Palestinian National Council (PNC). The PNC Ten Point Program declared the "right of return" (the first such use of this specific formulation by the PNC) "at the front" of the Palestinian people's rights (Khalidi 1992, 34; Klein

1998, 3). The PNC stressed that durable and just peace in the Middle East would not be possible without the restoration of the full Palestinian national rights and especially the right of return. At that time, the accomplishment of the right of return was still linked to the total liberation of Palestine.

The PNC document did not refer explicitly to UNGA Resolution 194, as well as to UN Security Council Resolution 242 and 338, not only because they called for a political solution of the Arab–Israeli conflict, but also because they referred to the refugee problem as a humanitarian issue on an individual basis.[5] The right of return became a crucial factor in the PLO's demand for recognition for Palestinian nationhood. Any rejection of the right of return was perceived as a denial of Palestinian collective identity and justification of its expulsion in 1947–49 (Klein 1998).

Correcting the injustice by the right of return

A significant change in the Palestinian attitudes regarding the correcting of the injustice was introduced in the Palestinian Declaration of Independence of November 1988. The declaration removed the references to liberation and the destruction of Israel that were presented in the Palestinian National Covenant of 1968. Instead, the declaration stated that the State of Palestine believes in the "settlement of regional and international disputes by peaceful means, in accordance with the UN Charter and resolutions." It further announces itself to be a peace-loving state, in adherence to the principles of peaceful coexistence … and it will join "with all states and peoples in order to assure a permanent peace based upon justice and the respect of rights." The right of return was mentioned among other several fundamental national rights, such as self-determination and establishment of a Palestinian state with reference to the UN Charter and its resolutions, but without explicitly mentioning UNGA Resolution 194.

The clear acceptance of Resolution 194 was made at the 20th PNC in September 1991 as part of the PLO confirmation of Palestinian participation in the Madrid Peace Conference (Klein 1998, 6). UNGA Resolution 194 has become since then the main international legal source for the Palestinian demand and justification of the right of return. Paragraph 11 of the Resolution adopted on 11 December 1948 refers to the resolution of the Palestinian refugee problem in the following way:

> [The General Assembly] Resolves that the refugees wishing to return to their homes and live at peace with their neighbors should be permitted to do so at the earliest practicable date, and that compensation should be paid for the property of those choosing not to return and for loss of or damage to property which, under principles of international law or in equity, should be made good by the Governments or authorities responsible.

Although the UNGA resolution is non-binding on UN member states and it did not mention explicitly *a right of return*, the Palestinians see it as a definitive and absolute right. The Palestinians ignore also the fact that the resolution mentioned the fact that the return of refugees was placed in the context of permission and practicability, so it was conditioned on the willingness of refugees to "live in peace" with their [Jewish] neighbors (Bowker 2003, 98).

The Palestinians claim that Resolution 194 represents the general consensus of the international community as the way to resolve the refugee problem. The Palestinians insist that their own interpretation of Resolution 194 has to be the only basis for the solution of the refugee problem, and Israel should acknowledge and accept it, irrespective of whether they intend to exercise the right of return or not. While the acknowledgment of the right of return is a sacred and a protected value there is no authoritative and unified Palestinian conception of what constitutes *in practice* that right. Hence, there are different meanings to implementation of the right, and they range from the right of all the refugees and their descendents to return to their homes in Palestine (inside Israel) or to a return of some of them to other places in Palestine, such as the future Palestinian state in the West Bank and the Gaza Strip (Khalidi 1992, 29, 35; Bowker 2003, 98–99).

The Palestinian definition of Palestinian refugees includes "all those Palestinians (and their descendents) who were expelled or forced to leave their homes between November 1947 (Partition Plan) and January 1949 (Rhodes Armistice Agreements), from the territory controlled by Israel on that later date" (Zureik 1996, 10).[6] In addition to this definition of Palestinian refugees, the Palestinians tend to include also the 1967 refugees who were expelled by Israel following the 1967 war and those who were expelled from their homes after Israel occupied the territories (Zureik 1996, 91).[7]

Khalidi maintains that, by accepting UNGA Resolution 194, the PLO has accepted certain crucial limitations on the exercise of the right of return. The first limitation is the acceptance of the principle of compensation for those refugees who will choose not to return. This option was rejected before and defined as an unjust *fait accompli*. The second limitation to the absolute return is the acceptance of the precondition that limits the return only to those refugees who will accept "to live at peace with their neighbors," and actually those who will fully accept Israel's jurisdiction and sovereignty. The third limitation on the right of return refers to the possibility that the Palestinian return will be to the Palestinian state rather than to Israel proper. Such a possibility has been mentioned in several Palestinian declarations although there is no official position on that limitation (Khalidi 1992, 35–36; Khalaf 1990). The PLO did not drop the right of return as a principle and a protected value, but it realized that this would not be an absolute return. Nevertheless, it insisted that Israel should accept the principle of the right of return, but the details of such a return will be left open for negotiations with Israel, and that the Palestinians should have a right to choose among several options (Khalaf 1990).

The Palestinian narratives as preconditions for conflict resolution

After the failure of the Oslo peace process and the erupting of the second *intifada* in September 2000, Palestinian scholars argued that the process actually derailed because of the parties' avoidance of discussing and resolving the broader question of the historical injustice done to the Palestinians by Israel in the Israeli–Palestinian conflict, especially in the 1947–49 war (Peled and Rouhana 2004; Dajani 2005; Rouhana 2006; Said 2006). According to this interpretation, the failure to discuss the Palestinian historical narrative was a key element for the breakdown of the negotiations. The peace process was perceived by the Palestinians as an opportunity not only to establish an independent state but also "to obtain recognition – and validation – of the legitimacy of their national narrative" (Dajani 2005, 69). However, the Israeli negotiators' refusal to discuss the past was perceived by the Palestinians as "unwillingness to grapple with their nation's past, and the debt owed to its primary victims" (Dajani 2005, 70). Nevertheless, Dajani admits that, "it is perhaps unlikely that discussions of the historical narrative would have altered the two sides' positions in fundamental ways, particularly on issues as contentious as refugee problem and Jerusalem, and it is unknowable how they would have affected atmospherics in the negotiations" (Dajani 2005, 70).

Furthermore, Palestinian scholars argue that the conflict cannot possibly be resolved without Israel's acceptance of the Palestinian narratives that were presented, including the following two demands. First, Israel should acknowledge its sole responsibility for the expulsion of the Palestinians from Palestine in the 1947–49 war (as an act of admission of transitional justice). Second, Israel should accept the Palestinian key demand for a just solution of this problem; i.e. the right of return of the Palestinian refugees to their homes in Israel (as an act of corrective and compensating justice).

At the heart of the demands for justice of the Palestinian cause remain the Israeli acknowledgment of its responsibility for the creation of the Palestinian refugee problem, as well as its acceptance of the refugees' political and moral right of return to Israel proper. A just solution to the conflict, or in Palestinian terms, a "just peace," is then contingent upon Israel's acceptance of these Palestinian demands (Khalidi 1997–98; Alpher *et al.* 1999; Peled and Rouhana 2004; Rouhana 2006; Said 2006). At the same time, more pragmatic scholars like Khalidi realize that a just solution is not a demand for absolute justice, because it is unattainable; therefore, a just solution should be termed only as an attainable one. In his own words, "justice within the realm of possible … justice within the limits of what is realistically attainable in current and future circumstances" (Khalidi 1995, 72).

Several scholars claim that the Palestinians' negotiators failed to include the demands for transitional and corrective justice in the peace negotiations, especially in the first stages of the Oslo process, because of their weakness due to the asymmetrical power relations between Israelis and Palestinians. Hence, the need for procedural justice that will balance the asymmetrical relation becomes a crucial precondition for just and honest negotiations with Israel (Khalidi 1997–98; Albin 2001).

While there is a full consensus among the Palestinian leaders and scholars about the demands for procedural, transitional, corrective, and compensating justice regarding the issues of Israeli responsibility and the right of return as principles of right and justice, there are different meanings and different ways as to the scope and magnitude of its implementation in practical terms (Khalidi 1995, 1997–98; Peled and Rouhana 2004; Rouhana 2006; Said 2006).

The demands for transitional justice and for compensatory justice in the Israeli–Palestinian conflict in the context of a Palestinian right of return were introduced in a sophisticated way in 1995 and in 1997–98 by a Palestinian scholar, Rashid Khalidi, and in 2004 by two Israeli scholars: Yoav Peled (a Jewish scholar) and Nadim N. Rouhana (a Palestinian one). The fact that they used the terminology of justice that mainly flourished in reconciliation studies, following the case of South Africa, was a deliberate attempt to make their argumentation for justice more scientific and probably more convincing and general.

Khalidi maintains that, whenever negotiations reach the final status talks, Israel

> will have to take responsibility for its conduct in the past, and accept that the deliberate actions of the state's founding fathers have played the major role in making more than half of the Palestinian people refugees between 1947 and 1949 ... Israelis will be asked to accept a proposition which in effect means that their country was born in original sin in 1948.
>
> (Khalidi 1995, 73)

In his view, Israel's acceptance of significant liability for creating the refugee problem "will inevitably be seen as the first step towards the wholesale return of the Palestinians" (Khalidi 1995, 73). Furthermore, Khalidi argues that Israel cannot avoid taking responsibility for the injustice, as a first step for real reconciliation and healing. Israel must accept that "all Palestinian refugees and their descendants have a right to return to their homes in principle," although most of them will not exercise their right to return for various practical reasons (Khalidi 1995, 76).

Similarly, Peled and Rouhana argue that,

> Recognition by Israel of the right of return would entail its assumption of responsibility for the uprooting of the majority of Palestinian society in 1948. This would satisfy a demand that has become a fundamental element in Palestinian national identity. Recognition would then enable the two parties to enter negotiations over restitution, in particular the implementation of the right of return.
>
> (Peled and Rouhana 2004, 318)

While recognition and responsibility are the basic principles of historical or transitional justice, they are also preconditions for compensatory justice; in other words, the implementation of the right of return.

Peled and Rouhana acknowledge that considerations of historical or transitional justice are essential for achieving reconciliation in intra-societal conflicts (domestic conflicts), but not necessarily in inter-societal (international) conflicts. However, they believe that the principles of transitional justice can also be applicable to the Israeli–Palestinian conflict because the conflict has features of both an intra-societal (Jewish–Arab relations within Israel) and inter-societal disputes as well.

Peled and Rouhana fully adopt the Palestinian historical narrative that the Palestinian catastrophe "was, indeed, an historic injustice," and that Israel is solely responsible for it. Israel, therefore, should recognize the refugees' right of return to Israel. This right cannot be denied and superseded because of the passing of time (Peled and Rouhana 2004, 325–26). In their view, the injustice can be rectified only through recognition of the refugees' right of return.

Having said that, Peled and Rouhana suggest the separation of the right of return (which is non-negotiable for the Palestinians) from the means and practical ways of its implementation, which could be negotiated between the two sides. The reason for that is their awareness that the implementation of the right of return is perceived by most Jewish–Israelis as an existential threat to the Jewish character of their state, if not to its very existence. Nevertheless, they maintain that

> the only right of return that can meaningfully [be] recognized by Israel is the right of the refugees to return to the State of Israel within the borders of its own sovereignty, whatever these borders may be following a future Israeli–Palestinian peace agreement. Since recognition of a right necessarily creates an obligation and since there is no moral value in creating an obligation for somebody else, Israel cannot meaningfully recognize the right of return to a third country, not even to the future state of Palestine.
> (Peled and Rouhana 2004, 327)

Peled and Rouhana believe that, if Israel will recognize the Palestinian right of return, this would satisfy the crucial demand of the Palestinians and would enable them "to recognize Israelis' (but not Jewish) acquired right to continue their national existence in their part of the disputed territory" (Peled and Rouhana 2004, 327). Moreover, since data based on polls conducted by Palestinians indicate that the number of refugees who would want to implement the right of return "is not as high as was originally expected" (Peled and Rouhana 2004, 331), then the implementation of the right of return will not necessarily endanger the Jewish character of Israel. For instance, Khalidi suggested in 1998 the return of 15 percent of the then approximately three million refugees and their descendants (about 450,000), and compensation for all the others (Khalidi 1997–98, 249).

Moreover, Peled and Rouhana differentiate between recognition and implementation of the Palestinian claim for the right of return. These claims are based on fully accepting the Palestinian narrative of the 1947–49 war and rejecting that of Israel. In other words, putting all the blame for the injustice on Israel, while ignoring the Palestinian and Arab refusal to accept the UN Partition Plan and initiating the 1947–49 war.

Khalidi admits that the issue of the Palestinian refugees is the most intractable problem to resolve, "more even than the formidably difficult question of Jerusalem" (Khalidi 1997–98, 233) because of the wide gap between the parties' narratives. However, "the refugee issue must be forthrightly addressed if there is to be a just and lasting peace" (Khalidi 1997–98, 234). Khalidi does not put all the responsibility for creating the refugee problem squarely on Israel and defines only its "share of responsibility" as primordial. He argues that the international community, the neighboring Arab states, and the Palestinians themselves are also responsible for creating the Palestinian refugee problem (Khalidi 1997–98, 240 and 245–46). Nevertheless, Khalidi does not regard the Palestinian and the Arab rejection of the UN Partition Plan and initiating the 1947–49 war as the major cause of the Palestinian plight.

Indeed, as Gans correctly maintains, "in order to provide comprehensive answers to questions concerning the responsibility of one party, one must provide answers to factual historical questions relating [to] the state of affairs in infinite points in time" (Gans 2004, 284). Unfortunately, Peled, Rouhana, and Khalidi arrive at their conclusions without doing so. For them, as well as for many others in both sides of the Israeli–Palestinian conflict, the issue is not necessarily a factual historical matter. Under the paramount influence of their respective historical narratives, both sides draw heavily from their collective memory rather than from more factual data.

Salim Tamari introduces a different and novel approach regarding Israel's responsibility on the Palestinian refugee issue. He differentiates between the refugee return and the refugee compensation. He suggests that, since Israel's position totally rejects any Palestinian refugee repatriation to Israel proper, and this position will not be changed soon, the Palestinians should insist that the right of return should be accomplished within territories to be annexed to/swapped into the future Palestinian state. As to the compensation issue, Tamari believes that Israel will most likely respond positively to Palestinian property claims because it wants to close the issue of the refugees more than any other issue. This is in accordance with the Israeli aim of bringing an end to claims and to conflict. In addition to that, Israel would like to legitimize its status in the Arab world and this will be impossible without resolving the refugee claims, especially for Jordan, Syria, and Lebanon which are populated by many Palestinian refugees (Tamari 2007).

The right, "yes," the return, "no"

Sari Nusseibeh, the president of al-Quds University, declared several years ago in many speeches, interviews, and articles in the international, Israeli, and

Palestinian media, that in a two-state solution, the Palestinians should give up the implementation of the right of return to the State of Israel. In his view, the idea of a two-state solution excludes a massive return of Palestinians to the State of Israel. The Palestinians cannot demand the return of Palestinian refugees to areas inside the State of Israel because this will infringe upon Israel's character as a Jewish state. "The Palestinians have to realize that if we were to reach an agreement on two states, then those two states will have to be one for the Israelis and one for the Palestinians, not one for the Palestinians and the other also for [the] Palestinians."[8] As a matter of fact, the Palestinian insistence that Israel must allow the refugees to return to their original homes and lands will prevent a peace agreement (quoted in *Haaretz*, 24 September 2001). The refugees should be resettled in a future Palestinian state "not in a way that would undermine the existence of the state of Israel as a predominantly Jewish state" (quoted in *Associated Press*, 23 October 2001).

Nusseibeh does not call for giving up the right of return in its symbolic terms, but points out that it is impossible to implement this right literally, particularly in light of the current peace process that sponsors a two-state solution. Moreover, Nusseibeh does not clean Israel from its responsibility for creating the refugee problem and for its resolution. In his own words, "Israel has to assume its historical responsibility, and compensating refugees and returning the possible number to their original homes." However, it is the role of the Palestinian leadership to establish a Palestinian state that will free the Palestinians from the occupation and resolve the tragedy of their refugees: "Establishing a free democratic state is a historical responsibility for the Palestinian leadership in order to solve the tragic situation of refugees" (quoted in *al-Quds*, 23 November 2001).

In a keynote address at the University of Chicago Law School in 2004, titled: "Right Versus Good: Palestinian Rights in Conflict," Nusseibeh maintained that the Palestinian claim for two rights, statehood and return, were in an inner conflict, if not contradiction. The Palestinians could not implement both rights, and therefore they should decide between statehood and freedom from occupation, and the right of return to Israel proper. Although there is a moral discontent with the principle of the trade-off itself that enforces giving up the natural right of return as the price to be paid for implementing another natural right of freedom, a political solution that will bring about the establishment of a Palestinian state holds a moral primacy.

> Choosing between two rights is not of itself wrong or morally reprehensible … the moral value of the choice itself would have to be determined by balancing between moral values or weights of the two potential actions. In our specific case, the balance would be between freedom and return … this could be viewed in terms of right versus good.

Hence, it is the responsibility of the Palestinian government to choose between the two rights in favor of right of freedom, i.e. independence.

The parallel Israeli concession to giving up the right of return on the Palestinian side should be a complete evacuation of the settlements in the occupied territories. In this political compromise, there is no need to redefine and unify the opposite narratives as a precondition for making peace. "The parameters for making such peace could have been reached by each side independently and on the basis of different, if parallel calculations."

Nusseibeh's position has been totally rejected by many Palestinians who perceive it as a threat to Palestinian identity, history, rights, morals, national consensus, and unity, as well as contradicting many UN resolutions, especially UNGA Resolution 194.[9]

Conclusions

The Palestinians' narratives of justice and injustice are part of the Palestinian identity and ethos. Throughout the Israeli–Palestinian conflict they became protected values that cannot be compromised. The Palestinians are very sensitive to the justness of their narratives and to the urgent need to correct the injustice perpetrated on them by Israel. The Palestinian claims for just peace are rooted in the outcomes of the 1947–49 war that prevented the establishment of a Palestinian state and led to the emergence of the refugee problem. The Palestinians put all the blame for these outcomes on the Israeli side, and they reject any responsibility for it.

The operational and practical ways to correct this injustice and reach a just peace have changed throughout the conflict, from the destruction of the State of Israel to a resolution of the Israeli–Palestinian conflict that will enable the establishment of a Palestinian state in the 1967 borders (including the West Bank, East Jerusalem, and the Gaza Strip). Nevertheless, the Palestinians also present two other conditions for the resolution of their conflict with Israel that can be defined as conditions for transitional justice: First, Israel has to acknowledge its sole responsibility for creating the Palestinian refugee problem. Second, Israel should accept in principle the right of Palestinian refugees to return to the state of Israel. Nevertheless, its implementation and the number of the refugees that will return to Israel could be "agreed upon" and negotiated with Israel.[10]

Notes

1 At the vote, 253 members of the Palestinian National Council voted in favor, 46 against, and 10 abstained. The virtual Palestinian state was recognized at that time by about 100 states.

2 This was the first time that the Palestinians invoked the UN Partition Plan as providing legitimacy to their statehood, probably indicating that they ultimately accepted it.

3 The declaration was accompanied by a political statement that explicitly mentioned UNSC Resolution 242. Furthermore, Yasser Arafat's statement in Geneva a month later was interpreted as an implicit recognition of Israel.

4 Harkabi summed up those attitudes in his excellent book, *Arab Attitudes to Israel*, which was published in English in 1972. A previous, Hebrew, version of the book appeared in 1966.

5 UN Security Council Resolutions 242 (1967) and 338 (1973) do not mention UNGA Resolution 194 and the "right of return." Moreover, UNGA Resolution 194 does not mention explicitly the term "right of return."

6 This definition was introduced by the Palestinian delegation at the first meeting of the Refugee Working Group (RWG) held in Ottawa, Canada on 13 May 1992.

7 The Oslo I Agreement ("Declaration of Principles") of September 1993 clearly distinguishes between the 1947–49 Palestinian refugees and those displaced by the 1967 war.

8 Nusseibeh's speech at the Hebrew University on 16 October 2001, cited by Joel Greenberg, "Palestinian Offers Idea: Get Israelis on Our Side," *The New York Times*, 17 October 2001.

9 Arafat dismissed Nusseibeh from his position as the Palestinian Authority's diplomatic representative in Jerusalem, following an al-Awda network petition addressed to Arafat calling for this.

10 Editor's note: This position is reflected in the Arab Peace Initiative adopted in 2002 and revised in 2007.

References

Abdel Jawad, Saleh. "The Arab and Palestinian Narratives of the 1948 War." In *Israeli and Palestinian Narratives of Conflict: History's Double Helix* (ed.) Robert I. Rothberg. (Indianapolis: Indiana University Press, 2006), pp. 72–113.

Abdel Jawad, Saleh. "Zionist Massacres: The Creation of the Palestinian Refugee Problem." In *Israel and the Palestinian Refugees* (eds) Eyal Benvenisti, Chaim Gans, and Sari Hanafi. (Berlin: Springer, 2007), pp. 58–127.

Abu-Nimer, Mohammed. "Conflict Resolution in an Islamic Context," *Peace and Change*, Vol. 21 (1996), pp. 22–40.

Abu Sway, Mustafa. "Roundtable Discussion; 1948: Independence and the Nakba," *Palestine-Israel Journal of Politics, Economics and Culture*, Vol. 15, 1 and 2 (2008), pp. 107–25.

Abu Zayyad, Ziad. "Seeking Justice," *Palestine-Israel Journal of Politics, Economics and Culture*, Vol. 2, 4 (1995), pp. 6–7.

Albin, Cecilia. *Justice and Fairness in International Negotiations* (Cambridge: Cambridge University Press, 2001).

Alpher Joseph, Khalil Shikaki, Herbert C. Kelman and Nadim N. Rouhana. "Concept Paper: The Palestinian Refugee Problem and the Right of Return," *Middle East Policy*, Vol. 6 (1999), pp. 167–89.

Barkan, Elazar. "Considerations Toward Accepting Historical Responsibility." In *Exile and Return: Predicaments of Palestinians and Jews* (eds) Ann Lesch and Ian Lustick. (Philadelphia: University of Pennsylvania Press, 2005), pp. 85–105.

Bowker, Robert. *Palestinian Refugees: Mythology, Identity, and the Search for Peace* (Boulder: Lynne Rienner, 2003).

Cattan, Henry. *Palestine, the Arabs, and Israel: The Search for Justice* (London: Longman, 1969).

Dajani, Omar. "Surviving Opportunities: Palestinian Negotiating Patterns in Peace Talks with Israel." In *How Israelis and Palestinians Negotiate: A Cross-Cultural Analysis of the Oslo Peace Process* (ed.) Tamara Cofman Wittes. (Washington, DC: USIP, 2005), pp. 39–80.

Gans, Chaim. "The Palestinian Refugees and the Right of Return: Theoretical Perspectives," *Theoretical Inquiries in Law*, Vol. 5, 2 (July 2004), pp. 269–304.

Greenberg, Joel. "Palestinian Offers Idea: Get Israelis on Our Side," *The New York Times*, October 17, 2001.

Harkabi, Yeoshafat. *The Arab Attitudes to Israel* (Jerusalem: Keter 1972).

Hassassian, Manuel. "Development of the Palestinian National Movement, 1919–39." In *Shared Histories: A Palestinian–Israeli Dialogue* (eds) Paul Scham, Walid Salem, and Benjamin Pogrund. (Walnut Creek, CA: Left Coast Press, 2005), pp. 92–100.

Khalaf, Salah (Abu Iyad). "Lowering the Sword," *Foreign Policy*, 78 (spring, 1990), pp. 92–112.

Khalidi, Rashid. "Observation on the Right of Return," *Journal of Palestine Studies*, Vol. xxi, 2 (1992), pp. 29–40.

Khalidi, Rashid. "The Palestinian Refugee Problem: A Possible Solution," *Palestine-Israel Journal of Politics, Economics and Culture*, Vol. 2, 4 (1995), pp. 72–78.

Khalidi, Rashid. "Attainable Justice: Elements of a Solution to the Palestinian Refugee Issue," *International Journal*, Vol. 53 (1997–98), pp. 233–52.

Klein, Menachem. "Between Right and Realization: The PLO Dialectics of 'The Right of Return,'" *Journal of Refugee Studies*, Vol. 11, 1 (1998), pp. 1–19.

Masalha, Nur. "The Palestinian Nakba: Zionism, 'Transfer' and the 1948 Exodus," *Global Dialogue*, Vol. 4 (2002), pp. 1–10.

Nassar, Issam. "The Pre-History of Palestinian Nationalism." In *Shared Histories: A Palestinian–Israeli Dialogue* (eds) Paul Scham, Walid Salem, and Benjamin Pogrund. (Walnut Creek, CA: Left Coast Press, 2005), pp. 68–74.

Nusseibeh, Sari. "Why Israel Can't Be a 'Jewish State'," *Al-Jazeera*, 30 September 2011.

Peled, Yoav and Nadim N. Rouhana. "Transitional Justice and the Right of Return of the Palestinian Refugees," *Theoretical Inquiries in Law*, Vol. 5, 2 (July 2004), pp. 317–32.

Qaymari, Ata. "The Holocaust in the Palestinian Perspective." In *Shared Histories: A Palestinian–Israeli Dialogue* (eds) Paul Scham, Walid Salem, and Benjamin Pogrund. (Walnut Creek, CA.: Left Coast Press, 2005), pp. 148–53.

Qurei, Ahmed. "Commemorating the *Nakba*," *Palestine-Israel Journal of Politics, Economics and Culture*, Vol. 15, 1 and 2 (2008), pp. 10–13.

Rabinowitz, Dan. "Beyond Recognition: Staggered Limited Return of Palestinians to Israel." In *Israel and the Palestinian Refugees* (eds) Eyal Benvenisti, Chaim Gans, and Sari Hanafi. (Berlin: Springer, 2007), pp. 411–32.

Rouhana, Nadim N. "Zionism's Encounter with the Palestinians: The Dynamics of Force, Fear, and Extremism." In *Israeli and Palestinian Narratives of Conflict* (ed.) Robert I. Rotberg. (Bloomington: Indiana University Press, 2006), pp. 115–41.

Rouhana, Nadim N. "The Jewish State is a Recipe for Continued Injustice," *Jadal*, 5 (December 2009), p. 1.

Sabet, Amr G. E. "The Peace Process and the Politics of Conflict Resolution," *Journal of Palestinian Studies*, Vol. 27 (1998), pp. 5–19.

Said, Edward W. "A Method for Thinking about Just Peace." In *What is Just Peace?* (eds) Pierre Allan and Alexis Keller. (Oxford: Oxford University Press, 2006), pp. 176–194.

Salem, Walid. "Paradoxes of the UN Partition Plan." In *Shared Histories: A Palestinian–Israeli Dialogue* (eds) Paul Scham, Walid Salem, and Benjamin Pogrund. (Walnut Creek, CA: Left Coast Press, 2005), pp. 182–87.

Tamari, Salim. "The Future of Palestinian Refugees in the Peace Negotiations," *Palestine-Israel Journal of Politics, Economics and Culture*, Vol. 2, 4 (1995), pp. 8–14.

Tamari, Salim. "The Local and the National in Palestine Identity." In *Israeli and Palestinian Identities in History and Literature* (eds) Kamal Abdel-Malek and David C. Jacobson. (New York: Macmillan, 1999), pp. 3–8.
Tamari, Salim. "Palestinian Refugee Property Claims: Compensation and Restitution." In *Israel and the Palestinian Refugees* (eds) Eyal Benvenisti, Chaim Gans, and Sari Hanafi. (Berlin: Springer, 2007), pp. 309–22.
Yahya, H. Adel. "The Birth of the Palestinian Refugee Problem in 1947–48." In *Shared Histories: A Palestinian–Israeli Dialogue* (eds) Paul Scham, Walid Salem, and Benjamin Pogrund. (Walnut Creek, CA: Left Coast Press, 2005), pp. 220–27.
Zoabi, Haneen. "The Concept of the Jewish State." *Jadal*, 5 (December 2009), pp. 1–5.
Zureik, Elia. *Palestinian Refugees and the Peace Process* (Washington, DC: Institute for Palestinian Studies, 1996).

5 Linking justice to peace in the Oslo process, 1993–2001

The Oslo peace process, from 1993 to 2001, was the first serious attempt to resolve the Israeli–Palestinian conflict. This was also the first attempt to link justice to peace in the peacemaking negotiations. It was clear for both sides that their respective narratives of justice and injustice will play a significant role in the negotiations, so the question was whether they would succeed in bridging the wide gaps between their conflicting narratives. From the beginning of the peace process, it was clear to the parties that a failure to bridge the gaps between their conflicting narratives will prevent them from reaching a peace agreement.

This chapter presents the role of the Israeli and the Palestinian narratives of justice and injustice throughout the negotiations at Track I, i.e. the Oslo process since its beginning in January 1993 in Oslo to the January 2001 meeting at Taba, as well as in the Track II initiatives – the "People's Voice" (Ayalon-Nusseibeh agreement of July 2002) and the Geneva Initiative of October 2003.

The historical narratives, and in particular the ethos of injustice and the Palestinian demands for justice, fairness, and equality, played a central role throughout the Oslo process. Although they did not prevent the initiation and pursuit of the peace process, these narratives did contribute significantly to its failure through the enormous divide that they generated between the parties.

The Oslo negotiations, 1993

The Palestinian negotiators presented their demands for procedural justice and for transitional and corrective justice during the unofficial talks that took place at the beginning of the Oslo process and during the official talks that followed suit. The Palestinians stressed their concerns that, in light of the asymmetrical power imbalance between the parties and the relationship of occupier versus occupied, they doubted that fair and just negotiations could be conducted, and that a fair and just agreement between the parties could be reached. Hence, they demanded a different and more equitable relationship, based on full equality and respect of their respective status as equal partners in the peace process. The Palestinians warned that they could not accept any agreement that exploited Israel's greater relative power, which would prevent realizing their own demands and just and fair rights and would impinge on their honor. This position was clearly expressed by Ahmed Qurei (alias "Abu-Ala"), head of the Palestinian delegation to the negotiations, who stressed the point to Uri Savir, head of the Israeli delegation, in saying,

> You may try to force your approach on Arafat. And if you use your strength to push him into a corner, he may have no choice but to accept your approach. But remember: If you do that, you will isolate him. A one sided agreement will not stand.
>
> (Savir 1998, 180)

Even at the signing ceremony when the Oslo Accords were initialized at Oslo on August 20, 1993, Abu-Ala emphasized the Palestinian demands for equality as a condition for the success of the peace process:

> Our two nations are equal, despite the differences in their material means. As long as cooperation is based on equality and respect, then we shall be able to overcome the obstacles of doubt and fear that have accumulated over the decades. Relations between us must reflect this equality.
>
> (Quoted in Hirschfeld 1999, 144)

The Palestinian demands for procedural justice were not acceptable to Israel. The Israeli negotiators certainly recognized that without Palestinian consent it would be impossible to advance the negotiations and reach an agreement. They also realized that it was necessary to embark on a new political relationship that would refer to the Palestinians as equal partners based on mutual dependence. Yet, in practice they found it very difficult to relate to the Palestinians as equals. The Israeli negotiators had a tendency to patronize, demonstrating their unwillingness to alter the basic conditions of inequality, as the Palestinians demanded, or to refrain from taking advantage of their relative power in the negotiating process and in the agreements signed: Oslo I (13 September 1993), the Cairo Agreement (4 May 1994), and Oslo II ("The Interim Agreement" of 28 September 1995). The obvious gaps in the positions of the parties and in the balance of power between them, as well as the nature of the prolonged conflict, the occupier–occupied relations, and the basic lack of trust, did not enable suitable conditions for negotiations along the lines of the classic requirements of procedural justice.

These were not negotiations between equals. While the Palestinians felt that Israel did not treat them as equals and, instead, took advantage of their weakness, the Israelis felt that, while they were granting the Palestinians real concessions (such as the gradual devolution of territories in the Gaza Strip and in the West Bank), the Palestinians did not reciprocate in any kind, since they were all the time driven by demands of honor, justice, and fairness, which could easily derail the process.

From the Palestinian standpoint, the Israeli offerings were condescending and seemed like dictates, leaving the Palestinians with the feeling that they were once again being dominated, rather than negotiated with.[1] Thus, Dajani asserts that "the Oslo process makes clear that Palestinians will not behave as equal partners if the attitudes of their Israeli counterparts or the terms of their proposals place Palestinians in a position of subordination" (Dajani 2005, 75–76). For instance, there were many contentious issues that the Oslo Accords would not address, adding to the list of grievances experienced by the Palestinians (Albin 2001, 150).[2] Therefore, it was difficult for the Palestinian negotiating team to regard the talks as legitimate; rather, they saw the negotiations as "unjust historically and legally and as an unfair exploitation of their weakness" (Albin 2001, 149).

The Palestinians felt that the negotiations largely reflected Israeli security interests and deferred all substantial issues to the final status talks, without any assurances of how and when these issues would be resolved (Albin 2001, 150). As the talks progressed, Israeli security needs took precedence and the Palestinians saw themselves being coerced and pressured to concede to Israeli demands. The asymmetries of the talks were so pronounced that "Palestinians risked being worse off than before negotiations started while Israel would have fortified its position" (Albin 2001, 150).

However, some of the Israeli negotiators do admit that they had adopted too patronizing an attitude and that the process could have been conducted on the basis of a more direct and egalitarian dialogue, respecting the Palestinians' honor, and not as an occupier dictating the terms to the occupied (Savir 1998; Sher 2005). Nevertheless, they maintain that the negotiations were fair and the agreements were agreed voluntarily by both sides, so they were mutually beneficial, and that "the Palestinians had already gained extensively from the Oslo peace process" (Albin 2001, 151).

In this context, it can be argued that in practice it was Israel that primarily determined the agenda of the Oslo process and its management as a process that was essentially an interim arrangement to establish Palestinian self-rule (autonomy) in the occupied territories for five years, while the discussion of core issues was postponed to the later stage of permanent arrangements (starting only three years after the initial implementation of the Palestinian autonomy in the Gaza Strip and the Jericho area). The Palestinians' failure to secure their status of an equal partner was characterized as unjust, unfair, and disrespectful peace, as described by Palestinian and Arab intellectuals. According to Fouad Ajami,

> There was no honor in this unequal peace, the true believers said. The language, the preserve of the intellectual class, came to the aid of the opponents of the peace. In a play on words, normalization, *tatbi*, was dismissed as *tatwi* (domestication) and peace, *salam*, as nothing other than surrender, *istislam*.
>
> (Ajami 1998, 274–75)

The Palestinian demands for transitional and compensatory justice were categorically rejected by their Israeli colleagues, who even conditioned the Oslo process on not engaging with issues of justice, claiming that they were there to deal with the future rather than the past, and that dealing with the past would create a barrier to peace. The Palestinian demands for the recognition of Israeli responsibility for the injustice perpetuated against the Palestinians during the 1947–49 war, and the insistence on the right of return were considered by the Israelis as entirely unacceptable. The latter claimed that peace negotiations required a pragmatic approach that should set aside the historical mutual charges of injustice. The Israelis argued that the negotiations should focus on the results of the 1967 war, rather than the outcomes of the 1947–49 war. Indeed Uri Savir, Israel's chief negotiator at Oslo, notes in his memoirs that he had already made this abundantly clear to the Palestinians at the first stages of the Oslo process:

> I am sure that we can debate the past for years and never agree. Let's see if we can agree about the future … . Never again would we argue about the past … . Discussing the future would mean reconciling two rights, not readdressing ancient wrongs.
>
> (Savir 1998, 15)[3]

Although the Palestinian negotiators felt from the outset of the negotiations that Israel's refusal to discuss past wrongs and the right of return was unjust and unfair, they felt compelled to agree to this approach. They correctly assumed that the Israelis would absolutely not agree to negotiate the outcomes of the 1947–49 war and that it would not be possible to coerce them to do so because of the power imbalance, whereas there was an immediate Palestinian interest in reaching an agreement that would lead to the establishment of a Palestinian state in the occupied territories. The Palestinians assumed that their insistence on recognition of the injustice and its remedy would immediately derail the negotiations and prevent any possibility of ending the occupation in the West Bank and the Gaza Strip. Thus, during the first phase of negotiations, the Palestinians considered the fact of not having an independent state a greater injustice than dealing with past wrongs (Hovdenak 2009).

Indeed, Ahmed Qurei (Abu-Ala) explained the Palestinian concession on the issue of injustice during the first phase of the Oslo process by pointing out the Palestinian weakness:

> The balance of power drastically favored Israel and worked against the Palestinians. This was reflected in the behavior of the Israeli negotiators on all issues and at every stage. For this reason, the Palestinian negotiators were obliged to use the few cards in their hand with patience, endurance and skill. We also needed to deploy logical argument. *We derived our power from the justice of our case, as*

> *opposed to the Israelis, who sought to define what was just on the basis of their power.*
>
> (Ahmed Qurei 2006, 296–97, my emphasis [the author, Yaacov Bar-Siman-Tov])

As the talks progressed, the Palestinian side came to believe that no just solution could come out of the Oslo Accords, so they were faced with choosing between a settlement that was "minimally acceptable and fair under the circumstances" or on insisting "on justice and risking losing even more" (Albin 2001, 150). Facing such a dilemma led to further fragmentation and disunity within the Palestinian negotiating party and the wider Palestinian community.

In sum, at the beginning of the Oslo process the Palestinians raised the issues of justice, causing several deadlocks and crises. Conversely, Israeli negotiators opposed the idea that the negotiations should focus on issues of justice because that would prevent reaching an agreement. Successful negotiations required a pragmatic approach rather than dealing with historical narratives and charges of injustice, which were perceived to be formidable barriers for reaching an agreement. Eventually, due to the asymmetrical power relations between the parties, the Palestinians realized that, if they would like to reach an agreement, they would have to concede on justice issues. As a result, the issues of justice became less significant in the negotiations. As Albin states, "Both Israeli and Palestinian negotiators admitted in interviews [with her] that considerations of justice were not the primary factor which ultimately determined the course and outcome of the talks" (Albin 2001, 177).

In addition to the power asymmetry, it seems that the Palestinian leadership failed to endorse the refugee issue as being at the top of the negotiations' agenda because until 1993 the PLO regarded the right of return as a principle, rather than being a policy or practical program. Thus, the PLO never spelled out in detail how the right of return should be implemented. Furthermore, the lack of a concrete program of return, and the 1974 PNC decision of linking the right of return to the right of self-determination, made the issue of self-determination much more significant in the talks than the right of return. Indeed, such linkage enabled the PLO to sign the Declaration of Principles (Oslo I) with Israel on 13 September 1993.

This potential link between the implementation of the right of return and the establishment of a Palestinian state enabled Israel to accept the parameters of the Oslo Agreement as well. Since Israel did not recognize in the Oslo Agreement the explicit Palestinian rights for self-determination and for establishing a Palestinian state, the issue of the right of return was not an obstacle for reaching the framework agreement in the first place.

By signing this agreement, the PLO and Israel agreed to divide the refugee problem into two parts. While the problem of the 1948 refugees was deferred to the permanent status negotiations and to the final agreement, Israel agreed in principle to let the 1967 refugees return to the West Bank and to the Gaza Strip. According to the Israeli–Palestinian Declaration of Principles on

Interim Self-Government Arrangements (DOP), a standing committee of the PLO, Israel, Egypt, and Jordan will be established in order to decide "on the modalities of admission of persons from the West Bank and Gaza Strip in 1967, together with the necessary measures to prevent disruption and disorder" (Article XII of the Oslo Agreement, quoted in Klein 1998, 10).

The Beilin–Abu-Mazen negotiations, 1994–95

A short time after the signing of the Oslo Agreement (the DOP), a new and unofficial second track channel regarding the final agreement negotiations was established. It was supervised by Israeli Deputy Foreign Minister, Yossi Beilin, and the Palestinian leader Mahmoud Abbas (Abu-Mazen), resulting in the Beilin–Abu-Mazen Agreement (October 1995) (Beilin 1997; Enderlin 2003). This channel was conducted secretly and parallel to the interim negotiations that led to the Cairo Agreement (4 May 1994) and to the "Israeli and Palestinian Authority: Interim Agreement on the West Bank and Gaza Strip" (Oslo II Agreement of 28 September 1995).

The Beilin–Abu-Mazen Agreement, though it was never formally recognized and adopted by the parties, presented a framework for the conclusion of a final status agreement between Israel and the PLO. The agreement aimed to achieve "a just, lasting, and comprehensive peace … based on the implementation of UN Security Council Resolutions 242 and 338." Interestingly enough, UNGA 194 Resolution was not mentioned in the agreement (quoted in www.jewishvirtuallibrary.org/jsource/Peace/beilinmazen.html; see also *Haaretz*, 21 September 2000).

The main points agreed upon included the establishment of a Palestinian state within agreed and secured borders with its capital as *al-Quds* (the Arab Eastern part of Jerusalem). Regarding the Palestinian refugees,

> the Palestinian side considers that the right of the Palestinian refugees to return to their homes is enshrined in international law and natural justice, it recognizes that the prerequisites of the new era of peace and coexistence, as well as the realities that have been created on the ground since 1948, have rendered the implementation of this impracticable.

The Israeli side, for its part, "acknowledges the moral and material suffering caused to the Palestinian people as a result of the war of 1947–49." Israel also "acknowledges the Palestinian refugees' right of return to the Palestinian state and their right to compensation and rehabilitation for moral and material losses." Israel also agreed "to continue to enable family reunification" and "to absorb Palestinian refugees in special defined cases, to be agreed upon with the ICPR (International Commission for Palestinian Refugees)." In addition, the agreement had detailed provisions for establishing an international fund, with Israeli contributions for financing compensation, resettlement, and rehabilitation of refugees. The PLO considered

> the implementation of the above a full and final settlement of the refugee issue in all its dimensions. It further undertakes that no additional claims or demands arising from this issue will be made upon the full implementation of this Framework Agreement.

The Beilin–Abu-Mazen Agreement was indeed a unique and exceptional document drafted in the peace negotiations. The agreement implied that the PLO accepted Israel's position on the refugee issue, as it was reflected also in the Oslo Agreement, as the basis for a peace agreement. The PLO agreed to an explicit trade-off between the Palestinian demands for transitional justice and the establishment of a Palestinian state. The Palestinians realized that, because of Israel's position regarding the refugee issue, the only way to establish a Palestinian state would be giving up their demands for Israel's acknowledgment of its responsibility for creating the refugee problem and accepting in principle the right of return to the state of Israel. Thus, in this agreement the PLO gave up the right of return in exchange for the establishment of an independent Palestinian state in the West Bank and the Gaza Strip. Conversely, Israel's two main concessions in the agreement included a readiness for the first time to establish a Palestinian state and dropping its previous demand that the number of refugees returning to the Palestinian state would be subject to negotiations with Israel.

The Palestinian criticism of the DOP and of the Beilin–Abu-Mazen Agreement

Following the signing of the Oslo Agreement in 1993 and the leaking to the press of the contents of the October 1995 Beilin–Abu-Mazen Agreement, Palestinian refugees, leaders, officials, and scholars blamed the Palestinian leadership for giving up the basic Palestinian demands for justice, including Israel's recognition of its full responsibility for creating the Palestinian refugee problem and accepting the right of return of the refugees to their original homes in Israel. Many of the 1948 refugees expressed their anger that the PLO did not regard their right of return as the most significant issue in the negotiations; quite the contrary, their right of return was bargained away for the establishment of a Palestinian state in the occupied territories. They stated that the right of return was a sacred and protected principle immune from negotiations and bargaining, and that the PLO was not authorized to bargain the right of return in exchange for obtaining territorial concessions from Israel (Aruri 2001; Hovdenak 2009; Said 1994, 1995, 2006; Zureik 1996).

The Palestinian concerns were even exacerbated following the Cairo Agreement of 4 May 1994 regarding the Gaza Strip and Jericho area, and the Israeli–Palestinian Interim Agreement of 28 September 1995 (Oslo II). Although both agreements were not supposed to refer to the refugee issue because its discussion was delayed to the permanent status (i.e. final agreement) negotiations, these interim accords were perceived by the Palestinian refugees and many others as an explicit neglect of the right of return in favor of establishing a Palestinian state and surrendering to Israeli dictates not to discuss the issue of refugees before the final agreement. Thus, the Palestinian critics of the Oslo process warned that the exercise of the right of return was essential for the resolution of the conflict, as a matter of principle and justice that could not be given up even for the sake of establishing a Palestinian state (Zureik 1996, 60–65, 90–95; Bowker 2003, 159–63).

Netanyahu's first administration, 1996–99

During Netanyahu's first administration (1996–99), the issues of justice, injustice, and fairness played some role in the negotiations between the parties, especially in the implementation of the Oslo Agreements. Both sides complained that their counterpart failed to implement the agreements. At the same time, both sides discussed the issues of justice and injustice in several meetings.

For instance, at a meeting on 17 February 1998, between Ariel Sharon, Israeli Minister of Infrastructure, and Ahmed Queri (Abu-Ala), Palestinian chief negotiator, Sharon raised the issue of injustice and suffering caused to the Jews by the Palestinians throughout the long conflict:

> The Jews in Israel faced injustice and oppression at the hands of the Palestinians. The Palestinians had unjustly rejected the claim of the Israelis to the land of their forefathers and had perpetrated massacres against the Jews, slaughtering even the survivors of the Holocaust.

Sharon referred specifically to the violent events initiated by the Palestinians in the 1921, 1929, 1936, and 1939 riots and to the war of 1947–49. The history lessons of the conflict made Israel realize that it had to rely only on itself and not compromise its security (quoted in Qurei 2008, 40 and 46).

For his part, Abu-Ala refused to accept Sharon's version of the injustice and defined it as "a blatant misrepresentation of the facts" and presented to Sharon "the story of the real victims … [and] the endless grievances of the Palestinians and enumerated the atrocities and massacres that the Palestinians had suffered at the hands of the Israelis" (Qurei 2008, 30). Abu-Ala maintained that, while the Palestinians understood the suffering and injustice caused to the Jews in Europe, Israel should understand as well the suffering and the injustice done to the Palestinians in their own land. In Abu-Ala's words, the Palestinians were the "true victims of the current situation" (Qurei 2008, 36–37). After a fruitless exchange of blames and recriminations, Abu-Ala suggested that "let us learn the lessons of the past instead of crying over it," and Sharon agreed: "I acknowledge your difficulties and your tragedy and I understand them fully. Therefore, we should look for realistic solutions" (Qurei 2008, 40) Indeed,

> both sides agreed to stop looking backwards, and to waste no further time or effort in rehearsing contradictory historical accounts on which we would never agree. Instead, we agreed to focus on the possibility that we could cooperate to build a better future.
>
> (Qurei 2008, 30)

Abu-Ala also raised the need for procedural justice in the negotiations because of the asymmetrical power relations between the parties. He stated that the Oslo Agreement was "a fair agreement," because "both sides took into consideration the balance of power and the underlying nature of the problem, the need for a solution fair to both sides and offering prospects for the future." However, Netanyahu's government exploited the asymmetrical balance of power in its favor:

> There is a wide gap at the moment between the Israel government and us, because Israel has the power on the ground and can impose its will on all issues. It imposes closures upon us and can freeze the implementation of the agreement. On our side, the only power we have is to insist on the agreement with all our might.
>
> (Qurei 2008, 39)

With the exception of this meeting, the issues of justice and injustice were not part of the negotiations that led to the Hebron (1997) and Wye (1998) interim agreements during Netanyahu's administration, as part of the implementation of the Oslo Accords.

Barak's era: turning to procedural, transitional, and corrective justice, 1999–2001

The severe criticism raised against the Palestinian negotiators for giving up the Palestinians demands for justice had a significant influence upon the Palestinian attitude in the negotiations with Israel from 1999 to 2001, during the administration of Israeli Prime Minister Ehud Barak. The Palestinian negotiators renewed their demands for procedural, transitional, and corrective justice because of the Palestinian domestic criticism of neglecting the issue of the refugees, and because of the approaching stage of reaching a permanent and final agreement, following the (delayed) timetable of the Oslo process.

The Swedish back channel track, 1999–2000

Between the end of 1999 and May 2000, 15 meetings were held in the region, two memorable encounters took place in Stockholm, and one meeting in Washington, as part of a "back channel" negotiation track (official but secret), that preceded the Camp David Summit of July 2000. These negotiations were supposed to lead to a framework agreement and to address the permanent status issues. The Palestinians presented their demands for procedural justice that meant fair and just treatment as equal partners in the negotiations. The Palestinians maintained in the talks that the asymmetrical power relations, and especially their economic and military weakness, did not mean that they were totally weak because they held the "key to war and peace in the Middle East." "Israel would never be accepted in the Arab world or in the broader Muslim community without establishing peace with the Palestinians, since the Palestinians exercise what amounts to a veto power on any peace" (Qurei 2008, 111).

Abu-Ala maintained that Shlomo Ben-Ami, at that time Israel's Internal Security Minister who led the Israeli delegation in the back channel talks, "was a cooperative negotiating partner." Ben-Ami seemed to realize the significance of the Palestinians' role in the Middle East and the need to resolve the conflict including the resolution of the most intractable issues that were deferred to the permanent status negotiations, such as borders, territory, Jerusalem, refugees, and settlements. Nevertheless, Ben-Ami stressed that the real asymmetrical power relations reflected an opposite constellation:

> You might think we stand for Goliath and you play the part of David. We think quite the opposite. We are David, the Israeli Jew who lives amid a vast Arab and Muslim world that, to this day, refuses to recognize the legitimacy of the existence of the Israeli state in this part of the world.
>
> (Quoted in Qurei 2008, 112)

From this standpoint, the resolution of the Israeli–Palestinian conflict, with all its significance, would not necessarily end Israel's basic security problems in the Middle East.

According to the Palestinian version of the negotiations, in respect of transitional and corrective justice Israel agreed to acknowledge only the suffering caused by the 1947–49 war, but without assuming any responsibility. The Palestinians stressed that the right of return was the most important issue for them. They requested that any discussion of this issue should be conducted in accordance with UNGA Resolution 194. They demanded that Israel should recognize the right of return and should agree to absorb a substantial number of refugees within its territory. Although the Palestinians refrained from presenting specific numbers, they were ready to discuss all the relevant details, including lists of names, numbers, and the question of possible reparations (Ben-Ami 2004, 20, 33, 40, 47; Qurei 2008, 102–6; Shavit and Bana 2001).

The Israeli position was to induce the Palestinians to make a historical renouncement on the right of return, in return for Israeli territorial concessions of the West Bank and Gaza, and to conclude a framework agreement that would be regarded as the end of the conflict. The Palestinians were also asked to refrain from reopening further issues relating to the history of the Israeli–Palestinian conflict. The Palestinians refused categorically to accept Israel's position (Qurei 2008, 103; Shavit and Bana 2001).

According to the Israeli version, Israel's positions on the issues of transitional and corrective justice did not change during the back channel track negotiations. Israel rejected the Palestinian claims regarding any responsibility for creating the refugee problem and the right of return, arguing that, "there is no turning the wheels [of time] back" (Sher 2001, 41). Nevertheless, the Israeli negotiating team did explore a number of new proposals to address the questions of responsibility and return of refugees. For instance, in order to share responsibilities regarding the fate of the Palestinian refugees, Israel proposed establishing an international commission and an international fund to develop a mechanism for compensation and resettlement of the refugees in the Palestinian state, in their host countries, or in other states. "We wanted a mechanism that would internationalize the issue instead of allowing it to serve as an eternal barrier between us and them, as the exclusive responsibility and burden of Israel" (Ben-Ami 2004, 47). Even so, Israel expressed willingness to absorb a limited number of refugees (perhaps a few thousand), over the course of several decades, in accordance with its sovereign judgment, and only on a humanitarian and family reunification basis.

Regarding compensation for refugees, Israel agreed to allocate a sum of money to be determined and disbursed over a number of years as part of an international effort to establish an international fund totaling US $20 billion dollars. Israel sought to set a final upper limit in advance, on the assumption that a third party would ensure the funds were raised. Although the Palestinians agreed to establish an international commission and international fund, they continued to demand the implementation of the right of return according to UNGA Resolution 194, which meant fulfilling the right to return to Israel proper, as well as demanding substantive compensation for the properties that were abandoned in Israel. The link that they sought to establish between "properties that were abandoned" and compensation was in their view principled and ideological, rather than economic and practical. Thus, the Palestinians wanted Israel to officially acknowledge that the country was built on the basis of abandoned property that belonged to Palestinian refugees.

According to the Palestinian version, the two sides agreed during the Swedish back channel track on the need for a just and humanitarian agreement based on international law that will lead to the implementation of UNGA Resolution 194, within the context of ending the Israeli–Palestinian conflict. Israel preferred that the solution should be based on Security Council Resolution 242. The sides disagreed on the number of refugees who would be allowed to return, and the justification for their return. While the Palestinians demanded basing it on the right of return, Israel insisted that this should be done only on a humanitarian basis. Nevertheless, both sides agreed to form an international committee that would address these issues. This committee would be drawn from Israel, the PLO, the regional host refugees' countries (Jordan, Syria, Lebanon, and Egypt), as well as the United States, Canada, the European Union, Japan, Russia, and Norway. This committee will develop a formula according to which each refugee could decide upon one of the following options: (1) to return to Israel with compensation, (2) to return to the State of Palestine with compensation, (3) to settle in the country of his or her present residence with compensation, and (4) to migrate to another country with compensation (Qurei 2008, 120–21). Furthermore, both sides agreed to establish an international fund managed by the international committee in cooperation with the World Bank. They will determine together the composition of the international institution that will manage the resources for the rehabilitation of Palestinian refugees and their compensation (Qurei 2008, 350).

Although the issues of responsibility and right of return were not resolved in the Swedish track, Israelis perceived that the Palestinians had relaxed their principled stance and that real progress had been made, so that a joint perspective had been developed regarding the practical aspects of resolving the refugee problem, the essence of which was compensation (Ben-Ami 2004, 47, 54; Sher 2001, 86, 104, 107–8, 142; Pressman 2003). On the eve of the Camp David Summit, the Israeli impression was that the question of the right of return had been satisfactorily resolved. The Israeli side also learned that most of the members of the Palestinians' senior echelon, with the exception of Abu-Mazen, had all given their assent to the understandings reached in the Swedish back channel (Shavit and Bana 2001).

It seems that this impression was a false one though, because, soon afterwards, during talks in June 2000 in Tel Aviv, it became clear to the Israeli team that the Palestinians had withdrawn from what the Israelis considered as joint understandings reached during the Stockholm talks. The Palestinians stressed that the principle of "family unification" was not acceptable to them and that Israel needed to acknowledge its responsibility for creating the refugee problem. Israel also should agree to the principle of right of return to be implemented through a quota of 5,000–10,000 refugees per year, "until the issue naturally dissipates" (Ben-Ami 2006, 77, 82) or, according to Abu-Ala, 10,000 refugees every year "until the issue of principle was resolved" (Qurei 2008: 129).[4]

In another meeting on 25 June 2000 with Arafat in Nablus, Ben-Ami tried again to reach an agreed formula for a joint solution to the refugee problem. According to Abu-Ala, Ben-Ami was aware of the Palestinian suffering, and that the Palestinians perceived the refugees' situation as a catastrophic problem. Ben-Ami added that he realized that, if both sides failed to reach an agreement on the issue, it would be difficult for the Palestinian leadership to mobilize the Palestinian people to support the agreement. While not denying the morality of the Palestinian demand for the right of return, Israel could not accept it because of demographic concerns. Therefore, Ben-Ami suggested that the right of return would become only a symbolic one, so that the refugee problem would be resolved in practical terms mainly by compensation, by setting up an international fund, and by a special reparations commission. Ben-Ami told Arafat that he had to give up the right of return: "You must understand that no one in Israel, not now, not tomorrow, not even fifty years from now, will accept the refugees' right of return" (quoted in Enderlin 2003, 167). Ben-Ami warned the Palestinians against being hostages to prejudices, legends, and myths that they had created throughout the conflict. Again, Ben-Ami failed to convince Arafat, who stated that most of the refugees would not return anyway (Qurei 2008, 150–51).

Following this meeting, Abu-Ala summarized both sides' positions on the refugee problem. The gap between the two sides remained unbridgeable on the right of return. While the Palestinians demanded that the right of return should be recognized and a mechanism of implementation should be agreed upon, Israel rejected these demands and accepted only the discussion of the idea of family reunification. At the same time, both sides agreed that a fair compensation should be awarded to every refugee, and to set up an international fund. The Palestinian further demanded that compensation for the long years of occupation should be acknowledged and estimated as well. In addition, the Palestinians wanted the refugees to receive special compensation from Israel for the property and the land they had left behind, even before they received compensation from the international fund that would be set up for this purpose. Israel vehemently refused even to discuss it (Qurei 2008, 158; Shavit and Bana 2001).

On the eve of the Camp David Summit, Yasser Arafat sent President Clinton a letter indicating the Palestinian position in preparation for the summit. Regarding the refugee problem, Arafat maintained that the refugee issue was for every Palestinian not only a matter of human rights, but also "a matter of right and conscience," so he would not sign an agreement that would not resolve the problem. UNGA resolution 194 remained the "principle, the basis, and the key for a just solution" (quoted in Qurei 2008, 163). The Palestinian refugees should be asked whether they wished to return to Israel, to move to the future Palestinian state, to remain in their host country and receive compensation, or to move to a third country and receive compensation. The number of the refugees willing to return to Israel should be specified, as well as the timetable for their return (Qurei 2008, 168).

The Camp David Summit, 11–25 July 2000

The Palestinian and the Israeli positions regarding the issue of Palestinian refugees were presented to American officials before the convening of the Camp David Summit. The Palestinians clarified that "any agreement that did not include a just solution to the refugee problem would engender an even stronger revolution [within the Diaspora refugee camps]" (Hanieh 2000).[5] The Israeli side presented its traditional position: "Palestinian refugees would not be granted the right of return to places under Israeli sovereignty, under any circumstances, nor would Israel accept any ethical or legal responsibility for the fact that a refugee problem exists" (Yatom 2005, 37).

It seems that the gap between the two parties was unbridgeable, preventing any possible agreement. At the same time, the parties believed that the other side would give up some of its positions in order to move forward towards peace.

While Israel hoped that the Palestinians would give up the issues of responsibility and the right of return and accept the idea of compensation, the Palestinians hoped that Israel would accept the right of return, in principle, and the discussion would then focus on the practicalities, such as the agreed numbers of returnees.[6]

As for the summit itself, the Palestinians claim that their demands for justice were not discussed substantively during the Camp David negotiations. Akram Hanieh, a Palestinian journalist and member of the Palestinian delegation at Camp David, asserts that the reason for this was "the absence of seriousness on the part of Israel" (Hanieh 2000) and due to "the lack of will on Israel's part." According to Hanieh, the refugee committee at Camp David, which was supposed to deal with this issue, "was the most difficult, strangest, and most unsuccessful" (Hanieh 2000), and became "the greatest failure of the summit" because of Israel's position (Hanieh 2001, 82).[7] In his words, the refugee committee at Camp David

> was the most difficult committee because it was the reality Committee, ruled by history, and because it placed Israel at the center of the Palestinian question. It placed Israel in front of her victims, in front of the witnesses of its crimes.
>
> (Hanieh 2000)

Hanieh, who presents the Palestinian version of the Camp David talks, holds that the discussions of the refugee issues focused mainly on the past, on the roots of the conflict, and on the Palestinian *Nakba*. The differences in the narratives of the two sides regarding the past and the solution to the problem remained vast. The Palestinians blamed Israel for their suffering because of the establishment of the State of Israel at their expense and for creating the refugee problem, and demanded both Israel's acknowledgment of its legal and moral responsibility for creating the refugee problem and its principled acceptance of the right of return.

Furthermore, the Palestinians argued that the right of return was the essence of the problem and the solution, so without the return there was nothing left to discuss. The demand of the right of return should be relevant for each refugee according to UNGA Resolution 194. The Palestinians also called for the establishment of a mechanism for implementation of this right and repatriation of the Palestinian refugees from Lebanon first, in light of their particularly difficult circumstances and family links with Palestinians living in the Israeli Galilee. The mechanism for fulfillment of the right of return had to include a timetable and a count of the number of Palestinians who wanted to implement their right of return. The Palestinians also argued that, after recognition of the right of return and establishment of a mechanism for its implementation, it would be necessary to set up a fund for compensation. They believed that the issue of compensation for Jews who left Arab countries was not part of the Palestinian issue and therefore not a subject for discussion (Hanieh 2001, 94; Meridor 2011).

According to Hanieh, Israel "continued to deny its crime." Israel not only categorically denied any legal or moral responsibility for the refugee problem but also blamed the Palestinians for being responsible for the 1947–49 war and its outcomes. Nevertheless, the Israeli negotiators were ready to express regret for the Palestinian suffering that resulted from the war.[8] Moreover, the Israeli delegation absolutely denied any right of return. Hanieh argues that every discussion of the right of return was a taboo subject for Israel because it meant a declaration of a war of annihilation against it. Therefore there could not be any meaningful discussion about a timetable for its implementation.

Abu-Ala maintains that Israel also denied the issue of the right of return on the grounds that the return to what was now a third country (Israel) could not find any justification in international law, so that the Palestinian state should be the logical destination for Palestinian refugees. At the same time, Israel expressed willingness to compensate the Palestinians, not directly but through the international community. Israel also demanded that some of the allocations from the international fund for compensation be granted to Jews from Arab countries that had come to Israel. Israel did, nevertheless, agreed to allow a few thousand refugees to return to Israeli territory over the course of ten years in the context of family reunification and humanitarian considerations (Hanieh 2001, 82, 94; see also Qurei 2008, 178–79, 181, 228, 237).[9]

In their version of the Camp David talks, Hanieh and Abu-Ala also present the negative impressions of the Palestinians regarding the lack of implementation of their demands for procedural justice. They claim that Israel tried to maximize fully its achievements during the negotiations, while completely ignoring the positions, rights, and demands of the Palestinians as equal partners in the peace process. With US support and acquiescence, Israel tried to impose its preferred schemes for an agreement upon the Palestinians, though the latter forcefully rejected this coordinated effort.

Abu-Ala argues that the Israelis

> underestimated the ability of the Palestinians to stand firm in the face of unfair demands over the fundamental issues relating to territory, Jerusalem, and the rights of the refugees, and had overestimated the extent of the concessions they might wring from us through orchestrated and insistent pressure.
>
> (Qurei 2008, 262)

The Israelis "had obstinately refused to accept the minimum requirements for an honorable peace that would not be rejected by the future generations" (Qurei 2008, 261). The Palestinians had an interest in concluding a peace agreement with Israel; however, "peace must be on a just basis, and cannot be the unjust peace that the strong can dictate to the weak … . No people can be expected to surrender more and more of their basic rights.

(Qurei 2008, 271)

According to the Palestinians, the United States took advantage of their relative weakness and put a lot of pressure on them to compromise, while it refrained from putting similar pressure on Israel. The Americans also tended to present the Israeli proposals as their own. Therefore, according to Hanieh and Abu-Ala, the failure of the Camp David Summit was directly attributable to Israel and the United States (Hanieh 2000, 81; Qurei 2008, 257, 259, 266).

The Palestinians also complained about Ehud Barak's treatment of Yasser Arafat. Arafat felt humiliated and overmastered by Barak, who dictated his positions rather than negotiated them. Arafat accused Barak of treating him at Camp David "as a slave" (Ben-Ami 2006, 253). Other Israeli negotiators noted as well that Barak indeed humiliated Arafat by ignoring him throughout the summit and by refusing to meet him (Meridor 2011; Sher 2001, 200).

The Israeli version of the discussion of refugees during the Camp David talks differs significantly from the Palestinian version. The Palestinians demanded that Israel acknowledge its responsibility for creating the refugee problem, recognize their right of return, and accept 10–20 percent of the refugees, amounting to about 400,000 to 800,000, back in Israel. The Palestinians primarily demanded the return of refugees from Lebanon to their homes in Galilee and they rejected Israel's demand for compensation for Jewish refugees who had fled Arab countries. Israel, for its part, made clear to the Palestinians and to the Americans that it rejected any responsibility for the creation of the refugee problem, as well as denying the right of return to Israel. Israel could not accept the Palestinian narrative, just as the Palestinians could not accept the Zionist narrative, so that recognizing the right of return would be a moral defeat for Israel. Nonetheless, Israel remained open to practical solutions to the problem of the refugees in the framework of compensation through an international committee and fund. Israel also agreed to recognize a right of return to a *Palestinian* state and even to receive within its territory a "modest number" (token) of refugees on humanitarian grounds over the course of an extended period of time (Ben-Ami 2004, 142, 205, 208; Ben-Ami 2006, 249; Meridor 2011).[10] From the Israeli standpoint, the Palestinians refused to discuss any modalities of compensation before Israel's acceptance of the right of return (Meridor 2011).

At Camp David, the Israeli negotiators were surprised by the intensity of the Palestinian demands on the issues of justice, first and foremost the right of return. They had assumed, or deluded themselves, that the Palestinians had accepted that they were not there to discuss the past and the right of return, having presumably internalized Israel's absolute opposition to this issue, and that the refugee problem could be resolved only through compensation. Sometimes, the Israelis wondered whether the Palestinian position on the refugee issue was only a tactical one in order to trigger Israel's concessions on other negotiation issues, such as Jerusalem, borders, and territorial scope of the future Palestinian state. However, very quickly the Israelis realized that the refugee issue was a real strategic and most emotional issue for the Palestinians. As Meridor describes, "It seems to me that the issue is very deep and emotional. There are hundred thousands of refugees who believe [in that issue]. It is difficult, very difficult" [to resolve] (Meridor 2011). Moreover, the Israeli negotiators realized that the Palestinians did not limit their demands for transitional and corrective justice, which were linked to the outcome of the 1947–49 war, but also expanded their demands for justice by questioning the very existence of Israel at their expense.[11]

In this context, Shlomo Ben-Ami describes his impressions as follows:

> The Israelis arrived ready to seek a compromise solution to the problems of 1967 and found themselves crashing into the wall of 1948 problems ... with the Israelis speaking of a dream come true through a process of reasonable compromise during which they relinquish some of their dearly-held myths about Jerusalem and the Land of Israel, while the Palestinians are refusing to abandon their perception of Israel as a state born in sin that needs to admit as much and pay the price. The apparently weaker side, the Palestinians, strove for Israel's moral defeat, to the point of dealing a fatal blow to her legitimacy as a Jewish state.
>
> (Ben-Ami 2004, 464)

Ben-Ami cites Hanieh who said:

> At Camp David we intended to make the Israelis face the tribunal of history, face the victims of their crime and sin. Israel wanted to silence for ever the voice of the witnesses to the crime and erase the proof of the Nakbah.
>
> (Quoted in Ben-Ami 2006, 249–50)

Thus, Ben-Ami reaches the conclusion that the Palestinian demands for justice were an obstacle to peace:

> We can say in all honesty that we tried everything and that we found, to our regret and sorrow, that the Palestinian leadership rejected the boldest possible proposals – including, in fact, a complete return of the territories – while trapped in myths of return, exile, and Islam, and that it is not capable of a compromise that would recognize a Jewish state's moral right to exist in this part of the world.
>
> (Ben-Ami 2004, 455)

According to Ben-Ami, at Camp David the Palestinian leadership was not searching for a practical solution but rather seeking justice. He states that on more than one occasion he warned the Palestinian negotiators that striving for justice would undermine the chances of peace, but they saw the peace process as

> a political journey to justice and to the sanctity of Islam, which – if it fails – becomes a violent journey intended to compel the Israelis to

> recognize and acknowledge the justness of the Palestinian cause and the Islamic claims of ownership in Jerusalem.
>
> (Ben-Ami 2004, 487)

Hence, Ben-Ami concludes that the question of the Palestinian ethos has been a determinant of the future of peace and normal relations between the parties. The question in his mind was whether the Palestinians will succeed in "letting go – which will not be easy for them – of the ethos of revenge and remedy for injustice directed against Israel, the state that – in collective Palestinian memory – murdered, expelled, and inherited" (Ben-Ami 2004, 506). Furthermore, Ben-Ami argues that Arafat refused to be the first and only Arab leader "to recognize the unique historical and religious roots of the bond of the Jews to their millenarian homeland and their holy shrines" (Ben-Ami 2006, 249).

Ehud Barak, who shared Ben-Ami's perspective, held that Arafat could not in his heart of hearts morally and legally accept Israel's right to exist as a Jewish state and that Arafat's obsession was not the establishment of a sovereign Palestinian state in part of the Land of Israel (Palestine) but rather to provide a remedy for the injustice of 1948 or, in other words, to bring about the ultimate destruction of the State of Israel (Interview of Barak by Ari Shavit, *Haaretz*, 6 September 2002).

Although the Israeli policymakers rejected Palestinian demands for justice, and especially the right of return, they understood that Israel needed to find a way to deal with these demands for justice in practical terms. During discussions within the Israeli team at the Camp David Summit, differences of opinion on the matter surfaced. Barak held that "we must distinguish between our justice and the patently clear observation that without some sort of satisfactory response to the other side, there will be no agreement" (Sher 2001, 164). Ben-Ami was also convinced that, given that the Palestinians were the main victims of the conflict,

> we must not shrink away from one fundamental, moral aspect of the conflict: we, a nation of victims, also insist on living within the culture of victimhood without a real ability to acknowledge that another nation was – even if mainly through the fault of its leaders – our constant victim. … We are obliged to give them back their dignity and compromise on their rights.
>
> (Ben-Ami 2004, 507)

He held that even if the agreement on refugees is "very narrow and measured," it must include some element of moral compensation (quoted in Sher 2001, 164). In contrast, Elyakim Rubinstein, the Legal Advisor of Israel's Foreign Affairs Ministry, denied the possibility of demonstrating any kind of empathy to the Palestinian narrative: "History cannot be rewritten. The State of Israel has an ethos and does not need to abandon it" (quoted in Sher 2001, 164). Rubinstein maintained that,

> on the historical level, we cannot agree to be held responsible for the refugee problem. What happened in 1948 is the subject of controversy, and the peace process should not be the arena in which historical truth is pronounced. … We do not consider ourselves to blame.
>
> (Quoted in Enderlin 2003, 196–97)

Similarly, Meridor warned that even financial compensation provided by Israel could indicate some acknowledgment of responsibility and blame and, therefore, Israel should insist at least that the compensation would also include Jewish refugees from the Arab countries (Meridor 2011).

The attitude of the Israeli negotiators towards "moral compensation" or "some sort of satisfactory response" to the other side was limited then to an Israeli willingness to recognize the suffering and hardship of the Palestinian refugees and the reality that the Palestinians were the primary victims of the bloody Arab–Israeli conflict, as well as a certain disposition to receive a few thousand refugees over the course of many years solely on a humanitarian basis but not on the grounds of a right of return, which would amount to an admission of injustice and recognition of this right (Barak 2005; Beilin 2002; Ben-Ami 2004, 277; Meridor 2011).

Sher maintained that, although Israel could not accept the right of return of the refugees to its territory, it could show some flexibility over the wording about it, so that would satisfy emotionally the Palestinians. Sher believed that the Palestinian negotiators realized that the refugees would not be allowed to return to Israeli territory but they considered it their duty to show at least "verbally that they were bringing an end to the tragedy of the refugees and that their dream of Return was about to [be] realized" (Sher 2005, 62). Sher assumed that all the talk about the right of return was just "empty propaganda and negotiating maneuver" and the right of return "was never the obstacle to reaching a permanent status agreement, neither at Camp David nor at any point thereafter" (Sher 2005, 67).

Although the issue of refugees was not the sole cause of the summit's failure (after all, it was not discussed in detail as compared to Jerusalem), it still played a major role in the breakdown of the talks. As Barak stated, "to be sure, the Palestinian Right of Return was one of the main causes of the failure" (Barak 2005, 145). At Camp David, for the first time, the historical narratives had played a major role in discussing the refugee issue. The issue of injustice became an integral part of the negotiations. Israeli negotiators realized that the formula of the negotiations was not limited only to the outcomes of the 1967 war, but also to the consequences of the 1947–49 war. Thus,

> there is no way to discuss an "end of conflict" without first going back to where it all began, which is when they [the Palestinians] lost their homeland in 1948, and not when Israel took the West Bank and the Gaza Strip in June 1967.
>
> (Susser 2005, 201)

After the Camp David Summit, the parties continued negotiating these issues, while each side kept its traditional position. The Palestinians continued to demand that Israel should recognize its moral responsibility in creating the refugee problem and should agree to a right of return, though implemented in a way that maintained the internal demographic balance (i.e. Jewish majority) within Israel. The Palestinians made it clear that, if Israel wanted to conclude the conflict and put an end to its demands, it should recognize their right of return. In practice "an authentic right of return" could be implemented in two ways: to the new Palestinian state and, according to a free decision of each Palestinian refugee, to live in any other place he or she might choose, including Israel. Priority for return to Israel should be given to refugees who were born in historic Palestine and to the refugees in Lebanon (about 250,000) because of their difficult situation (Qurei 2008, 252–54).

Israel, for its part, categorically denied the Palestinian demands and put forward another reason for its absolute resistance to the right of return. Israel held that the right of return should only be fulfilled within the territory of the Palestinian state because it was inconceivable that on the one hand a Palestinian state would be established and on the other hand Palestinian refugees would return to live within Israel. There was a clear and logical contradiction between the Palestinian aspiration for a state and their simultaneous demand for a massive return of several million refugees to Israel. Moreover, Israel's acceptance of an unrestricted return of Palestinian refugees to a Palestinian state amounted to a new and significant Israeli concession.

Israel also raised the idea, which President Clinton later adopted as one of his parameters, that refugees would be able to return to those territories that the Palestinian state would receive from Israel in the context of territorial exchanges (territorial "swaps"), so that the Palestinians could define this as an implementation of the right of return and the fulfillment of UNGA Resolution 194. In addition, Israel held that the foundation for a discussion of the refugee question was not UNGA Resolution 194 but Resolution 242. At the same time, Israel expressed willingness to adhere to the Stockholm draft and receive 15,000 refugees over the course of 20 years (Ben-Ami 2004, 277, 285, 372–73; Pressman 2003). Nevertheless, some of the Israeli negotiators realized that the Palestinians kept the issue of the right of return as their final card (and bargaining chip), so they would not give up their claims until agreements were concluded on all other issues (Enderlin 2003, 252).

The Clinton parameters, December 23, 2000: transitional and corrective justice

On 23 December 2000, US President Bill Clinton presented to the parties an outline regarding the resolution of the Israeli–Palestinian conflict. Just before the conclusion of Clinton's presidency, the US intermediary for the first time proposed a series of parameters about ways of resolving the conflict that addressed the questions of justice and resolution of the refugee problem, among other issues (such as territory, security, Jerusalem, and end of conflict). Under the heading "Refugees," President Clinton noted that he *believed* that Israel was prepared to acknowledge the moral and material suffering caused to the Palestinian people as a result of the 1948 war and the need to assist the international community in addressing the problem. This approach was not rejected by Israel, since it essentially limited the recognition to a "willingness to acknowledge the moral and material suffering" of the Palestinians, without acknowledging Israel's responsibility for the suffering or its remedy. Indeed, President Clinton stressed that the fundamental gap in the positions of the parties related to the right of return. The president noted that, being familiar with the history of the issue, he knew how hard it was for the Palestinian leadership to appear to be neglecting the principle of the right of return, but conversely, Israel could not acquiesce on this issue because a Palestinian right of return would endanger its Jewish character.

According to Clinton, the solution had to address the needs of both sides according to the perspective of "two states for two peoples": the Palestinian State as the homeland of the Palestinian people, and the State of Israel as the homeland of the Jewish people, a perspective on which both sides had agreed as a practical way to resolve the Israeli–Palestinian conflict. In the two-state solution, the Palestinian state would be the "focal point" for Palestinian return, without ruling out that Israel would accept some of these refugees. Regarding the right of return, the president stressed that he *believed* that the parties needed to adopt a formula that made it clear that there was no specific right of return to Israel itself, but at the same time it did not negate the aspiration of the Palestinian people to return to their homeland. In this context the president proposed two alternative formulae to the parties:

1 "Both sides recognize the rights of Palestinian refugees to return to historic Palestine";
2 "Both sides recognize the right of Palestinian refugees to return to their homeland."

(Clinton 2000, quoted in Laqueur and Rubin 2008, 564)[12]

In the president's opinion, the agreement between the parties should define the fulfillment of the right of return in a way that would fit the framework of the two-state solution. In this context, Clinton proposed five alternatives for permanent residence for refugees:

1 the State of Palestine
2 areas in Israel being transferred to Palestine in the land swap
3 rehabilitation in a host country
4 resettlement in a third country
5 admission to Israel.

(Clinton 2000, quoted in Laqueur and Rubin 2008, 564)

In noting these alternatives, the agreement would make clear that a return to the West Bank and Gaza, or to the territories that Israel would transfer to the Palestinian State in the context of territorial exchange (swaps), would encompass the fulfillment of the right of Palestinian refugees, whereas their rehabilitation in host countries, resettlement in third countries, or absorption into Israel would depend on the policies of these countries. Israel could indicate in the agreement its intention to establish a policy so that some of the refugees would be absorbed into Israel, consistent with its sovereign decision. President Clinton also noted that he believed that priority should be given to the refugees living in Lebanon. The parties would further agree that implementing these steps would be regarded as implementing UNGA Resolution 194 regarding Palestinian refugees into practice.

President Clinton's parameters on the matter of responsibility and the right of return addressed Israel's aspirations. Israeli recognition of the moral and material suffering of the Palestinian people as a result of the 1947–49 war and limited reception of refugees over a long period of time – not on the basis of a right of return but solely on humanitarian grounds of family reunification – were practical solutions that Israel had no difficulty in accepting. In contrast, Clinton's parameters generated a formula that did not address the Palestinian overall demands for justice. Indeed, rather than determining that Israel was responsible for the refugee problem, the president's formula only included Israeli recognition of the moral and material suffering of the refugees, and the right of return was limited to the Palestinian state only and to territories that Israel would transfer to the Palestinians in the context of territorial exchange. Israel's willingness to receive an undetermined number of refugees over a long period of time was not sufficient to address the principled demand for a right of return.

On 28 December 2000, Israel accepted Clinton's parameters as a basis for the continuation of the negotiations towards a permanent arrangement, on the condition that the Palestinians would accept them as well. At the same time, Israel had various reservations. Regarding the refugee issue, Israel emphasized that its position opposing the right of return to its territory was stronger than what appeared in the president's proposal (Sher 2001, 373).[13]

According to Abu-Ala, the Palestinians asked Clinton for certain clarifications but the President refused to elaborate unless the Palestinians accepted the general principles. Arafat told Clinton that he accepted the proposals with some reservations, and that he was ready to continue the negotiations, but Clinton refused to make any changes in his proposals. Initially the Palestinians intended to reject the Clinton parameters; however, the fact that Israel seemed to accept them, at least in part, made them decide "to give them serious consideration" in the hope of being able to modify the elements that they did not like (Qurei 2008, 285). At the same time, they prepared an internal working paper referring to the Clinton's proposals (see Palestinian Negotiating Team, 2 January 2001, quoted in Laqueur and Rubin 2008, 567–73).

The Palestinians maintained in their internal working paper that they could not accept any proposal that does not guarantee the "establishment of a Palestinian state and the return of refugees to their homes." The US proposals reflected the complete acceptance by the Americans of the Israeli position that the application of the right of return would be entirely conditioned on Israel's acceptance. Furthermore, while UNGA Resolution 194, which was regarded as the basis for a just settlement of the refugee problem, called for the return of the refugees to their "homes" the Clinton Plan mentioned the return to a "homeland" or to "historical Palestine." According to the proposals, Israel only acknowledged the "moral and material suffering of the Palestinian people as a result of the 1948 war" and this enabled it to claim that the Arabs were responsible for the refugee problem.

The Palestinians insisted that Israel should also admit responsibility for creating the refugee problem. The Clinton proposals suggested that Israel's role would be limited to "assisting the world community to resolve the problem," and this meant that Israel would not have a special role in this effort. The Palestinians could not accept the recognition of the State of Israel as the "homeland of the Jewish people" because the "religious or ethnic nature of a state is an internal affair of that state and therefore inappropriate for a third state to specify in an international treaty." For the same reason, the Palestinians could not accept the definition of the Palestinian state as a "homeland for the Palestinian people." The essence of the right of return consisted in a freedom of choice, including return to the original home, and this had to be respected.

> No historical precedent has existed under which a people has surrendered its basic right to return home, whether they have been driven out or whether they fled in fear. The Palestinian people will not be the first to establish such a precedent. The recognition of the right of return, and the offer of choice to the refugees, are prerequisites to an end to the conflict.
> (Qurei 2008, 289–91; see also Laqueur and Rubin 2008, 570–71)

Nevertheless, the Palestinians were ready to consider mechanisms for application of the right of return with Israel as they did in their discussions with them in order to end the "plight of the refugees and calm the Israeli fears." The American proposals, however, did not consider these ideas and adopted "the old Israeli negotiation positions." They also did not provide guarantees for the implementation of the right of return of the refugees, for the recovery of their property, or for compensation (Qurei 2008, 291).

The Americans stated that they had the impression that Arafat was willing in principle to consider the president's ideas in a positive light, although they were not certain of this (see Sher 2001, 375, 377). Later on, the Americans received the impression that Arafat retreated from and changed his position when he understood that without a right of return he could not face the refugees because return was not only a matter of right, but also of justice and honor.

The Taba talks, 21–27 January 2001

The Taba talks that began on 21 January 2001 and continued for six days failed to reach a peace agreement between Israel and the Palestinians, and were the last formal round of negotiations dealing with a permanent status agreement, until the Annapolis talks in 2007–08. The Taba talks included the first significant and serious negotiations on the refugee problem. In a meeting between Shimon Peres and Abu-Ala that preceded the talks, the gap between the two sides on the refugee issue remained unbridgeable. While Peres stated that Israel perceived the fulfillment of the right of return as bringing about its destruction, and therefore it could not accept it, Abu-Ala maintained that the Palestinian position on the issue remained unchanged (Qurei 2008, 298).

Although the Palestinians requested that Clinton's parameters would not serve as the only basis for the talks, it appeared that they did indeed serve as such a basis. Regarding the refugee issue, the negotiations in Taba were headed by Yossi Beilin, then Israeli Minister of Justice, and Nabil Sha'ath, PLO's Chief Negotiator. The Taba talks were in fact the most substantive negotiations on this issue since the beginning of the Oslo process. At Taba, the parties dealt with three issues: the contending narratives, Israeli willingness to receive a certain number of Palestinian refugees, and international institutional arrangements for personal compensation to Palestinian refugees through an international fund.

The first issue to discuss at Taba focused on the contending narratives. Beilin suggested a joint narrative for the tragedy of the Palestinian refugees. Beilin noted that the insight reached in the Taba talks was that it was possible to discuss the creation of the refugee problem without expressing willingness to receive the refugees back in Israel. Being able to discuss them and to respect both narratives was enough to satisfy each party that its narrative had not been neglected. Beilin recalled a formula that had been developed to address the Palestinians' demand for transitional justice and corrective justice, which included three elements: refraining from demands for recognition of responsibility for creating the refugee problem; refraining from demands for a declaration cancelling the right of return; and refraining from demands for recognition of a right of return. Instead, the parties could agree on a concise description of the evolution of the conflict as each side saw it, humanitarian recognition of the refugees' suffering and hardship, and different interpretations of UNGA Resolution 194, while agreeing that this right would be implemented according to the principles of the Clinton parameters (Beilin 2001, 208; Moratinus non-paper, quoted by Qurei 2008, 357).[14]

Regarding the absorption of a certain number of refugees – a topic discussed for the first time in Taba – Beilin (without consulting with Barak) expressed Israeli willingness to receive 25,000 refugees during the first three years in the context of a 15-year arrangement, unrelated to the Palestinian demand regarding the right of return (Beilin 2002, 12–17).[15] As for the third issue, the establishment of an international fund and personal compensation for refugees, it was agreed to adopt the principles that Clinton had proposed as to where they would be received. All the five options mentioned in the Clinton Plan (i.e. the Palestinian state; swapped areas; third countries; Israel; and current host countries), including compensation, would represent the implementation of UNGA Resolution 194, and with this the Palestinian demands would end.

Nabil Sha'ath presents the understandings about refugees reached at Taba in a different light. Sha'ath claims that it was agreed that the right of return was a principle that Israel should accept if it wanted to solve the problem because, without acceptance in principle of the right of return, a solution to the problem would never be achieved. Sha'ath holds that a conceptual understanding was indeed reached regarding Israel's responsibility for the suffering and problems of the Palestinian refugees, but that fulfilling the right of return would have to be agreed upon by both parties to the negotiations.

In a document that he submitted to the United States, Sha'ath indeed accepted including the term "agreed" as part of a just solution to the problem (Sha'ath 2002).[16] Even so, the Palestinians were not willing to compromise on the number of refugees to be received by Israel or on the timetable, as Beilin had proposed at the Taba meeting. Israeli sources noted that the Palestinians cited a total number of 1.5 million refugees to be absorbed over the course of ten years – 150,000 refugees per year (Interview of Ben-Ami with Shavit, *Haaretz*, 14 September 2001; Barak 2005, 145).[17] Other sources cite different numbers suggested by the Palestinians at Taba, such as between 100,000 and 300,000 refugees (see Pressman 2003, 32).

In his report to Arafat, Abu-Ala noted that the gap between the parties remained unbridgeable. The Palestinian position remained that the right of return was fundamental: "This is a red line for us, without which there can be no agreement." Israel rejected this position because it would "destroy Israel," and stressed that "no other state demands the right of return for its people to a third country." Nevertheless, despite the disagreement, there was some progress on the issue, because Israel accepted that there should be "a fair settlement" on the issue, in accordance with UN Security Council Resolution 242, and in a "manner that would lead to the implementation of the UNGA Resolution 194" (Qurei 2008, 322–23; Taba: the Moratinus non-paper, quoted in Qurei 2008, 357).

Although Ben-Ami was not the principal Israeli interlocutor at the Taba negotiations on the refugee issue, he notes that the principal demand that the Palestinians raised at Taba, that Israel should recognize the right of return and then discuss the details of its implementation, "infuriated me no less than when they mentioned numbers in this or that occasion" (Interview of Ben-Ami with Shavit, *Haaretz*, 14 September 2001). Barak was even more adamant:

> When we understood that Arafat is not willing to relinquish the Palestinian demand to allow refugees to return to the sovereign territory of Israel – something we realized at Camp David and Yossi Sarid realized at

> Taba – we informed Clinton and Arafat that even if we are willing, like previous Israeli governments, to receive thousands of Palestinian refugees in the context of humanitarian reunification of families, we cannot agree to Arafat's version of the right of return. Neither I nor any other Israeli Prime Minister would be willing to receive a single refugee on the basis of the principle of Right of Return, because that would undermine Israel's *raison d'être.*
>
> (Barak 2005, 145)

Ben-Ami maintains that the failure to reach an agreement at Taba stemmed from the lack of will or lack of capacity of the Palestinian leadership

> to process a positive founding ethos that would enable them to assume a reasonable compromise. The Palestinian leadership under Arafat did not prove that it was prepared to discard, once and for all, the paralyzing narrative of the underdog and the victim.
>
> (Ben-Ami 2006, 278–79)

Procedural, transitional, and corrective justice in Track II talks, 2002–03

With the failure of the Oslo process and the ending of the official negotiations after the Taba talks in January 2001, the discussion that focused on issues of justice and injustice turned to unofficial channels, such as the Ayalon-Nusseibeh agreement (the "People's Voice") of July 2002 and the Geneva Initiative ("Geneva Accord") of October 2003.

In the Ayalon-Nusseibeh informal agreement of 27 July 2002, the matter of justice and its remedy was not mentioned, although the right of return was spelled out. The document limited the Palestinian return to the Palestinian state only and it denied return to the State of Israel. Article 4 of the agreement – entitled "Right of Return" – stated

> Recognizing the suffering and the plight of the Palestinian refugees, the international community, Israel, and the Palestinian state will initiate and contribute to an international fund to compensate them. Palestinian refugees will return only to the state of Palestine; Jews will return only to the state of Israel. The international community will offer to compensate toward bettering the lot of those refugees willing to remain in their present country of residence, or who wish to immigrate to third-party countries.

Interestingly, the first article in this agreement, entitled "Two States for Two Peoples," stated, "Both parties will declare that Palestine is the only state of the Palestinian people and Israel is the only state of the Jewish people." (quoted in www.jewishvirtuallibrary.org/jsource/peace/peoplesvoiceplan.html).

Similarly, the Geneva Initiative of 19 October 2003 did not mention the injustice and its remedy, nor did it mention the term "right of return," or even the word "return." Yet Article 7, which dealt with refugees, in Clause 1, under the heading "Significance of the Refugee Problem" stated, "The Parties recognize that, in the context of two independent states, Palestine and Israel, living side by side in peace, an agreed resolution of the refugee problem is necessary for achieving a just, comprehensive, and lasting peace between them." Later on, in Clause 2, it stated:

> The Parties recognize that UNGAR 194, UNSC Resolution 242, and the Arab Peace Initiative (Article 2.ii) concerning the rights of the Palestinian refugees represent the basis for resolving the refugee issue, and agree that these rights are fulfilled according to Article 7 of this Agreement.

During the negotiations of the Geneva Initiative, the Israelis rejected not only the return of refugees to Israel but even mentioning the very word "return." They also denied the Palestinian idea of territorial compensation based on territories beyond those of 1967 (what was termed the "101 percent option") in exchange for Palestinian relinquishment of implementation of the right of return to within Israel. Moreover, the Israelis also turned down the Palestinian demand that the agreement would state that the parties recognized the right of Palestinian refugees to return to their homeland of Palestine and demanded that the word "state" be inserted before "Palestine" so that it would be clear that the return was limited to the state of Palestine only, in contrast to the ambiguous language of alternatives proposed in the Clinton parameters. The Geneva Initiative enabled the individual refugee to retain the right of return in his or her consciousness, but if he or she chose to reside permanently in Israel and if Israel agreed, then he or she would have to undergo an immigration process conditional on Israel's agreement. This distinction differed completely from the classic Palestinian conception of the right of return, which demanded of Israel that the right be granted to each and every refugee. Moreover, according to the Geneva Initiative, a refugee who wanted to fulfill the right of return that existed in his or her consciousness could not rely on international resolutions and decisions of UN agencies because these would be voided and the Palestinian refugee status no longer recognized (Klein 2007, 57–58).

Article 7 of the Geneva Initiative further stated:

> The solution to the PPR [permanent place of residence] aspect of the refugee problem shall entail an act of informed choice on the part of the refugee to be exercised in accordance with the options and modalities set forth in this agreement. PPR options from which the refugees may choose shall be as follows: (i) The state of Palestine … (ii) Areas in Israel being transferred to Palestine in the land swap, following assumption of Palestinian sovereignty … (iii) Third Countries … (iv) The State of Israel … [and] (v) Present Host countries.

Regarding the fourth option – the State of Israel – the initiative stated:

> Option iv shall be at the sovereign discretion of Israel and will be in accordance with a number that Israel will submit to the International Commission. This number shall represent the total number of Palestinian refugees that Israel shall accept. As a basis, Israel will consider the average of the total numbers submitted by the different third countries to the International Commission.
>
> (Quoted in www.geneva-accord.org)

As for the Palestinian recognition of Israel as a Jewish state, the Geneva Accord explicitly stated that, "this agreement marks the recognition of the right of the Jewish people to statehood and the recognition of the right of the Palestinian people to statehood, without prejudice to the equal rights of the Parties' respective citizens."[18]

Menachem Klein argues that, during the negotiations of the Geneva Accord, the Palestinians also raised the issue of the 1948 narrative, including the questions of whom to blame for the creation of the refugee problem and what should be the nature and rubric of the agreement regarding the resolution of the problem. Klein claims that both sides learned the lesson of the official negotiations' failure to agree on a joint narrative of the 1948 war (for example, at Taba). The Geneva Initiative then proposed giving this assignment to civil society, with the support of both governments, a proposal that was not really disputed.[19] Indeed, in February 2005, after the death of Arafat and the election of Mahmoud Abbas (Abu-Mazen) as President of the Palestinian Authority, a series of petitions signed by writers and other personalities was published at the initiative of author David Grossman (not on behalf of the Geneva Initiative), calling for the government of Israel to commence negotiations

> by addressing the Palestinian people and acknowledging their suffering, and recognizing that Israel bears partial responsibility for that suffering. We feel that, as Israelis, we today have the ability to make the first necessary step: to look directly at the neighboring Palestinian people and recognize their suffering, out of human sympathy and empathy … . We expect that the new Palestinian leadership will also express its empathy for the suffering that Israelis have known over the years of conflict and recognize its partial responsibility for that suffering.
>
> (Klein 2007, 60; *Haaretz*, February 9, 2005)

This initiative did not receive a significant or clear response from the Palestinian side.

In sum, the two above Track II agreements did not mention the issue of injustice, did not address the question of Israeli admission of responsibility for the injustice perpetrated on the Palestinians, and did not refer explicitly to the right of return. The Geneva Initiative, however, did include an Israeli commitment to receive a certain number of refugees as it saw fit. For both agreements, the issues of justice and its Palestinian interpretation did not pose a barrier to peace because the Palestinian representatives relinquished these demands following Israeli refusal to accept them.

It is difficult to say whether the Palestinians conceded because of the power imbalance between the two sides or because they understood that it would not be possible to establish a Palestinian state without concession on these demands. Although these agreements were the result of informal initiatives, their significance lies in their relatively large success in creating joint understandings about how to overcome the barriers of the past and bridge the gaps between the parties. Nonetheless, it is not clear whether policymakers as well as the public on both sides are ready at this stage of the conflict to accept the Ayalon-Nusseibeh Agreement or the Geneva Initiative as an agreed basis for their peace negotiations.

Conclusions

The relationship between peace and justice is at the heart of the Israeli–Palestinian conflict, particularly in light of the Palestinian demand for a just peace. The Palestinian demands for justice have two layers: a demand for procedural justice and a demand for transitional and compensatory justice. The demand for procedural justice relates primarily to Israeli recognition of the Palestinians as an equal partner in the peace process, given the asymmetry in their power relations, the condescending and patronizing attitude that characterized many of the Israeli negotiators vis-à-vis their Palestinian counterparts, and the occupier–occupied relations between them.

The demand for transitional and compensatory justice focuses mainly on Israel's acknowledgment of its responsibility in perpetuating injustice against the Palestinian people and providing a remedy for that. The Palestinian demand for procedural justice had been acceptable to some of the Israeli negotiators, but they had trouble carrying it out in practice, so the relations between the parties were never grounded in real equality.

After the outbreak of the second *intifada* in September 2000, Israel found it difficult to recognize Arafat or Abu-Mazen as legitimate negotiating partners, the former because of loss of trust in him and the latter because of his weakness. At the same time, the Palestinians sustain a veto power over the outcome of the negotiations, so there is no way of peacefully resolving the conflict without their agreement, unless Israel opts for an unilateral option in the West Bank that might manage the conflict in the short and medium terms.

The Palestinian demands for transitional and compensatory justice are principally linked to the outcome of the 1947–49 war and to the establishment of Israel as a state in what they considered as a Palestinian land. The Palestinians demand that Israel acknowledges its moral responsibility for the expulsion of the Palestinians and the creation of the refugee problem and that it agrees to implement the right of return within its borders. The Palestinians, for their part, do not acknowledge their responsibility for the outbreak of the Israeli–Palestinian conflict and specifically for the 1947–49 war and its outcomes. Similarly, they do not accept the Israeli view of justice, which is focused on the right of Jews to establish a Jewish state in the Land of Israel and/or to recognize Israel as the state of the Jewish people. In the Palestinian view, such acknowledgment would add to the injustice that the Zionist movement inflicted upon them through the establishment of Israel on their land, and it has the potential to deny their right of return and alienate the rights of Palestinians living in Israel.

The Palestinians presented their demands for procedural, transitional, and compensatory justice at the beginning of the Oslo process, but Israel completely rejected them. It conditioned the peace process on its focusing on the outcomes of the 1967 war and not those of the 1947–49 war. Israel objected to dealing with injustice and its remedy as defined by the Palestinians and, in fact, it imposed the negotiating framework that it wanted. This framework was based on a gradual and multi-phased process including an interim arrangement about Palestinian self-government ("autonomy") in the territories, to be achieved before the parties reach a permanent agreement over the core and most difficult issues, such as Jerusalem, settlements, security, and the Palestinian refugees.

The Palestinians were forced to accept the Israeli position at Oslo, recognizing that, in light of the power imbalance between them and Israel, their insistence on having their demands for justice met could be a barrier to peace and to the establishment of an independent Palestinian state. Nonetheless, they did not reconcile themselves to the removal of the justice issue from the agenda, so they saw the peace process as unjust and unfair, and a result of Israel exploiting its power during the negotiations. Their demands for justice were renewed more adamantly at the Camp David Summit in July 2000 because the massive domestic criticism leveled against Arafat and the Palestinian negotiating team by other Palestinians, especially intellectuals, for abandoning their demands for justice and particularly the right of return. Although the Palestinian demand for justice was not the only cause of the failure of this summit, it did contribute significantly to it.

The Israeli negotiating team at Camp David was surprised by the renewal of the Palestinian demand for justice and by its intensity, and they regarded it as a major barrier to peace. They had the impression that the Palestinian demands for justice included not only the right of return, which had the potential to endanger Israel as a Jewish state, but also in fact denied the very existence of Israel as the state of the Jewish people because its establishment was the primary source of injustice in the Palestinian view.

Nevertheless, changes in the Palestinian demands did take place between the beginning of the Oslo process in January 1993 and the Taba meeting and final round of negotiations in January 2001. While the Palestinians were insisting on transitional justice – that is, Israeli recognition of its responsibility for creating the refugee problem and Israel's willingness in principle to accept the right of return – they were willing to have the implementation of the right of return (corrective justice) – that is, determination of the number of refugees that Israel would receive – achieved through negotiations between the parties, while recognizing that a massive return of refugees could indeed endanger the Jewish character of Israel. Israel refused to accept the changes in the Palestinian demands for justice as substantive, because the latter were still focused on Israel's acknowledging its responsibility for the injustice and on the right of return to its territory. Israel expressed some willingness to receive a limited number of refugees on a humanitarian basis in the framework of family reunification but under no circumstances on the basis of a right of return. Similarly, Israel refused to accept any responsibility for the creation of the refugee problem.

The Track II initiatives, the People's Voice (2002) and the Geneva Initiative (2003) dealt in a different way with the Palestinian demands for justice. In both of these initiatives, the parties decided not to directly engage with the Palestinian demand that Israel acknowledge responsibility for the injustice perpetuated against the Palestinians. Instead, they linked the right of return solely to the territory of the Palestinian state and not to Israel proper. Even so, the Geneva Initiative included an agreement to receive some Palestinian refugees into Israel, though not on the basis of a right of return. The two initiatives dealt with a more practical solution to the refugees' problem outside of the framework of the right of return and thus removed the right of return as a barrier to the resolution of the Israeli–Palestinian conflict. It seems that, while Israel could accept this solution, it is doubtful whether the Palestinian policymakers and public are ready at this stage to abandon their demand for transitional and compensatory justice. This is because the demand for transitional and compensatory justice is a protected value that the Palestinians are not willing to relinquish, and any effort at such a concession on the part of Palestinian leadership will create a confrontation with the Palestinian public and especially with the refugees in the Palestinian Diaspora who base their current residence in exile on the ethos of return.

Notes

1 Editor's note: A clear expression of the asymmetry between Israel and the Palestinians derived from the fact that, on the basis of all the mechanisms established in the Oslo process, there was the need for a bilateral agreement between the parties, without the involvement of third parties, either by mediation or arbitration in case of disputes. Hence, the Israelis had a de facto veto power over the joint decision making, so the Palestinians had to acquiesce to their demands. The editor thanks Lior Lehrs for his comments on this point.

2 For instance, the Oslo Accords failed to take into consideration "Israeli practices in the territories occupied since 1967, illegal under international law and prevailing international opinion, notably the confiscation of land and natural resources for the purposes of Jewish settlements." Moreover, other issues important to the Palestinians that were not addressed in the negotiations included the right of return for Palestinian refugees and "their right to an independent state with Arab East Jerusalem as its capital." See Albin 2001, 150.

3 At the start of the Oslo process, Yitzhak Rabin was convinced that there was no chance of reaching an agreement with the Palestinians because of the core issues of Jerusalem and the Palestinian refugees (see Hirschfeld 1999, 153). At the same time Rabin did hope, as did other Israeli leaders, that eventually it would be possible to reach an agreement.

4 Ben-Ami holds that on the matter of Palestinian refugees there was a certain degree of regression between the Stockholm talks and the Camp David Summit of July 2000, essentially because of divisions within the Palestinian camp. He claims that Abu-Mazen persuaded Abu-Ala not to engage in any discussion about numbers, but rather to adhere to the right of return (see Interview of Ben-Ami by Ari Shavit, *Haaretz*, 14 September 2001). In a meeting with Ben-Ami on 25 June 2000, Arafat noted that he could not understand why Israel was not willing to recognize the Palestinian right of return, while at the same time wanted to annex 300,000 Palestinians from East Jerusalem (Ben-Ami 2004, 115). Another possible explanation for the Palestinian change in attitude is the leakage to the Israeli media of alleged Palestinian concessions on the issues of refugees, Jerusalem, and security arrangements (Qurei 2008, 123).

5 Akram Hanieh's *Camp David Papers* were published first in the Palestinian newspaper *Al-Ayyam* from 29 July to 10 August 2000. An edited and abridged version was published later in the *Journal of Palestine Studies* in the winter of 2001.

6 Israeli intelligence evaluated that the Palestinians would not change their basic positions regarding the right of return and the sovereign demands over the Temple Mount in East Jerusalem. However, these evaluations did not hinder the hope that Israel could convince the Palestinians to move "a little in our direction and narrow the gaps between us" (Yatom 2005, 39).

7 Abu-Ala also mentions that the refugee issue was never seriously discussed at Camp David, since Ehud Barak refused to take any responsibility for the refugee problem and its possible solution (Qurei 2008, 272).

8 Dan Meridor notes in his diary that he told the Palestinian negotiators that he would refuse to sign any agreement that would not include a Palestinian acknowledgment of responsibility for the emergence of the conflict, the wars imposed upon Israel, and the Israeli victims of the conflict (Meridor 2011).

9 Hanieh argues that the Israeli delegation tried to persuade the Palestinians that Israel had not undertaken a scare campaign and slaughter in the 1948–49 war, so there had not been any expulsions or destruction of Palestinian villages. According to the Israeli version, the Arab countries were responsible for the Palestinian *Nakba* since they called the Palestinians to abandon their homes and to await the Arab liberation of Palestine. Although many of these Israeli claims have long been denied by serious historians, including Israeli scholars, the Israeli delegation refused to withdraw from its stance. Moreover, the Israeli delegation was not ready to revise its view when the Palestinians presented memoirs and testimonies of Israeli generals who affirmed Israel's responsibility for the *Nakba* (Hanieh 2001, 82).

10 Israel implied that it would accept a few thousand refugees only over many years, but not more than 10,000 (Meridor 2011).

11 Editor's note: Not all the Israeli negotiators at Camp David agreed with Dan Meridor regarding the question as to whether the Palestinian demands on refugees were a strategic position or a tactical one. For negotiators like Gilad Sher, Amon Shakak, and Oded Eran, the issue of Jerusalem posed a more formidable barrier to peace than the refugee question. See, for instance, Sher 2001, 209. The editor thanks Lior Lehrs for his comments on this point.

12 It appears that both alternatives are problematic for Israel because both "historical Palestine" and "homeland" could include the State of Israel itself.

13 Interestingly enough, writers and intellectuals from the Israeli peace camp, including personalities such as David Grossman, Meir Shalev, Nissim Calderon, Amos Oz, Zeev Sternhell, and A. B. Yehoshua, published a petition in the newspaper

Haaretz in which they expressed unequivocal opposition to the acceptance of the right of return, since "acceptance of this right amounts to [the] elimination of the State of Israel" (quoted in Sher 2001, 376).

14 According to the Moratinus non-paper reflecting the Taba talks, although there was much progress, no agreement was reached in the attempt to develop a joint historical narrative.

15 According to a different version, Beilin agreed to 40,000 Palestinian refugees (Interview of Shlomo Ben-Ami with Ari Shavit, *Haaretz*, 14 September 2001). In his book, *Manual for a Wounded Dove*, Beilin notes that "the question of the number of refugees that Israel would be willing to accept symbolically was left to the decision of the leaders as part of the signing of a framework agreement" (Beilin 2001, 216).

16 In a press conference at the end of the Taba talks, Abu Ala declared that, on the matter of Palestinian refugees, it should be noted that the Palestinians demanded the right of return, which is sacred to them, and that it should be based on UNGA Resolution 194, while Israel refused to do that (Qurei 2008, 320). Although Beilin and Sha'ath claimed that this was not the case, and they asked him to relay the minutes of the significant progress that had been made on the issue, including identifying ways to present the problem so that neither side was offended, Abu-Ala refused to do that and said, "This is good for you [Israel] as well!" Beilin interpreted this as follows: "It is as if he said – why should you complicate things before elections through an agreement with us on the refugee issue? Better that each side sticks with its position" (Beilin 2001, 217). As a result, the impression created was that, in light of the conflicting demands of the parties on the issue of the right of return, a permanent agreement was not possible at that time.

17 Barak noted that he never heard these numbers from Arafat himself (see Barak 2005, 145).

18 Within Israel there was strong criticism of the initiative's handling of the refugee question. Two principal claims were voiced against the formulation of the accord. First, the Palestinians did not actually concede on demanding the right of return to Israeli territory. Second, the text cites UNGA Resolution 194 as one of the legal bases for the resolution of the problem, whereas many Palestinians interpret that resolution as a way of legitimizing their demands for a right of return to Israel. See Klein 2007, 189–91.

19 Editor's note: In article 14 of the Geneva Agreement there is specific reference to Reconciliation Programs, as follows:

> i. The Parties will encourage and promote the development of cooperation between their relevant institutions and civil societies in creating forums for exchanging historical narratives and enhancing mutual understanding regarding the past. ii. The Parties shall encourage and facilitate exchanges in order to disseminate a richer appreciation of their respective narratives, in the fields of formal and informal education by providing conditions for direct contacts between schools, educational institutions and civil society.
>
> (Quoted in www.geneva-accord.org/mainmenu/english)

The editor thanks Lior Lehrs for his comments on this point.

References

Ajami, Fouad. *The Dream Palace of the Arabs* (New York: Vintage Books, 1998).

Albin, Cecilia. *Justice and Fairness in International Negotiations* (Cambridge: Cambridge University Press, 2001).

Aruri, Naseer (ed.). *Palestinian Refugees: The Right of Return* (Sterling, VA: Pluto Press, 2001).

Ayalon-Nusseibeh Plan. *(The "People's Choice")*, 27 July 2002.

Barak, Ehud. "The Myths Spread About Camp David." In *The Camp David Summit: What Went Wrong* (eds) Shimon Shamir and Bruce Maddy-Weitzman. (Brighton: Sussex Academic Press, 2005), pp. 117–47.

Bar-On, Mordechai. "Conflicting Narratives or Narratives of a Conflict: Can the Zionist and Palestinian Narratives of the 1948 War Be Bridged?" In *Israeli and Palestinian Narratives of Conflict* (ed.). Robert I. Rotberg. (Bloomington: Indiana University Press, 2006), pp. 142–73.

Beilin, Yossi. *Touching Peace* (Tel Aviv: Yediot Ahronot, 1997) [Hebrew].

Beilin, Yossi. *Manual for a Wounded Dove* (Tel Aviv: Yediot Ahronot, 2001) [Hebrew].

Beilin, Yossi. "The Refugee Problem at Taba," (interview with Akiva Eldar), *Palestine-Israel Journal*, Vol. 9, 1 and 2 (2002), pp. 12–17.

Ben-Ami, Shlomo. *A Front Without a Rearguard: A Voyage to the Boundaries of the Peace Process* (Tel-Aviv: Yediot Ahronot, 2004) [Hebrew].

Ben-Ami, Shlomo. *Scars of War, Wounds of Peace* (New York: Oxford University Press, 2006).

Bowker, Robert. *Palestinian Refugees: Mythology, Identity, and the Search for Peace* (Boulder, CO: Lynne Rienner, 2003).

Dajani, Omar. "Surviving Opportunities: Palestinian Negotiating Patterns in Peace Talks with Israel." In *How Israelis and Palestinians Negotiate: A Cross-Cultural Analysis of the Oslo Peace Process* (ed.) Tamara Cofman Wittes. (Washington, DC: United States Institute of Peace, 2005), pp. 39–80.

Enderlin, Charles. *Shattered Dreams* (New York: Other Press, 2003)

Hanieh, Akram. "The Camp David Papers," *Al-Ayyam*, 11–25 July and 29 July–10 August 2000. See www.miftah.org/Doc/Reports/2011/CampDavidPapers.pdf.

Hanieh, Akram. "The Camp David Papers," *Journal of Palestine Studies*, Vol. 30, 2 (2001), pp. 75–97.

Hirschfeld, Yair. *Oslo: A Formula for Peace* (Tel Aviv: Am Oved, 1999) [Hebrew].

Hovdenak, Are. "Trading Refugees for Land and Symbols: The Palestinian Negotiation Strategy in the Oslo Process," *Journal of Refugee Studies*, Vol. 22, (2009), pp. 30–50.

Klein, Menachem. "Between Right and Realization: The PLO Dialectics of 'The Right of Return,'" *Journal of Refugee Studies*, Vol. 11, 1 (1998), pp. 1–19.

Klein, Menachem. *A Possible Peace Between Israel and Palestine: An Insider's Account of the Geneva Initiative* (New York: Columbia University Press, 2007).

Laqueur, Walter and Barry Rubin (eds) *The Israel–Arab Reader: A Documentary History of the Middle East Conflict*, 7th edition (New York: Penguin, 2008).

Meridor, Dan. "Meridor Diaries: Last Moments of Dialogue" *Haaretz*, 30 July 2011.

Pressman, Jeremy. "Visions in Collision: What Happened at Camp David and Taba," *International Security*, Vol. 28, 2 (2003), pp. 5–43.

Qurei, Ahmed. ("Abu-Ala"). *From Oslo to Jerusalem* (London: I. B. Tauris, 2006).

Qurei, Ahmed. ("Abu-Ala"). *Beyond Oslo: The Struggle for Palestine* (London: I. B. Tauris, 2008).

Said, Edward, W. *The Politics of Dispossession* (New York: Pantheon Books, 1994).

Said, Edward, W. *Peace and Its Discontents* (New York: Vintage Books, 1995).

Said, Edward, W. "A Method for Thinking about Just Peace." In *What Is a Just Peace?* (eds) Pierre Allan and Alexis Keller. (Oxford: Oxford University Press, 2006), pp.176–94.

Savir, Uri. *The Process: 1,100 Days That Changed the Middle East* (New York: Random House, 1998).

Sha'ath, Nabil. "The Refugee Problem at Taba," (interview with Akiva Eldar), *Palestine–Israel Journal*, Vol. 9, 1 and 2 (2002), pp. 17–23.

Shavit, Uriya and Jalal Bana. "Everything You Wanted to Know About the Right of Return but Were Too Afraid to Ask," *Haaretz*, 6 July 2001.

Sher, Gilead. *Just Beyond Reach: The Israeli–Palestinian Peace Negotiations 1999–2001* (Tel Aviv: Yediot Ahronot, 2001) [Hebrew].

Sher, Gilead. "Lessons from Camp David Experience." In *The Camp David Summit: What Went Wrong* (eds) Shimon Shamir and Bruce Maddy-Weitzman. (Brighton: Sussex Academic Press, 2005), pp. 60–67.

Susser, Asher. "The 'End of Conflict' Obstacle" In *The Camp David Summit: What Went Wrong* (eds) Shimon Shamir and Bruce Maddy-Weitzman. (Brighton: Sussex Academic Press, 2005), pp. 200–202.

Yatom, Danny. "Background, Process and Failure." In *The Camp David Summit: What Went Wrong* (eds) Shimon Shamir and Bruce Maddy-Weitzman. (Brighton: Sussex Academic Press, 2005), pp. 33–41.

Zureik, Elia. *Palestinian Refugees and the Peace Process* (Washington, DC: US Institute of Peace, 1996).

6 Linking justice to peace in the Annapolis process, 2007–08

The Annapolis Conference that took place on 27–28 November 2007 in Annapolis (Maryland, United States) aimed to revive the Israeli–Palestinian peace process and to enable intensive negotiations over a final status agreement. Since the last round of negotiation in January 2001 at Taba, no significant direct negotiations were held between the parties. US Secretary of State Condoleezza Rice organized and hosted the conference. Palestinian President Mahmoud Abbas (Abu-Mazen), Israeli Prime Minister Ehud Olmert, and US President George W. Bush attended the meeting.[1]

The Joint Understanding Declaration issued at the end of the conference explicitly stated that the objective of the negotiation process was "to conclude a peace treaty to resolve all core issues without exception, as specified in previous agreements." Both sides agreed to engage in continuous negotiations in an effort to conclude an agreement before the end of 2008. In the Joint Understanding Declaration, the parties also committed themselves to immediately implement their respective obligations under the Road Map of 2003.

The Annapolis process was conducted as a two-track negotiation process. The first track handled by both senior leaders, Abu-Mazen and Olmert, aimed to reach understandings in principle.[2] The second track included more detailed negotiations through 12 Israeli-Palestinian committees that dealt with many different issues, including core issues (except for Jerusalem), but also economics, peace culture, and environment. The negotiating teams were headed by Israel's Foreign Minister, Tzipi Livni, and former Palestinian Prime Minister Ahmed Qurei (Abu-Ala). The issue of Jerusalem was supposed to be out of the negotiations because of Olmert's commitment to his coalition partners to exclude the issue from the negotiation; however, it was actually secretly discussed at the Abu-Mazen–Olmert track. Both sides agreed that the guiding principle of the negotiations would be "nothing is agreed until everything is agreed" and that the content of negotiations would be kept secret.

All other issues of negotiations, including Palestinian refugees, were discussed at the second track headed by Livni and Abu-Ala. Until 14 July 2008, a special joint team on the refugee issue was managed by Dr. Saeb Erekat (Head of the Palestinian Negotiations Affairs Department) and Tal Becker (Political Advisor to the Israeli Foreign Minister). After that, Daniel Taub

(Deputy Legal Advisor at the Israeli Foreign Ministry) joined Tal Becker, while Ziyad Clot joined Dr. Saeb Erekat.

The Annapolis process, like the Oslo process before it, ultimately failed to reach a peace agreement. The refugee issue and its justice aspects were among the main causes for that failure. Nevertheless, while transitional and corrective justice issues dominated the negotiations, procedural justice was less relevant in them. It seems that, although there was no significant change in the asymmetrical power relations, it was not expressed in a disturbing way throughout the negotiations as in previous rounds.

Most of the information about these negotiations is based on three main sources: *al-Jazeera*'s leaking of internal Palestinian documents about the negotiations, including detailed minutes of the meetings of the negotiations themselves;[3] Olmert's speeches and memoirs; and the parties' interviews and declarations.

Throughout the negotiations' meetings, both sides presented their traditional positions regarding the issues of justice, especially concerning the problem of Palestinian refugees. Two issues were discussed in depth: the issue of responsibility and apology, and the right of return. Israel's negotiators, for the first time in the long peace process, introduced its request for Palestinian recognition of Israel as a Jewish state, in accordance with justice claims. The Palestinians re-introduced their traditional demands: Israel's acknowledgment of its responsibility for creating the refugee problem, expressing publicly its apology for it, accepting the right of return to Israeli territory, compensation for individuals, compensation for host countries, and establishing an international fund for compensation. The number of returnees to the State of Israel would be negotiated between both sides. The Palestinians demanded also that Saudi Arabia and the Arab League and countries that hosted the refugees (first and foremost Jordan), should be involved directly and indirectly in finding a solution.

Israel for its part rejected the Palestinian demands for taking responsibility and apology, and for accepting the right of return. It accepted only to express its sorrow for the Palestinian suffering in reciprocation for Palestinians expressing their sorrow about the Jewish and the Israeli suffering throughout the conflict years. Israel agreed to receive 5,000 refugees based on individual and humanitarian considerations, but not upon considerations of family reunification or invoking the right of return.

The refugee issue in the negotiations: the Palestinian version[4]

The issue of the refugees was discussed several times in the two tracks of negotiations, whereas the most detailed negotiations were conducted by the Plenary Committee of the Livni–Abu-Ala track. In the meeting of 22 January 2008, Abu-Ala maintained that the Palestinian position as to the refugee problem was the right of return and compensation for those who decided not to return in accordance with UNGA 194. Erekat asked directly about the number of refugees that Israel could absorb. Livni made it clear that Israel rejected any right of return: "I do not want to deceive anybody. There will be no Israeli official whether from the Knesset or the government or even the public who will support the return of refugees to Israel." In her view, the solution to the refugee problem resided in the establishment of a Palestinian state that would absorb the Palestinian refugees. As to the Jewish character of Israel, in a subsequent meeting on 27 January 2008, Livni stated, "The basis of the creation of the state of Israel is that it was created for Jewish people … [and the Palestinian state] will be the answer to all Palestinians including refugees. Putting an end to claims means fulfilling national rights for all" (quoted from http://transparency.aljazeera.net/files/2304.PDF and http://transparency.aljazeera.net/files/2309.PDF).

The issues of responsibility, apology, and the historical narratives were discussed in depth at the meeting of 24 March 2008 (see http://transparency.aljazeera.net/files/2347.PDF). Abu-Ala and Erekat insisted that the issue of "responsibility should be defined" and explained the significance of Israel's taking responsibility for the injustice: "There is the suffering of refugees. Where did it come from? We must show them that there are those to blame for their suffering." The Palestinians wondered why it was so difficult for Israel to acknowledge its responsibility for creating the refugee problem and to apologize for it. They justified their demands based on previous historical precedents in which sides in a conflict took responsibility for wrong doings and asked for apology. They indicated the example of Angela Merkel's speech of apology at the Knesset, although they recognized that there was nothing compared to the Holocaust.

Livni explained why Israel would not take any responsibility for creating the refugee problem. The issue of responsibility that the Palestinians asked for was based only on the Palestinian narrative of the events and this Israel could not accept. The Palestinians ignored the suffering of the Jewish people in the 1947–49 war and throughout the conflict itself.

> We need to understand sensitivities on both sides … . Both peoples in different ways suffered from the situation … I am sure that some of the people left because of the actions that were taken by Jews, but Jews were also attacked … . In 1948, Arabs and Jews died as result of acts of terrorism. History did not start in a Jihad of Jews against the Arabs. History led to some mistakes on both sides … I know when I celebrate [Israel's] Independence Day … it is very difficult for you. You call it Nakba … and I am sorry for that. In the past [the] two states' [solution] was rejected by the Arabs … [and that was] … a historic mistake.
>
> (Quoted from http://transparency.aljazeera.net/files/2347.PDF, p.5)

As to responsibility, Livni maintained:

> I did not take responsibility but I understand the facts that led to the fact that we have a state and you do not have … to speak about responsibility it is a waste of time … I know that talk about responsibility is wrong.

Livni maintained that Israel would not take responsibility for the creation of the refugee problem. Hence, Livni suggested changing the words from "responsibility" to "understanding the suffering". As to Merkel's speech of apology, "no one [in Israel] will ever forgive Germany for the Holocaust, in spite of Merkel's speech in the Knesset." Livni also mentioned that, although the Palestinians wanted Israel to apologize, they "will never forgive us." As to the right of return, Livni reformulated Israel's well-known position:

> There is no right of return for any individual or for a group. If the future Palestinian state absorbs them or not – it is not my business. Jews have a right of return to Israel, and Palestinians to Palestine ... I do not know if you want to open the door to Palestine.

To that Abu-Ala responded: "We want to open two doors – one to a Palestinian state, and a small door to Israel" (quoted from http://transparency.aljazeera.net/files/2437.PDF, pp. 5–6; pp. 7–9).

Two days after that meeting, the Palestinian Negotiations Support Unit (NSU) prepared a confidential policy document for Erekat on the wide gap between Israel and the Palestinians regarding the issues of responsibility/apology and the right of return as they were reflected in the discussion of the Plenary Meeting on 24 March 2008, and defined by the NSU as obstacles to the negotiations (see http://transparency.aljazeera.net/files/2370.PDF).

The policy document began by stating that both sides had a common interest in resolving the refugee issue in a just and reasonable manner for the following reasons:

1 Both sides agreed that there would be no peace without a just resolution of the problem that had been standing at the heart of [the] conflict since 1948.
2 It was their common interest to reach a satisfactory closure of the matter.
3 Both sides had a right to peace and security and the satisfaction of refugees was crucial in this regard.

(See http://transparency.aljazeera.net/files/2370.PDF, p. 1)

A just resolution of the refugee issue could provide Israel and the future Palestinian state with a historic opportunity to achieve a "true" peace for two reasons:

1 By recognizing the injustice caused to Palestinian refugees (that constituted the majority of the Palestinian population), Israel would be in position to ask for refugees' forgiveness and put an end to the corresponding Arab resentment.
2 Since the refugee issue was also a regional matter involving in particular Lebanon, Syria, and Jordan, it also provided Israel with a historical

chance to normalize its relations with other Arab countries, as stated in the Arab Peace initiative of 2002.

(See http://transparency.aljazeera.net/files/2370.PDF, pp. 1–2)

However, if the refugees' rights were not duly recognized, and if the adequate legal remedies were not provided to them, the refugee issue might lead to the failure of the peace process. Actually, the refugees would be the ultimate judges of the fairness of the agreement, because the options agreed upon by both parties will be submitted to their choice. Moreover, the Arab host states would accept cooperation and normalization of the situation of the refugees currently staying within their borders only if Israel endorsed its share of responsibility in the matter and showed a sincere commitment and efforts to reach a just solution (see http://transparency.aljazeera.net/files/2370.PDF, p. 2).

The NSU document presented two barriers that needed to be overcome at that "early stage" of the negotiations between both sides. The first barrier referred to Israel's willingness to accept only a limited number of returnees. The second barrier referred to Israel's refusal to recognize its responsibility and to endorse the right of return. Israel's position on these two issues was unacceptable to the Palestinians because it would cause a profound dissatisfaction and resentment amongst refugee communities in the Palestinian Diaspora. It was therefore crucial that the number of returnees should be substantial, and Israel's recognition of its responsibility and acceptance of the right of return would strongly be affirmed, in order to convince the Palestinian refugees of Israel's sincerity in the acknowledgment of their past suffering and historical rights (see http://transparency.aljazeera.net/files/2370.PDF, p. 2).

The NSU realized that the problem lay in the clash between both sides' narratives of the 1947–49 war. Israel refused to acknowledge the Palestinian narrative of the *Nakba* and the right of return because that would delegitimize Israel as a Jewish state. Conversely, the Palestinian leadership was convinced that only Israel's recognition of its own mistakes would help Israel to "become a State amongst others in the international community, integrated in the region, and willing to comply with international standards".[5] Due to the wide gap between both sides' narratives, the document suggested a solution that would accommodate Israel's concerns, recognizing that the discussion on the 1947–49 events could be counter-productive, as was reflected during the Camp David negotiations in July 2000. The NSU, therefore, suggested to the Palestinian leadership to consider one of two options, with a clear preference for the first one, and introducing the second option only in the case that Israel would refuse to discuss the first one (see http://transparency.aljazeera.net/files/2370.PDF, p. 3).

The first option called for re-initiating the discussions on the basis of the document presented by Israel at Taba on 23 January 2001. While the document was not acceptable to the Palestinians, "it had the merit to insist on the centrality of the refugee issue and [specified that] *a comprehensive and just solution is essential to creating a durable and morally scrupulous peace*" (emphasis in the original). This wording incorporated only limited historical references, in order to be acceptable to both parties. It also distinguished between the principles and the implementation of the solution, and addressed subtly the question of the responsibilities for the creation of the refugee problem. The NSU team concluded that, "if we want real peace to be achieved, this document can be used as a framework for discussion" (quoted from http://transparency.aljazeera.net/files/2370.PDF, p.3).

The second option would be offered in the negotiations only if Israel refused to recognize its moral responsibility in the creation of the refugee problem and stated its inability to resolve it, in conjunction with the international community. In such a case, the Palestinian leadership could offer that Israel recognize its legal responsibility as a result of various regulations ("statutes") passed by the Israeli Knesset (Parliament) since the late 1940s/early 1950s, "by which the Palestinians were legally disposed from their lands and prevented from returning to their homes." This option would then enable avoidance of any specific discussion over the 1947–49 period. At the same time, it should be legally emphasized that the original cause of the Palestinians' displacement remained irrelevant, and that an option of return remains "since anyone who leaves his home/country is entitled by law to return to it, irrespective of the purpose of his absence (forced displacement, holiday, etc.) (quoted from http://transparency.aljazeera.net/files/2370.PDF, pp. 3–4).

According to the NSU document, these options did not free Israel from recognizing its moral and legal responsibility, so it should officially apologize directly to the refugees because of their continued extraordinary suffering, losses, longstanding displacement, and miserable conditions of living. This apology remained a central element of the refugees' rights for reparation according to international standards. Israel should get the refugees' forgiveness because this was the central condition for the establishment of a durable peace. Hence, Israel's refusal to implement the right of return was a violation of international law and its most recent practice in places like Bosnia, Kosovo, and South Africa (see http://transparency.aljazeera.net/files/2370.PDF, p. 4).

The NSU suggested differentiating between recognition of refugees' rights (return, restitution, and compensation), which were non-negotiable because they were individuals, and their implementation (especially the right of return and, to some extent, the right of restitution), which could be adapted to the realities and the parameters of the two-state solution, namely, Israel as the homeland of the Jewish people, and Palestine as the homeland of the Palestinian people. Thus, in practice, returns of refugees would be limited to Israel's absorption capacity (see http://transparency.aljazeera.net/files/2370.PDF, p. 4).

Although it is not clear whether the NSU policy document had any impact on the Palestinian negotiation team, it is a fascinating document because it reflects thoroughly the Palestinian position on the issues of responsibility, apology, and the right of return. In addition, the document reflected the wide gap between both sides' narratives and positions on these issues, as the Palestinians understood it, and how the parties could try to bridge the gap, while taking into account Israel's concerns. However, it seems that the solutions suggested by the NSU were far from being accepted by Israel.

In another confidential internal document from 7 May 2008 that was named "Talking Points – Refugees," which was probably prepared for the Palestinian negotiation team, the issue of refugees was presented again. The document contained three parts: "Introduction," "Statistics," and "How to solve the refugee issue". The Introduction stated the traditional Palestinian positions:

1 "No real peace" [was] "possible without a just settlement of the refugee issue."
2 A just solution was a necessary condition for "the achievement of a just, lasting, and comprehensive peace in the Middle East."
3 A just solution of the refugee issue was possible only in a settlement that affirmed "all refugees' rights and provide[d] the framework for their implementation, including the right of return, in accordance to UNGA Resolution 194."

(Quoted from http://transparency.aljazeera.net/files/2530.PDF, p. 1)

The novel and most interesting part of the Introduction was the reference to the Arab Peace Initiative that called for a just solution to the refugee issue "to be agreed upon" in accordance with UNGA Resolution 194 as providing a historic opportunity and unique occasion to put an end to 60 years of suffering, dispossession, and displacement. The Introduction noted that the Palestinian position was in line with the Arab Peace Initiative of 25 March 2002,[6] combining the recognition of all refugees' rights with an implementation that would respect the refugees' choice, but would also "adapt to the legitimate interests and concerns of Israel, the Palestinian State, and Arab host states" (quoted from http://transparency.aljazeera.net/files/2530.PDF, p. 1).

In the section defined as Statistics, the Palestinian narrative of the *Nakba* was presented. It mentioned that, "more than 726,000 Palestinians were forced to leave their homes." The refugee problem was caused by Jewish attacks on Arab villages, by "the inhabitants' fears of such attacks, compounded by expulsions, atrocities and intentionally disseminated rumors of atrocities." After the war, Israel massively expropriated Palestinian land and most of it was designated only for Jewish inhabitants. Moreover, during the 1967 war, "another 400,000 Palestinians were displaced from the West Bank and the Gaza Strip". Dispossession and displacement have continued since 1967 until the present. Since 1948, Israel firmly refused to allow the refugees to return to their homes. Three-quarters of the Palestinians were considered to be refugees (by May 2008), and the overall number of refugees was over 7 million. More than 1.3 million refugees still lived in refugee camps, and many of them were stateless (quoted from http://transparency.aljazeera.net/files/2530.PDF, pp. 1–2).

In the third section of the document, defined as How to solve the refugee issue, it defined the solution as "complex" and stated that a successful solution had to be based on two pillars:

1 "The recognition of refugee rights and their implementation in accordance with the respect of refugees' individual choices."
2 "The conciliation of implementation of these rights with the relevant states' rights and legitimate interests." In this regard, the Arab Peace Initiative was defined as "the best framework for solving the issue" because it provided the formula of "a just solution to the refugee issue to be agreed upon in accordance with UN Resolution 194."
(Quoted from http://transparency.aljazeera.net/files/2530.PDF, p. 2)

In practice, Israel had to recognize formally its primary responsibility for the displacement and dispossession of the Palestinian refugees. "*This formal apology is a right according to international law and is essential for the satisfaction of Palestinian refugees*" (quoted from http://transparency.aljazeera.net/files/2530.PDF, p. 2, emphasis in the original).

The issue of refugees was discussed again in the Plenary Session on 21 June 2008. No real change in the positions of the parties was reported at the meeting. While the minutes of the meeting did not present the Palestinians' demands, Livni explicitly referred to them. Again, she suggested that, instead of dealing with responsibility, the sides should refer to the suffering of both sides. If the issue was about responsibility it should refer mainly to the Arab world's responsibility for keeping the Palestinian refugees in camps. Responsibility was not "just about the war, but what happened after for creating false hope". She emphasized that Israel would not accept the right of return. All that Israel could give the refugees was "suffering plus giving them compensation," but only in return for a previous Palestinian commitment "that this is the end of conflict." Livni also referred to the resolution of the Jewish refugees' compensation via an international fund. The Palestinian response to that issue was that this would not be part of the agreement because the Palestinians "never caused anything to the Jews, and all the Arab countries are ready to receive the Jews [back]" (quoted from http://transparency.aljazaeera.net/files/3027.PDF, pp. 9–10).

The issue of responsibility and apology continued to be crucial for the Palestinian negotiation team. The real question was how to convince Israel to accept the Palestinians' demands in this regard. In a memorandum sent on 25 July 2008 to Erekat, entitled: "State Declarations of Responsibility and Apology to the Palestinians," the NSU suggested some ideas about how to cope with Israel's refusal to accept responsibility and give apology. The NSU maintained that

> in the interest of justice, reconciliation, and building a relationship of trust between the parties, it is necessary for Israel to recognize its responsibility for placing the Palestinians in the position they are today

> and to apologize for the violations of their fundamental rights that have occurred daily since the establishment of the state of Israel.

The NSU stated that "throughout history, apologies that have acknowledged one party's responsibility in the mistreatment and oppression of another have served as tools for allowing both parties to leave the wrongs of the past behind and move into a future of coexistence and cooperation." Therefore, the NSU provided a long list of current and historical cases of taking responsibility and apology for resolving conflicts. Bringing them to the attention of Israel might help Israel to accept the idea of responsibility and apology, and this might be "a historic opportunity for Israel" (quoted from http://transparency.aljazeera.net/files/3002.PDF, pp. 1–2).

In accordance with another confidential document from the NSU entitled "Summary of Olmert's 'Package' offer to Abu-Mazen" from 31 August 2008, Israel offered the following conditions regarding the refugee issue:

1 "Israel would acknowledge the *suffering* of – but not responsibility for – Palestinian refugee … . In parallel, there must also be a mention of Israeli (or Jewish) suffering."
2 "Israel would take 1,000 refugees per year for a period of five years on 'humanitarian' grounds. In addition, programs of 'family reunification' would continue."
3 "Israel would contribute to the compensation of the refugees through the [international] mechanism and based on suffering" (it was not clear what "the heads of damage for compensation would be").
4 There would be "no acknowledgement of responsibility for the refugees, and not restitution or return (apart from the 5,000)."

(Quoted from http://transparency.aljazeera.net/files/4736.PDF, p. 1)

In a meeting of the refugees' committee on 14 September 2008 that the Palestinians defined as a "progress meeting on refugees," both sides discussed the points of agreement and disagreement. Under the points of agreement were the following:

1 a common understanding that the issue of responsibility was a major concern for the Palestinians;
2 different destination options would be offered to the Palestinian refugees (except return to Israel proper);
3 an international mechanism would have to be created and its mandate and goals would include the issues of compensation, rehabilitation, and settlement choices (except return). The International Mechanism (IM) "should be the exclusive forum";
4 there was an urgent need to bring about a definitive end to the issue;
5 UNRWA should be gradually dismantled;
6 the establishment of an International Fund;

7 the principle that Israel would contribute to this fund;
8 the principle that there would not be any further obligation beyond what is stipulated in the peace treaty;
9 some of the textual differences were narrowed (without specifying which of them).

(Quoted from http://transparency.aljazeera.net/files/3651.PDF, pp. 3–4)

The points of disagreement included the following arguments:

1 As for the preamble, the Palestinians insisted on the reference to UNGA Resolution 194 and the Arab Peace Initiative, whereas Israel wanted a reference to "two States for two peoples."
2 Israel wanted: "in the context of a complete resolution of the refugee issue, a sign has to be given to Israel's domestic audience regarding the Jewish refugee matter. The article on refugees has to be sold to an Israeli opinion."
3 While Israel understood that the issue of responsibility was very important for the Palestinians, it could not accept it, though there was a possibility to find an acceptable wording suitable to both sides.
4 From the Israeli standpoint, "all Palestinian refugees should be provided with Palestinian citizenship according to Palestinian law."
5 Regarding compensation, there were two main issues of disagreement: "restitution is a non-starter for Israel." Israel had a strong legal case to prove this. Regarding compensation, Israel decided "not to make a counter proposal on different forums of indemnification." Nevertheless, Israel preferred that "the priority should remain to use the funds for rehabilitation."
6 While Israel did not oppose the idea of a US-led detailed mechanism regarding compensation, the Palestinians rejected that proposition.
7 Both sides disagreed as to whether to "refer to the Custodian of Absentee Property."
8 Both sides also disagreed on "the way to refer to the Israeli financial contribution."
9 Israel did not accept compensation for host states (of the refugees), although it did not oppose compensation for future rehabilitation.

(Quoted from http://transparency.aljazeera.net/files/3651.PDF, p. 4)

On 16 September 2008, in an internal document entitled: "Talking Points and Questions," the Palestinians referred to Olmert's specific proposals. Regarding the issue of refugees, they raised the following questions and qualifications for Israel:

1 "What does it mean to acknowledge the suffering of refugees, without reference to responsibility? How is that different from acknowledging the suffering of people as a result of … a natural disaster?"
2 How did Israel propose to deal with the issue of responsibility?
3 "Why is the suffering of Israelis relevant to the refugee issue?"

4 As to Israel's proposal of accepting 5,000 refugees in five years, the Palestinians defined the offer as "not serious and cannot be accepted." They maintained that it was agreed to negotiate the number of returnees "in consideration of Israel's capacity of absorption." Hence, was Israel's proposal under the right of return, or on humanitarian grounds under Israeli discretion? Who will decide and what would be the criteria for deciding who is included among the returnees? "What does it mean to continue family reunification, and how is this linked to the refugees?" How did Israel propose to deal with restitution and with the assets of the "Absentees"?
5 How did Israel envisage its "participation and contribution to the international mechanism?"

(Quoted from http://transparency.aljazaeera.net/files/3294.PDF, pp. 2–3)

In another confidential policy document from 25 October 2008, for internal Palestinian preparations, entitled: "Progress on the Refugee Negotiations," the NSU summarized both sides' positions regarding the issues of responsibility and refugees. The document presented the wide gaps between both sides regarding the following issues: framework and principles, recognition of responsibility and apology, right of return and relocation options, reparation and compensation, international mechanism, international fund, and the UNGA Resolution 194 (see http://transparency.aljazaeera.net/files/3518.PDF).

On the framework and principles issues, both sides sustained common positions, including the need for "a comprehensive, just and agreed resolution of the Palestinian refugee issue," and that "the solution should ensure closure/end of claims". At the same time, the Palestinians wanted to do that "in accordance with international law and the Arab Peace Initiative", whereas Israel liked to do it "in accordance with the vision of two States for two peoples" (quoted from http//transparency.aljazaeera.net/files/3518.PDF, p. 9).

On the recognition of the responsibility/apology issue, the Palestinians demanded Israel's recognition of its "moral and legal responsibility/apology as a core element of refugees' rights and reparations." Conversely, Israel opposed recognizing any responsibility (quoted from http://transparency.aljazeera.net/files/3518.PDF, p. 9).

On the right of return/relocation options the Palestinians requested that refugees should be "provided with reparation, resettlement and integration options. They shall have a choice that will include: return to Israel, return/resettlement to the Palestinian state (at Palestine's discretion), and resettlement/integration in consenting third countries and host states." In contrast, Israel maintained that, "refugees shall be entitled to Palestinian citizenship and integration options only," without return to Israel (quoted from http://transparency.aljazeera.net/files/3518.PDF, p. 9).

On the issue of reparation/compensation, the Palestinian position stated that "refugees shall be granted restitution and compensation for the material and non-material damages they have suffered (including loss of livelihood and opportunities and human suffering, as a result of refugees' protracted displacement)." In addition, "states that have hosted Palestinian refugees shall be entitled for remuneration." Israel argued that refugees should be granted compensation only (quoted from http://transparency.aljazeera.net/files/3518.PDF, p. 9).

On the International Mechanism issue, the Palestinians demanded that,

> an IM shall be established to enable implementation of all Palestinian refugee rights. Palestine, Israel, the host countries and other relevant countries and entities should be represented in the mechanism. [The] IM comprehensive mission will include the repatriation, resettlement and integration of the refugees and the management of their claims for restitution and compensation.

Moreover, "the resolution of the refugee issue shall bring an end to the Palestinian refugee status and enable the phased termination of UNRWA in parallel with the implementation of the solution and in coordination with the IM". Furthermore, the "IM will also provide rehabilitation assistance to Palestinian refugees and to relevant states." Israel also agreed to an IM mechanism, "but which would be established and led by the US, in coordination with Israel and Palestine." In addition, from the Israeli standpoint, the IM mission would "extend to all aspects of the agreed solution, bringing to an end the Palestinian refugees' status and enabling the phased termination of UNRWA, in parallel with the implementation of the solution and in coordination with IM." Like their Palestinian counterparts, the Israeli negotiators also agreed that the "IM would also provide rehabilitation assistance to Palestinian refugees and to relevant states" (quoted from http://transparency.aljazeera.net/files/3518.PDF, pp. 9–10).

On the International Fund issue, the Palestinians maintained that,

> an International Fund shall be established to finance the restitution and compensation claims process and the process of repatriation, resettlement, integration, and rehabilitation of the refugees. Israel shall commit to contribute financially to the fund as necessary to cover restitution and compensation claims. International stakeholders will also contribute to the funding.

As a general principle, "all financial contributions should be based on responsibility." Similarly, Israel agreed that, "an International Fund shall be established to enable IM to fulfil, its mission. Israel will make a fixed financial contribution to the fund (the level of the contribution [remained] unclear), together with contribution from stakeholders" (quoted from http://transparency.aljazeera.net/files/3518.PDF, pp. 9–10).

Finally, on UNGA Resolution 194, while the Palestinian position was that it did not represent all of the refugee rights, Israel argued that it did not recognize the validity of that resolution.

Looking at the gaps between both sides' positions, the NSU document concluded that Israel wished to reach an agreement about an "end of claims" of the refugee issue at the lowest possible cost, "while deferring the practical resolution to third parties." Israel wanted the solution to be on the basis of two ethnically defined states: one Jewish and one Palestinian/Arab, invoking only humanitarian considerations. Moreover, Israel's positions regarding return, responsibility, and restitution remained very rigid and similar to those presented at the Camp David Summit of July 2000 or even before (see http://transparency.aljazeera.net/files/3518.PDF, p. 3).

The document noted also some of the main domestic problems within the Palestinian side regarding negotiation of the refugee issue and it suggested suitable means to overcome them. The main problems included:

1 the lack of coordination on the Palestinian side because of the parallel two tracks of negotiations, the Abu-Ala–Livni and Abu-Mazen–Olmert;
2 no clear Palestinian "red lines" on the refugee issue that gave "the impression that the PLO is ultimately ready to make unsustainable compromises."

(Quoted in http://transparency.aljazeera.net/files/3518.PDF, p. 2)

The gaps between the parties on the refugee issue and the ways to cope with them were underlined in an internal document entitled "Talking Points" for the Refugee Committee that was supposed to be convened on December 14, 2008. The main objective of the Palestinian negotiating team was to secure Israeli agreement to discuss and negotiate the refugee issue thoroughly and in detail, including the key sensitive issues: responsibility, return, restitution, and compensation. The Palestinian side should "*convey the message that without a serious willingness on the Israeli side to consider in a reasonable manner the issues of responsibility, return and their contribution to refugee rights for reparations, Israel cannot expect to see any sign of flexibility from the PLO and Arab host states.*" At the same time, the NSU analysts emphasized that they "were confident that both sides will be able to agree on all of these issues, especially if they adopt an interest-based approach rather than a positional one." In fact, both sides had a common interest to reach

> a just and comprehensive solution on the Palestinian refugee issue which will have to:
>
> 1 meet the satisfaction of Palestinian refugees;
> 2 permit reaching an end of claims status; and
> 3 ensure the security of the States of Israel and Palestine as well as the establishment of a durable peace in the region.
>
> (Quoted from http//transparency.aljazeera.net/files/3629.PDF, pp. 1–2, italics in the original)

In a comprehensive summary of the negotiations written by Dr. Saeb Erekat entitled: "The Political Situation in Light of Developments with the US Administration and Israeli Government and Hamas' Continued Coup d'etat: Recommendations and Options" (December 2009), Erekat also reconstructs the traditional and wide gaps between both sides on the refugee issue as they were presented before in the various documents of the NSU. However, the document is less detailed in comparison to the previous documents, but its uniqueness is due to its publicity in the media. According to the document, Israeli positions were the following:

> 1 "The return of 1,000 refugees to Israel annually and for a period of five years," on the basis of humanitarian considerations.
> 2 "Return to the state of Palestine would be an internal Palestinian affair."
> 3 "An international compensation fund would be established, on which Israel would be a member."
> 4 "Israel rejected to bear any liability for the calamity caused to the Palestinian refugees."
> 5 "Israel would bear a special liability for the compensation of refugees."
>
> (Quoted from http://prn.mcgill.ca/research/papers/erekat.pdf, pp. 2–3)

The positions of the Palestinian side included the following:

1 "Solution for the refugees' properties would be discussed."
2 "The right of return is safeguarded by the international law and UNGA Resolution 194."
3 "The return to Israel of 15,000 refugees per year for 10 years, renewable thereafter at the agreement of both parties".[7]
4 "Return to the State of Palestine shall be subject to Palestinian law only".
5 "An International compensation fund shall be incorporated, whereby all refugees would be compensated regardless of their choice. The right is for the return and compensation, not return or compensation."
6 "Host countries would be compensated."[8]

(Quoted from http://prn.mcgill.ca/research/papers/erekat.pdf, p. 3)

A more detailed and confidential document from 1 January 2009, entitled "Current P/I (Palestinian–Israeli) Positions – Reflecting Discussion Up to January 2009," presented again the wide gaps between both sides on the refugee issue as were brought up in the document of 25 October 2008 (see http://palestine-studies.org/~ipsdc/positionmatrix.pdf).

Recognition of Israel as a Jewish state

The Israeli side, first and foremost the Israeli Foreign Minister Tzipi Livni, introduced the issue of the Palestinian recognition of Israel as a Jewish state throughout the Annapolis negotiations of 2007–08. For the first time since the beginning of the Oslo process the Israeli negotiating team insisted on this issue.[9] Although the recognition was not presented as a precondition for concluding an agreement, it became a cornerstone in the Israeli claim for justice, especially by Binyamin Netanyahu, since his re-election as Prime Minister in 2009 and entry into the current negotiations mediated by the United States. This issue would become not only the main expression of the Israeli claim for justice but also a test case of the sincerity of the Palestinian interest in ending the conflict with Israel.

Although it is not clear why Israel raised the issue only so late in the peace process with the Palestinians, the Palestinians rejected the Israeli demand and even defined it as a formidable barrier to conflict resolution. The issue was discussed in-depth by the NSU. In a confidential document from 16 November 2007 submitted to the Palestinian Drafting Team, titled "Strategy and Talking Points for Responding to the Precondition of Recognizing Israel as a "Jewish State," the NSU suggested that the Palestinian negotiators should maintain their position not to recognize or characterize the state of Israel as a "Jewish state" or "state for the Jewish people," or "homeland for the Jewish people."

The Palestinian negotiation team should refuse to engage on the issue of recognizing the Jewish character of Israel and argue that, "the traditional terms of reference of the peace process and existing agreements shall serve as the basis of peace. These terms of reference and agreements do not contemplate Palestinian recognition of Israel as a Jewish state as a basis for peace at all." Moreover, the recognition of Israel as a "Jewish state" was never a part of any of the previous negotiations between the parties and Israel never insisted on it as a precondition for establishing peace. Moreover, none of the peace agreements signed between Israel and Arab states referred to this issue. In addition to that, there is no practice of recognizing the demographic character of states. Israel was admitted to the UN as a "state" and not as a Jewish state (see http://transparency.aljazeera.net/files/2021.PDF, pp. 1–3).

In addition to these arguments for the rejection of the Israeli demand, the NSU added that the Palestinians could not recognize Israel as a Jewish state because it discriminated against the Arab population in it, so that any recognition of it as a "Jewish state" would only legitimize this discrimination and give the Arab citizens in Israel second-class status. Interestingly enough, the document did not refer to the traditional Palestinian argument against recognition of Israel as a "Jewish state" that any such recognition meant a political and ideological surrender to the Zionist ideology and to the Zionist occupation of Palestine. Nevertheless, if Israel insisted on the recognition of it as a Jewish state, then the Palestinian team should insist that, "the whole status of Mandate Palestine should be opened for discussion because the demand to base the agreement on two ethnically-defined national entities subverts the traditional terms of reference" (quoted in http://transparency.aljazeera.net/files/2021.PDF, p. 1).

The refugee issue in the negotiations: the Israeli version

The Israeli version of the negotiations in general, and of the refugee issue in particular, was given by former Israeli Prime Minister Ehud Olmert in a public speech in a conference of the Geneva Initiative on 19 September 2010 and in his own memoirs that were published in part in *Yeidot Aharonot* newspaper on 28 January 2011. In his speech, Olmert maintained that, in the general historic context, the refugee problem could not be resolved within the State of Israel. Nor does anyone who was serious about resolving the conflict believe that this should be considered a relevant option. In all of his meetings around the world, including with the British Prime Minister, the US President, the Quartet Envoy Tony Blair, the German Chancellor, and India's, China's, and Russia's leaders, there was no one that thought that the resolution of the refugee problem had to be solved within the borders of sovereign Israel. Nevertheless, Olmert stated that he was the first Israeli Prime Minister in 60 years to publicly acknowledge the suffering of Palestinian refugees:

> We, the Israeli government, the people of Israel feel a deep empathy to the suffering of those who used to be the inhabitants in the area that became the State of Israel, and to the reality that imposed on them a status of refugees. However, I would not recommend mentioning this without acknowledging the terrible suffering that was caused to the Jewish people because of the wars [with the Arabs]. Why we could not to say that we see and feel their sufferings as they should feel our suffering too?
>
> (See http://heskem.org/il/activity_detail.asp?id=2375& meid = 19)[10]

As for the resolution of the refugee problem, Olmert said that he suggested to the Palestinians that the refugee issue could be resolved in accordance with the Arab League Initiative. Olmert added that he told Abu-Mazen that Israel would be prepared to absorb inside Israel a minimal number of refugees, as an acknowledgment of their suffering based on humanitarian and individual considerations, but not those of family reunification, and neither according to UN resolutions or the right of return. This would be done on an annual basis in five years and the numbers would not be 50, 40, 30, or even 20,000 refugees. Moreover, Israel would carry out this humanitarian idea only in exchange for a written commitment of an authorized Palestinian authority, accepted by the Palestinian people, that the agreement reached represented the end of the conflict and the end of claims.[11] Furthermore, Olmert added new information that was never publicized, according to which the United States had agreed to absorb 100,000 Palestinian refugees in a framework of permanent Israeli–Palestinian agreement.[12]

In his memoirs Olmert mentioned specifically the exact number of Palestinian refugees that Israel would agree to accept: 5,000 in five years,

1,000 per year. Olmert maintained again that the Israeli acceptance to absorb these refugees was conditional on a written Palestinian commitment that this would be the end of the conflict and of the Palestinian claims. Olmert stated that the agreement should explicitly state that this sensitive part of the accord was concluded in accordance with the spirit of the Arab Peace Initiative and as a way to address and repair the suffering caused to the Palestinian people, part of whom were uprooted from their original homes because of the violent conflict between them and Israel for so many years. At the same time, the agreement should also include similar wording with respect to the suffering caused to the Israeli citizens and to the Jewish people because of the continued wars that were part of their life since the creation of the state.

In addition, both sides should act in cooperation with international actors in their contribution to establishing an international fund that will generously compensate the Palestinians, the Jews, and the Israelis who suffered because of the long Israeli–Palestinian conflict and regional wars. Olmert noted also that it was clear to him and to Abu-Mazen that the budget of the international fund would come from other states that had the financial means and the willingness to contribute to the end of the conflict.

Conclusions

The Annapolis conference of 27 November 2007, and the intensive negotiations that followed it were probably the most detailed negotiations between Israel and the Palestinians since the beginning of the peace process about 20 years ago. However, they ultimately failed to reach an agreement because of the gaps that remained between the two parties, as well as other factors such as Olmert's investigation for corruption in the Fall of 2008 that led to his resignation and the war in Gaza that suspended the negotiations in January 2009.

The issue of linking justice to peace remained dominant in these negotiations as in the previous ones. No significant change happened in both sides' positions regarding the issue of responsibility and the right of return for Palestinian refugees. Nevertheless, it seems that both sides became more aware of the other's difficulties in accepting the other's position. The transcripts of the Plenary Negotiation Committee as well as the NSU documents reflect the wide gaps between the two sides' positions and narratives, and their difficulties to reconcile the gaps. The Palestinian side turned to other historical cases of taking responsibility/apology as a means to convince the Israeli side about the necessity to comply with their demands. Furthermore, both sides agreed to turn to the Arab Peace Initiative as a potential framework for resolution of the refugee problem. In addition, based on both sides' documents and reflections, there were no longer Palestinian complaints as to their traditional claims for procedural justice, or at least they were not mentioned specifically in the various Palestinian documents.

Notes

1 The United States invited 49 countries and many international organizations to send representatives to the conference. Attendees included China, the Arab League, the European Union, Russia, the United Nations, the International Monetary Fund, and the World Bank.

2 Editor's note: It should be pointed out that over the course of almost two years, from December 2006 to mid-September 2008, Olmert and Abbas met 36 times! See Avishai (2011).

3 These are the so-called *Palestinian Papers* published in *al-Jazeera* (n.d.). They can be freely accessed on the web at http://transparency.aljazeera.net/en/search-english.

4 Editor's note: The Palestinian version of the talks is mostly based upon *The Palestinian Papers* and the memoirs of Abu-Ala. The quotations from *The Palestinian Papers* are from the relevant website, in text.

5 This rationale is quite extraordinary, since it seems that the Palestinians would like to enhance Israel's international status and legitimacy. The document offers the examples of major countries that recognized that they had committed legal wrongs in the past, without jeopardizing their existence or identity, like the United States, France, Germany, and Australia. These examples should be an encouragement for Israel.

6 Editor's note: The Arab Peace Initiative was launched by the Arab League in Beirut on 25 March 2002, and reaffirmed at the Riyadh Summit in April 2007. In the revised version of the initiative, article 2 (ii) refers to "achievement of a just solution to the Palestinian refugee problem *to be agreed upon* in accordance with UN General Assembly Resolution 194" (editor's emphasis).

7 This paragraph is not mentioned in the confidential documents disclosed in *The Palestinian Papers.*

8 The document does not present the Palestinian demands for Israel's responsibility and apology.

9 Editor's note: On the Israeli demand for the recognition of Israel as a Jewish state and the origins of this demand, see the document redacted by Tal Becker, www.washingtoninstitute.org/uploads/Documents/pubs/PolicyFocus108.pdf.

10 Editor's note: At the Annapolis international conference of November 2007 Olmert had similar remarks:

> I know and acknowledge the fact that alongside the constant suffering which many in Israel have experienced because of the history, the wars, the terror and the hatred towards us – a suffering which has always been part of our lives in our land – your people [the Palestinians] have also suffered for many years, and some still suffer.
>
> For dozens of years, many Palestinians have been living in camps, disconnected from the environment in which they grew, wallowing in poverty, neglect, alienation, bitterness, and a deep, unrelenting sense of deprivation.
>
> I know that this pain and deprivation is one of the deepest foundations which fomented the ethos of hatred towards us.
>
> We are not indifferent to this suffering. We are not oblivious to the tragedies you have experienced. I believe that in the course of negotiations between us we will find the right way, as part of an international effort in which we will participate, to assist these Palestinians in finding a proper framework for their future, in the Palestinian state which will be established in the territories agreed upon between us. Israel will be part of an international mechanism which will assist in finding a solution to this problem.
>
> (See www.cfr.org/israel/prime-minister-olmerts-speech-annapolis-november-2007/p14925.)

11 Palestinian sources maintained that the Palestinians demanded that Israel absorb hundreds of thousands of refugees in its territory.
12 Olmert's claim was quickly denied the next day by former Bush Administration officials. See www.jpost.com/International/Abrams-Bush-never-agreed-to-take-100000-refugees.

References

al-Jazeera. The Palestinian Papers. Access at http://transparency.aljazeera.net/files/ (n.d.).

Avishai, Bernard. "A Plan for Peace That Still Could Be", *The New York Times Magazine*, 7 February 2011. Access at www.nytimes.com/2011/02/13/magazine/13Israel-t.html?pagewanted=1&_r = 2.

Erekat, Saeb. "The Political Situation in Light of Developments with the US Administration and Israeli Government and Hamas' Continued Coup d'etat," December 2009. Access at http://prn.mcgill.ca/research/papers/erekat.pdf.

7 Linking justice to peace in the Israeli–Palestinian conflict

Looking for solutions

The two rounds of the peace process in the Israeli–Palestinian conflict, Oslo (1993–2001) and Annapolis (2007–08) failed to bridge the gap between each side's narratives of justice and, specifically, the Palestinian demands for linking justice to peace. This concluding chapter has two aims: (1) to summarize the role of the parties' justice narratives in the peace process and to argue that the gap between the contending narratives has been a major barrier for resolving the conflict; (2) to look for alternative solutions for linking justice to peace, among them linking justice to reconciliation, to a two-state solution, and to a one-state solution.

Linking justice to peace as a barrier to conflict resolution

The Palestinian demands for justice have two layers: a demand for procedural justice and a demand for transitional and corrective justice. The demand for procedural justice relates primarily to the Israeli recognition of the Palestinians as an equal partner in the peace process, despite the asymmetry in the power relations between the two parties and the occupier–occupied relations between them. The demand for transitional and corrective justice focuses mainly on the Israeli acknowledgment of its responsibility in perpetuating injustice against the Palestinian people and its remedy by implementing the right of return for Palestinian refugees.

The Palestinian demand for procedural justice was acceptable to some of the Israeli negotiators in the Oslo process, though they had trouble in carrying it out in practice, so that the relations between the parties were not grounded in real equality. Moreover, after the outbreak of the second *intifada* in September 2000, Israel found it difficult to recognize Arafat or Abu-Mazen as sincere and reliable negotiating partners, the former because of the loss of trust in him and the latter because of what was perceived as his weakness. Indeed, the Israeli unilateral disengagement from the Gaza Strip in August 2005 was a direct outcome of Israeli disappointment about the possibility of resolving the conflict through peaceful negotiations. Nevertheless, the resumption of the peace negotiations via the Annapolis process in 2007–08 took place after Israel recognized Abu-Mazen as a serious partner. Hence, it seems that the relations between the Israelis and Palestinians, especially between Ehud Olmert and Abu-Mazen, were grounded in a better sense of equality and a certain degree of empathy. However, the asymmetrical power relations persist nowadays, so they will continue to influence the current and future negotiations. In this sense, most of the burden is on the Israeli side and especially on the US as a mediator to balance the asymmetrical power relations in the peace negotiations.[1]

The Palestinian demands for transitional and corrective justice are principally linked to the outcomes of the 1947–49 war and less so to the outcomes of the 1967 war. The Palestinians require that Israel acknowledges its responsibility for the expulsion of the Palestinians and for the creation of the refugee problem, and that it agrees to the implementation of the right of return within its borders. The Palestinians, for their part, do not acknowledge their responsibility for rejecting the Partition Plan of November 1947 and for initiating the 1947–49 war. Similarly, they do not accept the Israeli standpoint on justice, which is focused on the right of Jews to establish a Jewish state in the Land of Israel and/or to recognize Israel as the state of the Jewish people. In the Palestinian view, such acknowledgment would add to the injustice that the Zionist movement inflicted upon them through the establishment of Israel on their land, and it has the potential to deny their right of return and undermine the rights of Palestinians living in Israel.

The Palestinians presented their demands for procedural, transitional, and corrective justice at the beginning of the Oslo process, but Israel completely rejected them. The Israelis conditioned the peace process on its focusing on the outcomes of the 1967 war rather than those of the 1947–49 war. Israel objected to dealing with injustice and its remedy as defined by the Palestinians and, in fact, imposed the negotiating framework that it wanted, based on a gradual and multi-phased process including an interim arrangement (Palestinian self-government for five years in the occupied territories), before the parties engage in reaching a final and permanent peace treaty, with the core issues postponed to the permanent status negotiations. The Palestinians were then forced to accept the Israeli position at Oslo, recognizing that, in light of the power asymmetry between the parties, their insistence on having their demands for justice fulfilled could be a barrier to peace and to the establishment of an independent Palestinian state. Nonetheless, the Palestinians did not reconcile themselves to the removal of the justice issues from the agenda, and they saw the peace process as unjust and unfair, and the result of Israel exploiting its power during the negotiations.

The Palestinian demands for justice were renewed more adamantly at the Camp David Summit in July 2000 following the massive criticism leveled against Arafat and the Palestinian negotiating team by other Palestinians, especially the intellectuals, for abandoning their demands for justice, and particularly the right of return. Although the Palestinian demands for justice were not the only cause for the failure of this summit, it did contribute significantly to it.

The Israeli negotiating team at Camp David was surprised by the renewal of the Palestinian demands for justice and by their intensity, and they saw it as a barrier to peace. They had the impression that the Palestinian demands for justice included not only the right of return, which had the potential to endanger Israel as a Jewish state, but also in fact denied the very existence of Israel as the state of the Jewish people because its establishment, on 14 May 1948, was considered the primary source of injustice perpetrated against the Palestinians. Israel refused to accept any responsibility for the creation of the refugee problem, though it expressed its sorrow for the Palestinian suffering, and it was ready to receive a limited number of refugees on a humanitarian basis in the framework of family reunification, but under no circumstances on the basis of a right of return. From the Israeli standpoint, the right of return should be implemented only within the Palestinian state.

Some changes in the Palestinian demands for justice did take place between the beginning of the Oslo process in January 1993 and the Taba talks of January 2001. While the Palestinians were insisting on transitional justice – that is, Israeli recognition of its responsibility for creating the refugee problem and Israel's acceptance in principle of the right of return – they were willing to have the implementation of the right of return (corrective justice) – that is, determining the number of refugees that Israel would receive – reached through negotiations between the parties, while recognizing that a massive return of refugees could endanger the Jewish character of Israel. Israel refused to accept those changes in the Palestinian demands for justice as substantive ones, because the Palestinians were still focused on Israel's acknowledging its responsibility for the injustice and accepting the right of return to its territory.

At the Annapolis process in 2007–08 no significant change took place in the position of the parties, regarding the links between justice and peace. While the Palestinians continued to insist on their demands regarding Israel's acknowledgment of its responsibility for the creation of the refugee problem and accepting in principle the right of return to the State of Israel, Israel refused to accept them. The most that Israel was ready to accept was to express its sorrow for the Palestinian suffering, but only on a reciprocal basis. Israel agreed to receive a limited number of refugees on a humanitarian basis but not within the framework of family reunification, and under no circumstances on the basis of a right of return.

The Track II initiatives, the "People's Voice," and the Geneva Initiative, coped in a different way with the Palestinian demands for justice. In both of these initiatives, the parties decided not to engage with the Palestinian demands that Israel should acknowledge its responsibility for the injustice perpetrated against the Palestinians. Moreover, these informal initiatives associated the right of return solely with the territory of the Palestinian state. Even so, the Geneva Initiative included an agreement to receive Palestinian refugees into Israel, though not on the basis of a right of return. The two initiatives dealt with a solution to the refugee problem outside of the framework of the right of return; that is, they removed the right of return as a barrier to the resolution of the Israeli–Palestinian conflict. It seems that, while Israel could accept this solution, it is doubtful whether the Palestinian policymakers and public are ready at this stage to abandon their demand for transitional and correcting justice. This is because the demand for transitional and corrective justice is a protected value that the Palestinians are not willing to relinquish, and any effort at such a concession on the part of Palestinian leadership will create a confrontation with the Palestinian public and especially with the Palestinian refugees living outside of the West Bank and the Gaza Strip, who base the justification for their exile on the ethos of return.[2]

The failure of the Israeli–Palestinian peace process so far can be attributed mostly to the failure of both sides to reach an agreed formula for linking justice to peace. Thus, the relationship between peace and justice has been at the heart of the peace process. As a matter of fact, the peace process sharply reflected and even enlarged the wide gap between both sides' narratives and the difficulty if not the impossibility of bridging the gap between them. Both parties continue to be guided by their historical narratives, which are protected values, that is, sacred and mystical values intertwined with national identity and therefore not subject to negotiation, bargaining, or compromise of any sort. Each side continues to be guided by their perceived injustices committed by the other side, and by a high sense of justice and righteousness in its cause, while de-legitimizing the justice of the other side (Caplan 2010, 221–22).

The peace process so far has demonstrated the old and basic assumption that the Israeli–Palestinian conflict is a clash between two narratives of justice. The problem lies not only in the fact that the two national narratives vary so much, but that both "Palestinians and Jews each believe that acceptance of the other's identity [will] negate their own case and their own identity" (Bar-Tal and Salomon 2006, 20). Along the same lines is the belief that historically speaking "acknowledging the other's nationhood" meant accepting that group's access to the contested land while weakening "one's own claim for the same land" (Bar-Tal and Salomon 2006, 20).

The issues of justice and injustice are deeply embedded in the conflict and they have been clearly reflected in the negotiations. They probably will continue to remain like that for a long time, if not permanently, in the narratives of each side and in the current and future negotiations. "They may remain hidden or become explicit but are always present and guide thinking and judgment" (Belaief 1997, 331). Belaief defines this kind of situation as a tragedy and as a "tragic justice," characterized by

> the clash between two rights, neither of which can be satisfied without harm to the other's self-view of its rights. Justice will have to include the recognition of tragedy and to take into account that any peace arrangement will contain elements of injustice since the tragedy is permanent.
>
> (Belaief 1997, 331)

The basic conclusion of this complex reality is that justice cannot be absolute, but relative, and that it will be permanently incomplete. Any demand for linking justice to peace based solely on one's narrative is impossible and becomes a formidable barrier to conflict resolution. The central problem in the case of two conflicting views of justice is that both sides are partly right, in terms of one or another aspect of their claims, and therefore it cannot be expected that a peace agreement will fully and satisfactorily address all of the problems related to justice. Justice has then to be compromised if the sides have an interest in resolving the conflict.

Balancing between justice and peace: between theory and practice

It would appear that the theoretical arguments we presented in the first chapter regarding the possibility of finding a formula to compromise between peace and justice could help in dealing with the problems of justice in the Israeli–Palestinian conflict, as follows:

1 *Reviewing the different approaches that consider the linking of justice to peace suggests that an explicit concern for justice must be included in the peace negotiations and in the peace agreement.* Considerations of justice cannot be excluded from a successful peace process. Although including the issue of justice in the peacemaking can undermine the prospects of concluding peace, it cannot be simply ignored.

   At the same time, both Israelis and Palestinians should be aware that there is no ideal solution to the question of justice in peacemaking, especially when two claims of justice confront each other and no one of them has the monopoly of truth. The question is therefore how to find a common formula that satisfies both sides' conception of justice, while recognizing that both have to compromise some of their just claims for the sake of peace. In the absence of a certain measure of agreement between the sides on what and who is just and unjust, it is clearly more difficult if not impossible for the sides to conclude a peace agreement. Without a shared conception of justice the sides may fail to resolve the conflict. In such a case, linking justice to peace may foil the possibility of concluding a peace agreement, so justice might become a significant barrier to conflict resolution.

   The two sides should agree that justice, like other issues, needs to be among the issues subject to discussion as part of the negotiations in the peace process. The two sides should develop a joint framework regarding matters of justice that are linked to the peace process and practical ways of dealing with them. Nevertheless, it would appear that the theoretical arguments we presented in the first chapter regarding the possibility of finding a joint compromise formula between peace and justice can only be of limited help in dealing with the problem of justice in the Israeli–Palestinian conflict. This is due to the fact that, even if both sides agree that justice is one of the topics for negotiation in the peace process, it is doubtful whether today they are ready to develop a joint framework regarding the issues related to justice and how to handle it.

2 *Given that every peace process includes concessions, compromises, and costs, these should apply to questions of justice as well.* The real issue that the parties need to confront is not only whether the peace agreement is just, but whether the concessions made – including the issue of justice – are mutual, reciprocal, balanced, and bearable, and whether the benefits of peace outweigh its costs, including those linked to the issue of justice. Moreover, the parties need to consider whether the benefits of peace outweigh the sense of incomplete justice. Any Israeli–Palestinian peace agreement will require concessions of what is termed as justice for the sake of peace and, therefore, there is the need for a wide domestic legitimacy for it. Any concession of justice for peace will be perceived by different groups in each society as an act of betrayal of a protected value, and this will require therefore an effective argumentation of both political leaderships that will justify it, in terms of domestic legitimacy. Both leaderships should frame positively the benefits of peace for the interests and the values of each side. Compromising justice because of weakness or historical necessity will not secure a wide domestic legitimacy and durable peace. When the sole justification of a peace agreement is legitimized by arguments such as that there was "no other alternative" or "no other choice" then there is no real motivation to respect such an agreement. This kind of a peace agreement will be likened more to a truce or an act of appeasement, rather than genuine peace (Margalit 2010, 77–79).

3 *Dealing with the current injustice of the Israeli occupation and the fact that the Palestinians still do not have an independent state is more urgent and significant than the injustice linked to the past.*

4 *The accepted tenets in the theoretical literature, that there is a trade-off to make between protected values as a compromise that combines justice with peace, has been so far formally rejected by the Palestinians.* The Palestinians had rejected an Israeli proposal for an exchange of protected values that had been raised during negotiations after the Camp David Summit that included Israel relinquishing sovereignty over the Temple Mount in exchange for Palestinian concessions on the right of return. The Palestinians were unable to concede the right of return, given its status as a protected value, and it is surprising that the Israeli negotiating team raised the possibility of giving up the Temple Mount, considering that it would be unlikely to receive religious, political, and public legitimacy for it (Ben-Ami 2006, 367, 377). This proposal could present an apparently fair compromise, but it is doubtful whether it will be reiterated, since it ignores the difficulty for both sides in exchanging protected values.[3]

5 *Issues of justice should be framed in terms of interests rather than values.* Such framing is likely to make the possibility of compromise easier and

turn the concessions necessary for resolution of the conflict into a matter of interests, which, unlike values that are not subject to compromise, can be subjected to bargaining and compromise.

6 *Another reasonable compromise would involve distinguishing between the Palestinian demands for transitional justice and their demands for corrective justice.* A moderate Palestinian demand for transitional justice, such as Israel's willingness to acknowledge the suffering of the Palestinian people (without taking responsibility), as proposed in the Clinton parameters of 23 December 2000, could serve as a compromise to the demand for transitional justice. Alternatively, both sides could adopt a formula acknowledging their joint responsibility for the injustice that each side inflicted upon the other during the course of the conflict, apologize to each other, and forgive each other.

Peacemaking and linking justice to reconciliation

In a situation where the parties are unable to reach an agreement regarding justice, but they are still interested in reaching a peace agreement based on a two-state solution, they should consider postponing engagement with the issue of justice to the phase of reconciliation. In so doing, they would agree, within the framework of a peace agreement, that the issue of justice is very important to them and that peace cannot be established and maintained between them until they have fully dealt with the question of justice in their relations. Delaying the matter to the reconciliatory phase could make it easier for the parties to overcome the justice barrier in the peace process and enable them to examine this issue after they have resolved the conflict in formal terms and established some form of trust. The parties would then be better prepared to engage in this issue, which is very value-laden and difficult to resolve through compromise.

It is possible that the parties had failed in their efforts to formulate a joint framework linking justice with peace and that the demands for justice generated a strong barrier to peace, yet the parties might still be interested in reaching a peace agreement. In such a case they should consider postponing efforts to address the issue of justice to the reconciliation phase. This would entail that the parties should agree, within the formal peace accord that they would sign, that they consider the question of justice to be very important and that the peace between them cannot be stabilized until this question is addressed. Delaying the discussion to the reconciliation phase, however, could make it easier for the parties to overcome the justice barrier in the peace process and enable them to examine the issue of justice after building trust and reaching a stage of readiness to engage in a difficult and value-laden issue, after formally concluding peace.

In order to secure addressing the issue of justice in the reconciliation stage, the sides should consider its formal inclusion in the text of the peace agreement itself. A paragraph stating a mutual commitment to look for a compromise solution to the justice issue following the implementation of the peace agreement may help the sides to overcome the barrier to a peace agreement. The concluding of a peace agreement and its implementation to the satisfaction of both sides will enable the sides to build trust and to ease the process of reconciliation that will require them to cope with issues of justice. Nevertheless, even at the reconciliation stage, it is unrealistic to expect that one side's justice concept will be accepted as the single and objective truth, so the parties will probably need to negotiate different kinds of justice: substantive (fundamental needs of both sides), future (just institutions, arrangements and relationships), procedural (fair and reciprocal process of negotiation), and emotional (a significant degree of a just outcome) (Kelman 2004, 123).

Reconciliation will also require consideration by each party of its responsibility for the wrong done to the other in the course of the conflict, as well as the need for an acknowledgment of the injustice and its implications in terms of apology and compensation. Nevertheless, as Kelman maintains, "The acknowledgment of responsibility cannot be based entirely on an objective set of legal or moral norms, but requires a process of negotiation in different types of responsibility [that] are identified and agreed upon" (Kelman 2004, 124). This is true especially when both sides are responsible for the injustice done, so they share the blame. Therefore, a mutual process of reconciliation based on mutual acknowledgment and apology is required.

A failure to reach reconciliation to the satisfaction of both sides may endanger the durability of the peace agreement, so the sides should consider this possibility as a constraint on the peace prospects over time. This might encourage them to moderate or to reduce their claims of justice or to be more responsive to each other's claims in order not to endanger the peace. Much depends also on the material benefits of the peace relations. If they appear to be substantial, then the sides will prefer not to endanger them. However, if the dividends of peace are low and they do not satisfactorily answer the initial expectations, the issue of the past injustice may serve as an excuse for ending the peace relations or remaining at the negative, precarious, or "cold" levels only.

In order for the two parties to reach reconciliation some re-interpretation and review of their narratives is in order. There is a need for both sides to review and be critical of their own narratives, not just critical of the other side; there is a need for historical self-examination. This exercise could potentially lead to "self-critical revisions exposing a prevailing narrative's nationalistic ideology, transcend simplistic generalizations, and attempt to understand the rationale of the other's behavior and narrative" (Rotberg 2006, 10). The bridging of these narratives becomes a central issue when reconciliation is desired in that "the focal point for reconciliation attempts becomes the attainment of the legitimization of the other side's narrative, including the acknowledgement of its history" (Bar-Tal and Salomon 2006, 40), or at least "in the sense of acknowledging the legitimacy of the other's narrative without necessarily fully agreeing with that narrative" (Kelman 2004, 119).

The two-state solution as a form of compromised justice

With respect to the demands for corrective justice, the two-state solution and the establishment of an independent Palestinian state alongside Israel should be seen as an Israeli and Palestinian fair compromise, and as a fulfillment of the demands for corrective justice. Furthermore, the Israeli and American proposals – that the Palestinian refugees will be also relocated to territories that Israel would exchange ("swap") with the Palestinians and that relocation would then be considered as realizing their right of return – can also be regarded as a kind of compromise.

The establishment of a Palestinian state would not only put an end to the current Israeli occupation of the West Bank and to the Palestinian suffering, but it would also allow the fulfillment of the right of return within the Palestinian state. So far, the Palestinians have rejected solutions that did not in their view address their demands for a right of return (to Israel itself). Yet, the Palestinian demand for a right of return to Israel proper conflicts with the idea of establishing a Palestinian state. While returning Palestinian refugees to Israel is not possible, the establishment of an independent Palestinian state could offer a rational, moral, and reasonable solution to the refugee problem. Palestinian insistence on the right of return to Israel will not only prevent the achievement of a peace agreement and the creation of a Palestinian state, but will also cause more suffering to refugees and residents of the West Bank and Gaza Strip and would increase the sense of grievance and injustice among Palestinian refugees in the Palestinian Diaspora. The Palestinian demands for transitional and corrective justice in the form of demanding a comprehensive right of return are, therefore, a formidable barrier to peace.

The basic principle of a compromised justice should be based on mutual recognition of the rights of both sides for self-determination, nationhood, and statehood. The only possible solution that can accomplish this basic principle is the "two-state solution," which calls for "two states for two peoples." This solution is not a new one and was proposed first by the Peel Commission in 1937 and then by the 1947 UN Partition Plan. The Jewish side in the conflict accepted both proposals, whereas the Arab side rejected them. The Arab side initiated the 1947–49 war in order to prevent the implementation of the UN Partition Plan and the establishment of a Jewish state. Following the war, Israel as the Jewish state was established, while the Palestinians lost their opportunity to establish their own independent state.

Following the 1947–49 war and until 1988, the Palestinians continued to oppose the two-state solution. The Palestinian Declaration of Independence of November 1988 could be considered as the beginning of a sea change; it was interpreted as an indirect recognition of the State of Israel and expressed support for a two-state solution. Israel, which had occupied the West Bank and the Gaza Strip after 1967, opposed that solution, maintaining that the establishment of a Palestinian state alongside of Israel in the West Bank and Gaza Strip could pose an existential threat to it.

The Oslo process of 1993–2001 opened the road for the two-state solution, although the Oslo Accord did not explicitly refer to it. The main Palestinian goal during the Oslo process was to promote a two-state solution that will bring about the establishment of an independent Palestinian state in the West Bank and in the Gaza Strip within the pre-1967 war borders (i.e. the Armistice lines or "green line" of 1949), including East Jerusalem as the capital of the Palestinian state and implementation of the right of return to the State of Israel. This Palestinian goal has remained constant throughout the peace process and has formally not changed substantially until today.

During the Oslo process, Israel's position remained ambiguous vis-à-vis the establishment of a Palestinian state; in formal terms, the most that Israel was ready to accept was the establishment of a Palestinian entity which would be less than an independent state in the Gaza Strip and in part of the West Bank, while keeping Jerusalem unified under Israel sovereignty and rejecting the right of return. Only at the Camp David Summit, in July 2000, Israel accepted for the first time the two-state solution, making it conditional upon the demand that the right of return will be implemented only in the Palestinian state. In the 2000s, both Israeli Prime Ministers Ariel Sharon and Ehud Olmert also accepted the two-state solution. Even the current Israeli Prime Minister, Binyamin Netanyahu, endorsed the two-state solution in June 2009. Nevertheless, the parties have failed so far to reach an agreement on the two-state solution because they have been divided on several core issues, including borders, Jerusalem, refugees, and settlements. It seems that both parties are not ready yet to make the necessary concessions for reaching the two-state solution.[4]

In our view, a two-state solution, despite all the difficulties involved in its realization, is probably the best compromise and just solution for the two sides. This solution requires both sides to make very painful concessions. Israel has to recognize the right of the Palestinian people to have their own state, while the Palestinians have to recognize the right of the Jewish people to have their own state. Furthermore, the formula of the two-state solution requires Israel to give up its dream of Greater Israel (*Land of Israel*) and its occupation of the Palestinians.

The occupation of the Palestinians is not only an injustice and humiliation by itself, but it also denies the right of the Palestinians for self-determination, nationhood, and statehood. The occupation of the Palestinians is perceived by the international community as an act of territorial expansion that violates international law and basic principles of justice, so it also de-legitimizes the existence of the state of Israel itself as a Jewish and democratic one. If the interest of Israel remains in keeping its essence as a Jewish and democratic state, then the continuing occupation of the Palestinians endangers these characteristics.

The formula of a two-state solution requires also from the Palestinians that they accept Israel's existence not only de facto, but also *de jure* (Belaief 1997, 334). In other words, the Palestinians have to give up their demand for a massive implementation of the right of return to the State of Israel because it might threaten the very existence of Israel as the Jewish state. The Palestinians can keep their narrative of the right of return but they have to give up its implementation within the State of Israel. Thus, the right of return should be implemented solely within the Palestinian state.

There is no way to accomplish one's demand for justice in the two-state solution by creating injustice for the other side. If the Palestinian concept of just peace is the disappearance of the Jewish state by changing its Jewish character, then this is a demand for their absolute justice, and this demand will ultimately prevent the fulfillment of the two-state solution. Thus, the Palestinians cannot establish their own state and also demand to make Israel into another Palestinian state (Belaief 1997, 334). Moreover, the Palestinians should realize that their demand for the right of return to the State of Israel is totally unacceptable in Israel and will remain as such. As Shimon Peres argued,

> The claim to the "right of return" is [a] maximal claim; if accepted, it would wipe out the national character of the State of Israel, making the Jewish majority into a minority. Consequently there is no chance it will be accepted, either now or in the future. No Israeli government would agree to a strategy that entailed the destruction of our national entity.
>
> (Peres with Naor 1993, 189)

Indeed, the Palestinian insistence on the demand for a right of return will actually prevent the two-state solution and specifically the establishment of an independent Palestinian state. A peace with Israel that includes recognition of the Palestinians' national rights to establish their own state and putting an end to their long suffering and misery is a fair and just solution. Otherwise, Palestinian self-determination and statehood will be definitely postponed again. Indeed, as Belaief notes, "It is [the] irony of such situations that at a certain point the victim can become responsible for perpetuating his own suffering by failing to rise beyond tragedy into genuinely practical and political proposals and actions" (Belaief 1997, 336).

One-state solution as a just solution

The one-state or the bi-national solution was proposed several times by people on both sides and by outsiders throughout the long Israeli–Palestinian conflict. Proponents of that solution advocate a single state in Mandatory (Western) Palestine that will include the State of Israel, the West Bank and the Gaza Strip. In general, this solution refers to the establishment of a unitary, federal or confederate Israeli–Palestinian state in the entire territory west of the Jordan River. This solution will provide citizenship and equal rights for all the inhabitants in the combined entity, based on the principle of one person, one vote. The advocates of the bi-national solution are mainly intellectuals, whereas this proposed solution is not very popular in both societies, not in the official circles and not with the general public. This solution gains some momentum mainly in periods of crisis and stalemate in the peace process, as a default and as an inevitable outcome of the failure of reaching a two-state solution (Hermann 2005).

The idea of a bi-national state emerged during the British Mandate period.[5] Since the 1967 war, and especially after the recent failures of the Oslo and the Annapolis rounds of negotiations in the peace process, it became a kind of default option with the prolongation of the occupation and without a significant change in the status quo. Sometimes, the idea appears as a strategic solution; otherwise, it is regarded as a tactical warning to both sides that a failure of reaching the two-state solution will bring them de facto to a one-state solution, even against their will.

Some analysts and activists suggest that the one-state solution is the best, just, and fair possible outcome for moral reasons. This solution would enable Israel to claim all of the Land of Israel (*Eretz Israel*), while the Palestinians could claim all of historic Palestine as well. Both parties could then argue that they had accomplished their national narratives and identities. Such a solution would reflect the mutual recognition of the rights of the two parties to the same piece of land, which has to be shared. This solution would also allow a full recognition of the right of return of both sides to the Land, including the Palestinian refugees (Baraka 2005; Bishara 2003; Ghanem 2005; Said 2006; Khalidi 2011).

Other observers point out that the one-state solution is the only practical one because of the realities developed on the ground since the 1967 war, when Israel occupied the Palestinian territories. This solution appears to various people from both sides as the only feasible one, as the irreversible and inexorable outcome of the continuous expansion of the Israeli settlements in the West Bank and in East Jerusalem. This development prevents a viable, contiguous, sovereign, independent Palestinian state with East Jerusalem as its capital. Moreover, Israel and the Palestinian territories already function as a single political unit. They share the same resources, such as aquifers, the same highway network, the same electricity grid, and the same international borders, which can no longer be separated (Abu-Odeh 2001/2002; Benvenisti 2003; Shavit 2003; Tarazi 2004; Hermann 2005; Khalidi 2011).

In addition to the advocacy within both parties for the one-state solution, there is also an external, international advocacy for that option claiming that it is moral, just, and achievable. At the same time, that advocacy is often based on denying the right of Israel to exist based on a mixture of different political and demographic arguments. First, it is argued that Israel has been founded on religious and ethnic principles and not on democratic and pluralistic ones, which are improper by themselves. Therefore, Israel cannot continue to exist in such a way, so it should be radically transformed and eventually dismantled. Second, a demographic argument refers to the fact that the Arab population soon will exceed the Jewish population in the area of Mandatory (Western) Palestine; therefore, the Arab population, as the majority, has the right to rule. According to these two arguments, the establishment of a unitary, democratic, and pluralistic bi-national state with equal rights for Jews and Palestinians in the entire area of Mandatory Palestine *instead* of the State of Israel is a fair and just solution to the Israeli–Palestinian conflict (Tony 2003; Tilley 2005).

In contrast, the one-state solution is perceived by most of the Israeli Jews and by the Jewish people around the world as a nightmare development that would bring about the end of the Jewish state. Within a few years, there will be a Palestinian majority between the Jordan River and the Mediterranean Sea, and the result will be another Arab state, in which the Jews will remain a small minority. Thus, the majority of the Israeli Jews and the Jewish people in the Diaspora interpret the one-state solution as a suicidal act and as the end of Zionism. Moreover, such a solution is defined as an injustice by itself for the Jewish people (Hermann 2005).

In contrast, the Palestinian citizens in Israel generally support the one-state solution because they perceive it as the only option that can equalize their status in Israel. They maintain that, because of the existence of a significant Arab minority in Israel (about one-fifth of the population), Israel is already a bi-national state. They also prefer Israel to be a democratic state, "a state of all its citizens," rather than a Jewish and democratic state (as the Jewish majority in Israel prefers to be defined), because they see an inherent contradiction between its Jewish and democratic characteristics. From their standpoint, a Jewish state cannot be a democratic one because it treats the Arab citizens as non-equal citizens. A bi-national state that will also include the Palestinians in the West Bank and Gaza will make the Palestinians the majority in the new bi-national state (Ghanem 1999; Khalidi 2011).

Although not termed as such, the first formal Palestinian support for a bi-national state appeared in February 1969 with a resolution adopted by the fifth National Council of the PLO that called for establishment of a "secular and democratic state" in the entire territory west of the Jordan River, including the Gaza Strip, instead of the State of Israel. In that secular and democratic state Muslims, Christians, and Jews will enjoy equal civilian rights. Over the years, this idea failed eventually to attract substantial support on both sides, so in the 1988 Palestinian Independence Declaration, the PLO gave up the idea of one-state solution in favor of the two-state solution.

Other Palestinian analysts and activists adopt the one-state solution only as a tactical threat to exploit the Jewish apprehension about the bi-national state in order to push Israel in the direction of the two-state solution. Others seek to exploit the model of "one-person, one-vote" in order to establish a bi-national state with a Palestinian majority. Equal voting rights for millions of Palestinians in Israel and in the territories would ultimately bring an end to the Zionist project of Jewish self-determination and of the Jewish state (Khalidi 2006). Therefore, the one-state solution enjoys more support among the Islamic fundamentalist movements who refuse to accept any territorial compromise

(Khalidi 2006). Nevertheless, Palestinian mainstream, like the Jewish Israeli mainstream, opposes the idea of a bi-national solution because it undermines the Palestinian identity and narratives and will force the Palestinians to adjust to a solution that will recognize the dominance of Zionism. Moreover, it is doubtful if such a solution can be imposed on Israel (Khalidi 2006).

In sum, the one-state solution is perceived by most of the Israelis and Palestinians as a negative solution because it threatens the idea of self-determination and the rights for national independence. In a joint Israeli–Palestinian poll of March 2010 a majority of Israelis and Palestinians preferred a two-state solution as the most feasible and acceptable solution to the Israeli–Palestinian conflict, as opposed to a single bi-national state or a Palestinian–Israeli confederation. Seventy-one percent among Israelis and 57 percent of Palestinians polled supported the two-state solution, i.e. the establishment of an independent Palestinian state alongside of Israel. Only 24 percent of the Israelis and 29 percent of the Palestinians supported the solution of a bi-national state, in which the West Bank and the Gaza strip were integrated into Israel to establish one single state in which Palestinians and Israelis would have equal rights. As to a Palestinian-Israeli confederation, only 30 percent of the Israelis and 26 percent among Palestinians supported this option.[6]

This poll only confirms the well-known assumption that both sides still prefer to live in separate national states. It seems also that both parties realize that the bi-national solution cannot necessarily resolve the conflict and secure a peaceful coexistence between Israelis and Palestinians. Indeed, most of the proposals do not present concrete specific formulas regarding the future constitutional arrangement of the one-state solution, or its implications for both sides living in a single state. For instance, how will a single state resolve the mistrust and the mutual negative feelings between the parties? How will such a solution cope with the national aspirations, narratives, and identities of both sides? (Avineri 2003; Khalidi 2006).

Moreover, the historical experience has shown that bi-nationalism has been a severe source of violent conflict between ethnic groups around the world. The bloody breakdown of Yugoslavia in the 1990s is just one recent example of the tragic failure of ethnic groups to live peacefully. Even the Czechs and Slovaks preferred a peaceful separation after many years of unity. It is doubtful that, after such a protracted and violent conflict, Israelis and Palestinians could overcome the grievances of the conflict and live peacefully in one single state. Indeed, even Meron Benvenisti, one of the Israeli advocates of the one-state solution as the only viable one, expressed his pessimistic view about the prospects of that solution to bring peace: "We are not going to have peace here. Even if there is some bi-national arrangement, it can only manage the conflict. At its outskirts, however, violence will always prevail" (quoted in Shavit 2003).

Nevertheless, it seems that a failure to reach a two-state solution in the foreseeable future, together with the continuing massive expansion of Israeli settlements in the West Bank and East Jerusalem will intensify the calls, among Palestinians and in the international community as a whole, for a one-state solution. Indeed, senior Palestinian figures including Abu-Mazen, Abu-Ala, Qaddurah Fares, Jibril Rajoub, Ziad Abu Zayyad, and Seri Nusseibeh have warned recently that they would rescind their support for the two-state solution, call for the dissolution of the Palestinian Authority, and adopt the one-state solution for the Israeli–Palestinian conflict as the only feasible outcome (*Haaretz*, 31 July 2008: *Atlantic Magazine*, May 2008; The Reut Institute, August and September 2008; *New York Times*, 4 September, 2008; www.maannews.net, 20 December, 2011; www.amad.ps, 17 March 2012).

Conversely, senior Israeli politicians like former *Knesset* Speaker, Reuven Rivlin, and former Defense Minister and Minister of Foreign Affairs, Moshe Arens, as well as several *Knesset* members from the *Likud* ruling party have expressed their support for a one-state solution in order to prevent the partition of the land and retain the Land of Israel as a single political unit. There are many Israeli settlers in the West Bank who support such a solution if the alternative is their removal from their settlements.[7]

At the same time, the fear of realizing the scenario of a one-state solution as the only feasible one, which might endanger the survival of Israel as a Jewish and democratic state, might encourage Israel to advance more firmly the two-state solution, or even to endorse a unilateral disengagement from the West Bank, as previously happened with the Gaza Strip in the summer of 2005. Indeed, the increased concern at the impossibility of the two-state solution, on the one hand, and Palestinian statements that the Palestinians are no longer interested in the two-state solution, on the other hand, have pushed some Israelis in the recent past to turn to Track II channels with Palestinian partners (People's Voice and the Geneva Initiative), in order to advance the two-state solution option.[8] This concern was also a major factor in pushing the late Israeli Prime Minister, Ariel Sharon, to initiate the unilateral disengagement from the Gaza Strip and from the northern part of the West Bank. The joint concerns of losing the Jewish demographic majority, and the Palestinian calling for a one-state solution based on the principle of one person, one vote, motivated Sharon to carry out the idea of the unilateral disengagement (Bar-Siman-Tov 2009). Nowadays, this idea is still valid with reference to a possible unilateral disengagement from about 85 percent of the West Bank if the current Israeli–Palestinian negotiations to bring about a two-state solution ultimately fail.[9]

Conclusions

The negotiations in the Israeli–Palestinian peace process have demonstrated that narratives of justice on both sides played a significant and negative role in foiling the conclusion of a peace agreement. Both sides are motivated by the shadows of the past and being victims of them. Thus, narratives of justice proved to be formidable barriers to peace if both sides sustain clashing narratives.

The major lesson and conclusion of this book is that the only way to conclude a peace agreement requires that both sides should put aside the pursuit for a just peace according to their absolute narratives of justice and strive for peace in the first place. In other words, *justice should be compromised for the sake of peace*. A two-state solution is the only solution that can be defined as an imperfect but relatively just peace, since it reflects both sides' right for self-determination on the one hand, while easing or even ending the long suffering of both parties throughout the conflict on the other hand. Unfortunately, time is not working for the benefit of any of the parties, as new rounds of violence will just accelerate the grievances and lead to new victims in the name of "just peace."

Notes

1 Editor's note: The indefatigable efforts of US Secretary of State John Kerry to bring about a breakthrough in the peace negotiations since July 2013 include a deliberate attempt to balance this asymmetrical power relationship between the two parties.

2 Editor's note: In November 2012 Abu-Mazen expressed in an interview to the Israeli TV his readiness to somehow give up the "right of return" to his place of birth, Safed (nowadays Israel) on a personal level. He was harshly criticized by other Palestinian politicians and Palestinian public opinion for that. At the same time, according to many Israeli analysts, his position regarding the "right of return" has remained ambiguous until today. See www.timesofisrael.com/abbas-says-he-has-no-right-to-live-in-safed-and-has-no-demands-on-pre-1967-israel.

3 Editor's note: In a meeting at Hebrew University on 17 February 2002 with Israeli scholars sponsored by Prof. Bar-Siman-Tov and the Leonard Davis Institute within a project of oral history, Yossi Beilin also referred to a possible solution to the Israeli–Palestinian conflict in terms of an exchange between two "virtual rights"; namely, the Palestinians would give up the right of return in exchange for Israel's surrendering of the Temple Mount. For an account of the Israeli narratives during the Oslo process, see Kacowicz (2005).

4 Editor's note: It remains to be seen whether the current efforts of US Secretary of State John Kerry to bring the parties together to pursue that solution are effective; this is considered the last significant chance for a negotiated peace based on the two-state solution.

5 The idea of a bi-national state or one-state solution was first proposed by Jewish groups during the British Mandate, such as *Brit Shalom* (Covenant of Peace) and *Ihud* (Union), and Jewish intellectuals such as Martin Buber and Judah Magnes, the first rector of the Hebrew University of Jerusalem, as the best possible solution to the Arab–Jewish conflict in Palestine. The bi-national solution was based on a parity regime, in which both sides would enjoy equal rights irrespective of their relative size at any given time (Hattis 1970, Hermann 2005). This bi-national solution was based on a combination of moral and pragmatic considerations. Yet, the original bi-national solution failed to attract any serious support. While the majority of the Jewish side preferred the two-state solution, the Arab/Palestinian side, because of its numerical majority in the territory of the Mandate, had no interest in a parity-based regime.

6 The Palestinian sample included 1,270 adults interviewed in person in the West Bank, East Jerusalem and the Gaza Strip between 4 March and 6 March 2010. The Israeli sample included 501 adult Israelis interviewed by phone in Hebrew,

Arabic, and Russian between 1 March and 10 March 2010. The joint Israeli-Palestinian poll was planned and supervised by Prof. Yaacov Shamir of the Harry S. Truman Research Institute for the Advancement of Peace, and the Department of Communication and Journalism at the Hebrew University of Jerusalem, and by Prof. Khalil Shikaki, director of the Palestinian Center for Policy and Survey Research (PSR), based in Ramallah.

7 Editor's note: The Israeli settlers in the West Bank encompass a powerful political lobby, represented in the current government by Israeli Economic Minister Naftali Bennet and his *Habayit HaYehudi* (Jewish Home) Party, as well as by many politicians from the *Likud* party. For a comprehensive review of the Israeli political right's support for the one-state solution, see www.haaretz.com/weekend/magazine/endgame-1.302128.

8 Editor's note: The most recent example of an Israeli-Palestinian partnership to advocate a two-state solution is the "Breaking the Impasse" (BTI) initiative sponsored by the World Economic Forum in 2012 by major Israeli, Palestinian, and international leaders from business and civil society for renewing the wider momentum for peace and supporting the Kerry mediation in the current negotiations.

9 Editor's note: This is the official recommendation from the Institute for National Security Studies in its annual strategic assessment for 2014. On 28 January 2014, the Head of the Institute, former Military Intelligence chief Amos Yadlin, urged that Israel should unilaterally withdraw from 85 percent of the West Bank – between the security barrier and the Jordan Valley – if the diplomatic process with the Palestinians fails. See *Haaretz*, 28 January 2014.

References

Abu-Odeh, Lama. "The Case for Binationalism," *Boston Review*, December 2001/January 2002.

Avineri, Shlomo. "A History of Conflicts," *Ma'ariv Online*, September 19, 2003.

Baraka, Mohammad. "Between the One-State and the Two-State Solution," *Al-Majdal*, 28, winter 2005.

Bar-Siman-Tov, Yaacov (ed.). *The Disengagement Plan: An Idea Shattered* (Jerusalem: The Jerusalem Institute for Israel Studies, 2009) [Hebrew].

Bar-Tal, Daniel and Gavriel Salomon. "Israeli–Jewish Narrative of the Israeli–Palestinian Conflict: Evolution, Contents, Function, and Consequences." In *Israeli and Palestinian Narratives of Conflict* (ed.) Robert I. Rotberg. (Bloomington: Indiana University Press, 2006), pp. 19–46.

Belaief, Lynne, "Tragic Justice." In *Philosophical Perspectives on the Israeli–Palestinian Conflict* (ed.) Thonis Kapitan. (Armonk, NY: M. E. Sharpe, 1997), pp. 331–56.

Ben-Ami, Shlomo. *Scars of War, Wounds of Peace* (New York: Oxford University Press, 2006).

Benvenisti, Meron. "Which Kind of Bi-national State?," *Haaretz*, November 20, 2003.

Bishara, Marwan. "One State for Two Peoples," *International Herald Tribune*, 12 November, 2003.

Caplan, Neil. *The Israel–Palestine Conflict: Contested Histories* (West Sussex: Wiley-Blackwell, 2010).

Ghanem, As'ad. "A Binational State-Palestinian-Israeli." In *Seven Options: For the Status of the Arabs in Israel* (eds), Sara Ozacky-Lazar, As'ad Ghanem, and Ilan Pappe. (Givat Haviva: The Institute for Peace Research, 1999) [Hebrew], pp. 271–302.

Ghanem, As'ad. "The Binational State is a Desired Palestinian Project and Demand," *Al-Majdal*, 28, winter 2005.

Hattis, Suzan L. *The Binational Idea in Palestine during Mandatory Times* (Haifa: Shikmonan, 1970) [Hebrew].

Hermann,Tamar. "The Bi-National Idea in Israel–Palestine: Past and Present," *Nations and Nationalism*, Vol. 11, 3 (2005), pp. 381–401.

Kacowicz, Arie M. "Rashomon in Jerusalem: Mapping the Israeli Negotiations' Positions on the Israeli–Palestinian Peace Process, 1993–2001," *International Studies Perspectives*, Vol. 6, 2 (2005), pp. 252–73.

Kelman, Herbert C. "Reconciliation as Identity Change: A Social-Psychological Perspective." In *From Conflict Resolution to Reconciliation* (ed.) Yaacov Bar-Siman-Tov. (New York: Oxford University Press, 2004), pp. 111–24.

Khalidi, Rashid. *The Iron Cage: The Story of the Palestinian Struggle for Statehood* (Boston, MA: Beacon Press, 2006).

Khalidi, Rashid "An Interview with Chemi Shalev," *Haaretz*, 5 December 2011.

Margalit, Avishai. *On Compromise and Rotten Compromise* (Princeton, NJ: Princeton University Press, 2010).

Peres, Shimon (with Arye Naor). *The New Middle East* (New York: Henry Holt and Company, 1993).

Rotberg, Robert I. "Building Legitimacy through Narrative." In *Israeli and Palestinian Narratives of Conflict* (ed.) Robert I. Rotberg. (Bloomington: Indiana University Press, 2006), pp. 1–18.

Said, Edward W. "A Method for Thinking about Just Peace." In *What is a Just Peace?* (ed.) Pierre Allan and Alexis Keller. (Oxford: University Press, 2006), pp. 176–94.

Shavit, Ari. "Forget about Zionism," *Haaretz*, 8 August 2003.

Tarazi, Michael. "Two Peoples, One State," *New York Times*, 8 October 2004.

Tony, Judy. "Israel: The Alternative," In *The New York Review of Books*, Vol. 50, 16, 23 October 2003.

Tilley, Virginia. *The One-State Solution* (Ann Arbor: The University of Michigan Press, 2005).

Index

Note: Page numbers followed by "n" refer to notes.

Printed in Dunstable, United Kingdom

9eb42eb9-3c8c-45c0-9451-dbf184091971R01